UNIX® System Security

How to Protect Your Data and Prevent Intruders

Rik Farrow

Addison-Wesley Publishing Company, Inc.

Reading, Massachusetts   Menlo Park, California   New York

Don Mills, Ontario   Wokingham, England   Amsterdam   Bonn   Sydney

Singapore   Tokyo   Madrid   San Juan

Many of the designations used by manufacturers and sellers to distinguish their products are claimed as trademarks. Where those designations appear in this book and Addison-Wesley was aware of a trademark claim, the designations have been printed in initial capital letters.

ISBN 0-201-57030-0

Managing Editor: Amorette Pedersen
Set in 10.5-point Palatino by Benchmark Productions

ABCDEFGHIJ-MW-943210
First Printing, December, 1990

Table of Contents

Acknowledgments

I got the idea for this book in 1987, when one of the other speakers at UNIFORM asked me if there was a book that explained the basics of UNIX system security. There was not. So I decided to write "the little book of UNIX security," based on the course material I had gathered over the years. Every time I spoke or taught about UNIX security, I would learn something new from my audience. I am sorry that I cannot remember all the people who gave me tips, but would like to mention a few:

Mike Carroll of Ohio Bell explained dialup passwords, Joe Klein shared stacks of material he had gathered, Becca Thomas passed on System V Release 4 shadow information, Dave Flack sent all security-related information he came upon, Cliff Neuman explained how Kerberos worked.

Matt Bishop offered both encouragement and his paper. The editorial staff at *UNIXWorld* magazine and SL Corporation provided many examples of real user behavior. My family, Rose Jasmine and Canyon, supported me through the trying period of writing, and finally, the people at Benchmark Productions: Chris Williams, Amy Pedersen, and Jean Garvey.

My thanks to all of you and those whose names I have forgotten.

Chapter 1

Introduction to UNIX System Security

Overview

The UNIX system is now the environment of choice for multiuser computers. UNIX system security, therefore, has become a crucial issue. With the UNIX system becoming a widely used operating system, it has expanded beyond its initial arena in education into business and government computing, areas where security is critical. The spectacular invasion of the Internet in November 1988 by the Morris worm further served to push UNIX system security to the forefront.

UNIX and Its Reputation

The UNIX system has acquired a rather notorious reputation when it comes to security. This reputation was earned, not only through misadventures like the Morris worm, but also because of a certain background in the educational community. What has made UNIX security a laughing matter for some people is not so much the design flaws inherent in the system, but the way in which the system is used.

Let's examine the past history of the UNIX system and trace the roots of this reputation. UNIX was born in Bell Labs as a platform for single user programming. Multics, the predecessor to the UNIX system, was designed with security as a priority and is one of the few top-rated secure operating systems available today. The UNIX system, although based on some of the concepts in Multics, was designed to be much simpler. UNIX was converted from a single user operating system to a multiuser operating system almost overnight.

As word about this simple, clear, and useful system was published and lectured about, universities began to acquire the source for the system. Within six years after the UNIX system was born, two books were published (*UNIX Operating System Source Code Level Six* and *Commentary on the UNIX Operating System*, J. Lions, University of Wales, June, 1977), providing a copy of annotated source to the UNIX system kernel, the heart of the security mechanism. This two volume set was a popular underground commodity in the UNIX programming community. (*Source* is the term used to described the C computer language files/listings that are used to create the UNIX system. Having a copy of the source is like having a blueprint of a bank vault. Any flaws or weaknesses of the kernel and ways to get around them are revealed to a programmer.) This book is less useful today because the UNIX kernel has changed so much since it was published in 1977.

The source for an IBM mainframe, by comparison, fills a small library. Each notebook's cover contains dire warnings against perusal by unauthorized personnel. The warnings are repeated within the notebook. You could certainly say that sharing information about IBM operating system internals is neither easy to do nor encouraged. Today, UNIX source is also officially protected. However, information about UNIX internals can be obtained by reading any of several books.

Some of the UNIX system's poor security reputation is just plain unfair. Some mainframes are sold with less default security than a microcomputer running an old version of Xenix. One of the largest minicomputer vendors trains its field engineers in a half dozen methods for obtaining system privileges, with or without passwords. The most common computers, personal computers, have no security at all. Yet, somehow it is the UNIX system that gets labeled as the "insecure" operating system.

The UNIX programming community is an open one, with many conferences and much sharing of information. This atmosphere of openness is extended to the environment on many computers, where almost every user has access to any file or resource. Although programmers like working with a non-secure system, moving that same system into a business environment, or connecting network devices to it, does not work well without security. Often, the wide-open system used by programmers would be delivered as-is with new UNIX systems. An installer of the new UNIX system would follow instructions which did not include making the system secure. Security was not a concern of the programmers that configured the system because their environment did not demand security.

Today, there is greater awareness of the need for security. Most UNIX systems are delivered in a more restrictive configuration, and instructions are included for maintaining a basic level of security while installing the system. What is still lacking is information on maintaining secure UNIX systems.

This book will help you learn about UNIX system security features and their problems. Over 90 percent of all UNIX security problems are caused by mistakes made by users and system administrators. This book is about learning how to avoid these mistakes. It is also about understanding the methods crackers use to bypass security on any computer so attacks can be, if not prevented, at least detected. Whether you are new to UNIX, or a seasoned hand, there are things in this book you need to learn.

Organization

The first chapter presents a background for understanding computer security. This background will be referred to later in the book, and it provides an important conceptual framework. The second chapter deals with user issues, that is, information that everyone using a UNIX system must know and follow. Together, Chapters 1 and 2 are sufficient material if you are a user of a secure UNIX system, and not a system administrator or programmer. For advanced users, the information in these chapters will fill in important gaps in your security knowledge.

Chapter 3 covers controlling access to your system. If you cannot keep unauthorized users out, then you have already lost half the battle. There are known weaknesses in the password file and methods for cracking passwords. You will learn effective countermeasures for controlling login access and defending against bad passwords. You will also learn about correct ownership and permissions for systems files, and how problems with system files can be taken advantage of. This chapter provides examples of scripts for creating security watchdogs, means of monitoring your system after you have correctly adjusted ownership, scripts, and permissions.

Modems and networks can make your system harder to defend. Because of remote access, your system extends beyond the physical domain you can control and watch over. You can use techniques to make modems use more secure and improve the security of the UUCP system. Chapter 4 also explains basic Internet security: what files permit passwordless logins, which services to provide for a secure connection, configuration of NFS, and how to set up anonymous **ftp** correctly. The final portion of this chapter covers so-called restricted environments—what are your options, how to set up a restricted environment, and how secure each environment can really be.

Chapter 5 explores techniques for watching for and detecting any suspicious activities. The focus here is on determining if your system is under attack and, if so, what to do next. Also, if you have discovered evidence of a past attack, this chapter will show you how to track down the abuser. Moment-to-moment monitoring of your system, along with stories of how other administrators discovered attacks, fill out this section. Finally, you will learn the rules of evidence necessary for you to begin the prosecution of alleged invaders and abusers of your system.

Chapter 6 covers the future of UNIX system security. Several secure versions of the UNIX system exist today, and their security features will be explored. Improved password protection, mandatory access controls, access control lists, secure logins, and auditing form the basis for increased UNIX system security. The final lesson, however, is that if users do not comprehend and follow the basic security issues discussed in the earlier chapters, then even the certified-secure versions of UNIX system will not be safe.

Computer Security

Computer security does not consist of guards, alarm systems, and infrared detectors. These things are considered physical security. Computer security is concerned with protecting information within the computer and access to the resources of the computer. The two forms are similar whenever there are assets that need to be protected against theft, vandalism, and accidental damage.

In particular, computer security involves three different areas: accountability, system protection, and data protection.

- **Accountability**—making it possible to discover who has done what, by identifying users and recording the activities of programs started by users. The recorded activities can be examined for suspicious activities, or to determine which person violated system security.
- **System protection**—preventing any user from tying up resources, thus denying service to other users, and preventing unauthorized use of computer resources.

- **Data protection**—control over access to data for reading, copying it, altering it, or removing it.

In computer security, the computer and its software are the only witnesses. For accountability to work correctly, each user must be identified uniquely as the user logs in. After logging in, the unique identification must follow the user, identifying accounting records, the ownership of new files and directories, and determining access rights to files and directories.

System protection has two focuses. If the bad guys cannot log in, the battle has been won. *Keeping unauthorized users out is the first line of defense*. If an intruder never sees more than a login prompt, you cannot lose any information. The other focus of system protection is often called *denial of service*. Denial of service means that a user is abusing the system by taking more than a fair share of resources, for example, using large amounts of disk space or starting many programs at once. In a denial of service attack, the system may become swamped by the attack, and unable to perform real work, even to determine the nature of the attack.

Data protection controls how users of a system interact with the files and directories. The system must decide, based on the unique identification of each user and the permissions associated with each file, whether the file can be read, written, or executed. The UNIX file permission scheme appears simple, but has twists and turns that can make it as devious as a grand masters' chess match. Once the sneak attacks around the permission scheme are understood, the UNIX system permissions work well for one level of security.

How Much Security Is Enough?

Before embarking on a project to increase your system security, you should evaluate the costs involved. There is a rule of thumb for evaluating the cost of security—the cost of securing your system must be less than the cost involved if your system is compromised. Some data is invaluable, such as the code phrases used to release nuclear weapons. Marketing data about future product lines has a more easily determined value. Medical and psychological information about individuals has value, in that disclosure of these records could damage someone's reputation. The smooth operation of computers monitoring stock prices obviously has value because a delay of only minutes could cost a broker millions of dollars.

In determining how much should be spent in securing your system, you must also look at the other side of the equation—ease of use. The UNIX system became popular because it made it easy to exchange information among users of the same computer, users of other computers running the UNIX system, and even computers using totally different operating systems. An inevitable side effect of increasing security is to reduce the easy exchange of information so dear to UNIX system users. If security is increased without serious motivation, users will revolt and work against the system, trying to bypass the added security. If increased security makes a computer too difficult to maneuver, no one will use it. The ease-of-use must be balanced against the need for security.

Of all the UNIX system users, programmers are probably the worst when it comes to security. Programmers labor long hours to create their software, which, if they are lucky, will be marketed and provide the financial backing for their next creations. While working, programmers are annoyed by even the slightest thing that interferes with getting the job done, and security definitely interferes. Even though a competitor could easily use the same network that the programmers use and steal the programmers' ideas, programmers prefer to keep the network unfettered by security. A *Permission denied* message can cause an explosion of wrath against the person who dared protect a file. Worst of all, these same programmers have been responsible for setting up the default security on both the operating system and the software that gets delivered to unsuspecting users. The good news is that security awareness has definitely improved among programmers, with a little help from system breakers.

Computer Security and Ethical Behavior

While in the speakers' lounge at a computer show, several people asked me how many systems I had broken into. After all, I was speaking about UNIX system security. I had to answer that I had never "broken into" someone else's computer. Entering and using a computer without permission is like breaking into someone's home or office. Just because they left a window open doesn't mean you are welcome to crawl in and look around.

Even while working on a system where I am welcome, I don't go poking through other peoples' directories without invitation. A home directory tree is the equivalent of a desk drawer. The usual assumption is that you keep things in a desk drawer because they don't belong out in plain view. How would you feel if you walked into your office and found someone, even an associate, rifling through your drawers?

Some of the information in this book can be used to "break into" computer systems where people haven't taken the time (or understood how to) "close their windows." There is nothing in this book that provides a method for breaking into a secured UNIX system, but there is certainly information that could be used on poorly protected ones. My position is that you must understand the dangers involved in poor security practices before you will stand up and do something about it. And I was personally frustrated by the vagueness of the advice when I began studying security. So I am giving you the information that I wanted for myself, that I had to dig up or discover on my own.

I am not inviting anyone to undertake criminal activities. The days when high school students invaded computer systems and got a scolding are over. Computer cracking is viewed as a serious crime, whether you are browsing files, making an unauthorized entry, or trying to get in. I will talk about how to catch a wrong-doing employee or even someone coming in over the modem, and how to collect evidence for criminal prosecution. Federal laws cover many computer-related crimes, and many states have passed laws protecting against computer misuse. In California, all the computer equipment at a site where a modem has been used to make an unauthorized login attempt is impounded awaiting actual prosecution. The user gets out on bail, but not the computer.

There is a strong computer underground today. For these people, breaking into computers is a game, and its criminality just makes it more exciting. Some of these same people are programmers whose livelihood depends upon keeping the source to their own software secret. Others see computer crime as simply an opportunity to make money, just as drug cartels import large quantities of drugs. After all, cartels don't make people buy drugs, and computer criminals don't force people to use computers. One group takes advantage of addicts, the other, one of the most useful tools ever developed.

The choice is up to you. If you are a "good guy," pay attention. Much of the information presented here is the result of someone's successful penetration of UNIX system security. If you want to be a "bad guy," see if you can join a "red team" instead. A member of a red team plays the part of the bad guys, and attempts to break system security. Breaks in security are reported and fixed, and the game continues. Some companies reward members of the red team for their successes because they have done the company a great favor.

A Model for Computer Security

Computer security is a relatively new concept. The first research on computer security was done in the late sixties and early seventies. Researchers needed to develop new ways of thinking about security. Then, in the existing models of security, you needed to protect information on paper, film, or tape, any of which could be viewed by people unaided by devices or with relatively simple equipment. To secure your secrets, you use physical security, for example, a locked safe in a guarded room. With computer security, you are protecting electronically encoded information that cannot be viewed without the intervention of a computer. You still can use physical protection to control access to the computer itself. But how do you control the people who use the computer? What does a "safe in a locked room" correspond to inside a computer?

Not surprisingly, many of the methods used for computer security parallel what has been done by the military in protecting information. This parallel helps us because we can examine a model that is easier to visualize and understand than what goes on inside a computer. I will refer to this allegory later in the book, so let's spend a minute watching the fictitious CIA agent who I call Jack.

It's 8 o'clock as Jack pulls into the parking lot at CIA headquarters in Northern Virginia. A guard looks at Jack's identification card and compares the picture on the card with Jack's face before allowing him to drive into the lot. Again, at the entrance to the building, Jack stops in front of guard behind a glass barrier, and presents his identification for verification. Satisfied that the identification matches the face, the guard presses a button that releases the lock on the door. Actually, Jack knows the guard, and they exchange greetings before Jack continues to his desk. As the door closes behind Jack, the guard notes in a log the time of Jack's arrival.

Later that same day, Jack needs to examine some photographs that are classified as Secret. Jack approaches the custodian of the photographs, explains his reason for needing to see the photographs. The custodian checks a list of persons permitted to view these photos, finds Jack's name, and has Jack sign a log before the photographs are taken from a safe. Jack remains in the custodian's presence while examining the photographs, and after returning the photos, the custodian marks in the log that he has witnessed the return of the items to the safe. As the sun sets over the Beltway, Jack leaves the building where he works, and the guard (a different one this time) notes the time of his departure.

Note that all the elements of computer security are present in this story. Before Jack can even enter the parking lot, he must present identification showing that he has permission to enter the parking lot—system protection. The guard compares the picture on the id with Jack's face. The id card provides identification, and the picture authentication, additional proof that the person and id card identify the correct individual. At the front desk, additional authentication takes place. The guard recognizes Jack personally (something computers are not so good at).

When Jack goes to see the photographs, he encounters an access control mechanism—data protection. Before he can get access to the photos, his permission to do so is checked by the custodian. When he signs the log, he has become accountable. The custodian is witness to the event and also is accountable for returning the photographs to the safe.

With a computer, things work very differently. This time we can follow Jill, as she logs in to work on her UNIX system. Jill works at home so she commands her modem to dial the UNIX system, and responds to the "login:" prompt by entering her user name—identification. In response to the "Password:" prompt, Jill enters her secret password—authentification. Although the elements are similar to the previous story, you can detect the difference immediately: anyone could be using Jill's user name and password.

When Jill logged in, information was recorded as data in the computer. As she works, more information about her activities is also recorded. Unlike Jack, who must present his id card as he moves around the building, Jill's identification accompanies her as she moves through the UNIX system. As part of her job, Jill must examine some sensitive information. To do so, she uses a special command and enters another password. Her success (or failure) at entering the password is noted, and she can now access the sensitive data. Once she has finished with this task, she resumes her normal user identity. At the end of her work day, she logs out, creating another record in the UNIX system.

The Trusted Computing Base

The task of identifying a computer user, recording the user's activity, and controlling access falls to the computer's hardware and software. The hardware consists of the physical electronics, the processors, memory, busses, and I/O devices, that execute software. The trusted portion of the hardware includes a mechanism for segregating regions of memory, and preventing software executing in one region from interfering with software or data in other regions. The operating system is the only software that is trusted. The combination of hardware and operating system software responsible for enforcing a security policy is called the *Trusted Computing Base*.

For now, we are going to ignore the role of the hardware in protecting memory and focus on the operating system and a few programs. This software replaces the guards and the custodians used in the CIA example. For example, the login program takes a user name as an argument and requests a password to authenticate that the person entering the user name is the correct user. The password entered must match the password in the user database file, **/etc/passwd**. Thus, the login program and **/etc/passwd** file take the place of the guard at the front desk.

It's time to define two terms that are often used in describing computer security, subjects and objects. *Subjects* are active entities, either persons or programs operating on behalf of users. In the UNIX system, active programs are called processes, so processes are subjects. The *objects* are passive entities that contain information—the files, devices, and the system itself. For example, if a user wants to read a file with the editor **vi**, the **vi** process is the subject attempting to access the file, the object.

The reference monitor software mediates the connection between subjects and objects. The reference monitor is not the same as the UNIX system kernel. The reference monitor is a small section of a program responsible for controlling access. The reference monitor must be small so that it is easy to analyze. If the reference monitor were large and complex, it would be difficult to tell by examining its code how well it does its performed task. Thus, the reference monitor is a small portion of a program entrusted with a particular access control task.

The reference monitor uses two other resources, the control database and the audit file. The control database contains the access information about objects. The control database will also hold information about which subjects have access, and what type of access, to the objects. The audit file is used by the reference monitor in order to record its actions. The amount of auditing done may range to none, to changing a date stamp, to keeping a complete record of which subject requested access of which object, when the request occurred, and whether the request was granted. The interaction between the subject, reference monitor, control database, and the audit file is diagrammed in Figure 1-1.

Figure 1-1: The reference monitor mediates the subject's request to access the object by reading the control database, and records the results in the audit file.

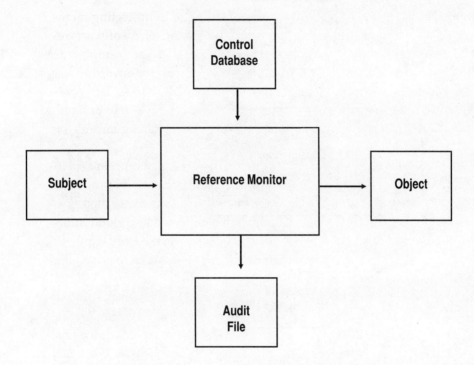

Several portions of the UNIX system kernel perform as reference monitors. For example, the user Jay wishes to view the contents of the **/etc/passwd** file. Jay starts the **more** process, giving the name of the object, **/etc/passwd**, as an argument. The **more** process, the subject, makes a system call to open the **/etc/passwd** file for reading. The access control code in the kernel, one of the reference monitors, examines the file permissions (the control database) for **/etc/passwd**, determines that the **more** process has read permission, and returns the open file to the process. The reference monitor also changes the audit file for **/etc/passwd** by updating a time stamp to reflect the granting of read access (Figure 1-2).

Figure 1-2: The UNIX system kernel's access control mechanism forms the reference monitor when the process **more /etc/passwd** *attempts to open* **/etc/passwd** *for reading. The control database is the object's permissions, and the audit file comprises of a time of access date stamp.*

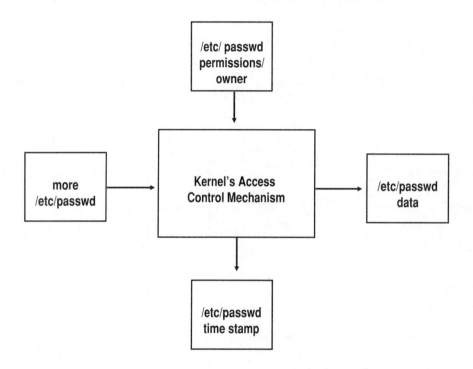

The Orange Book

The U.S. government is the largest user of computer systems requiring security. Security sensitive branches of the government follow directives enacted into law by Congress for the handling of sensitive materials. Usually, these materials are documents, but they may also be films, tapes, or other evidence. Procedures for protecting sensitive materials include descriptions of the physical barriers, such as guards, locked doors, alarm systems, and safes, and a security classification system.

The security classification system defines levels of security and categories. Levels of security haves familiar names, for example, Top Secret, Secret, Confidential, and Unclassified. Rules for who may view what materials follow simple, common sense, concepts. If you have been cleared to view Secret documents, you may also view Confidential documents, but not Top Secret documents.

The security categories work somewhat differently than the levels, but conceptually are as simple. A category contains information related to a single topic. Examples of categories are the Middle East, Naval Ships, and Central America. Oliver North worked for the National Security Agency and dealt with fundraising for the Nicaraguan Contra's and the Middle East hostage problem. His activities fall into two of our example categories, Middle East and Central America, but not the third, Naval Ships.

The idea of categories also corresponds to another security principle, the need-to-know. The need-to-know is more common sense—the more people know a secret, the more likely it is that the secret will become known. Even if Oliver North belongs in the Middle East category, he would not be permitted to see documents that do not relate to his missions.

The problem tackled by the National Computer Security Center (NCSC) was to define criteria for determining how well a computer and its software matched the existing paper security system. The paper system had easily recognizable parts, and well-established procedures. Computer systems, on the other hand, are very complex, and most of what happens exists in the form of electronic signals and magnetic residues. Even worse, there already exists a somewhat antagonistic relationship between some of the programmers who designed software and the security establishment. Some programmers feel that information should be free, or that they should always have access to the systems that they have designed. Having programmers responsible for policing themselves is like having rustlers herd your cattle.

So the NCSC designed a document, the *Trusted Computer System Evaluation Criteria*, to serve as a basis for rating computer systems. (The author of the book didn't want it to be lost on peoples' shelves, so he had an orange cover put on it, leading to the shortened name, the *Orange Book*.) The Orange Book was published by the Department of Defense in 1985, and has become the standard for rating computer systems for security. And, although the Orange Book is not a design specification, current secure versions of computer systems are composed with the Orange Book in mind.

Orange Book Definitions

The Orange Book is not pleasant, after dinner reading. It establishes criteria for the following:

- A clear, precise, well-documented security policy
- The ability to properly identify all users and to audit security-related events (authentication and auditing)
- The assurance that the system performs its trusted functions correctly
- Guidelines for administrative and user documentation for supporting the correct use and maintenance of the system.

Testing of systems for a security rating from the NCSC involves both the system's hardware and software. The entire process is very expensive for the vendor and takes years to complete. A system is submitted for a particular level of security, and must meet *all* of the requirements for that level before it can be certified.

The Orange Book makes an interesting assumption—that the trusted system can contain untrusted software and malicious users. By placing the burden of trust on the trusted system, application software need not be written specifically to work in a secure environment. The trusted system must also control the activities of users, preventing them from accidentally or intentionally reading or writing data for which they do not have the correct privileges.

The Orange Book focuses on preventing compromise of sensitive information, much like the paper system that it imitates. Ignored are attacks on computer security such as denial of service, where a malicious user takes more than a fair share of the system resources. The Morris worm (see Appendix) was a denial of service attack, in that it so overloaded infected systems that they could not function. A denial of service attack could be use to cripple a computer at a critical time.

The Orange Book follows the Bell-LaPadula model of computer security, which comes close to the paper model of security. The Bell-LaPadula model defines the relationship between subjects and objects. This relationship is based on the levels and categories used in the paper system, and introduces a new term, *dominates*. A subject *dominates* an object if the subject's level is greater than or equal to the object's level, and the subject's categories includes all the categories of the object. In other words, if your **vi** process is operating at the Secret level and within the Middle East category, you could read a file at level Secret or lower in the Middle East category.

There are two basic rules in the Bell-LaPadula model, one dealing with reading, and the other with writing. For reading, the subject must dominate the object, following the example used to demonstrate the term dominate. This principle is called *read-down*; that is, you can read objects at your own level and lower. Read-down is also known as *simple security*. For writing, the object must dominate the subject. As an example, you cannot write to a file labeled as Secret when your **vi** process is operating at the Top Secret level or is working within a different category. Write-up prevents a user from purposely or accidentally declassifying information by writing the data in a less secure file. Write-up is also called the *-property (star property), because the Bell-LaPadula paper neglected to name this property and instead left an asterisk to remind themselves to do it later.

Much of the Orange Book deals with the problem of assurance. *Assurance* is the proof that the trusted system components will always work as specified. Assurance gets more difficult as the level of security classification increases, so that it is easier to produce trusted systems at the lower classifications.

The Orange Book does not follow all the conventions of military security. For example, some sensitive information can only be viewed while accompanied by one or two other persons. The multiple witnesses for reviewing information is called *dual custody*, and a means for accomplishing dual custody within a computer has not been developed. It is also possible to declassify portions of a document so that a single document can exist a multiple levels of security. The Orange Book and the Bell-LaPadula model have no means for working with multiple level objects.

Divisions and Levels

The Orange Book defines four divisions, from division D (Minimal Protection) to division A (Verified Protection). Within these four divisions there are a total of seven levels. Each level includes *all* of the security provisions of the preceding levels, so that levels build upon each other. Levels are named by using the division level followed by a number, with higher numbers denoting more security. Thus, B2 security is greater than B1 and A1 is greater than all the other levels (Figure 1-3).

- D—Minimal Protection
- C1—Discretionary security protection
- C2—Controlled access protection
- B1—Labeled security protection
- B2—Structured protection
- B3—Security domains
- A1—Verified design

Figure 1-3: Divisions and levels for the trusted computer system evaluation criteria.

D - Minimal Protection   *A system that fits in at the D division would not be rated. These systems have essentially no security beyond physical security. Anyone who has physical access to the system has access to the resources and files of the system. Personal computers running MS/DOS, Macintoshes not running UNIX, and Atari Amigas (also not running UNIX) all fit in this division. There are some security packages that can increase the protection on personal computers, but not enough to get a rating at the next division.*

C1 - Discretionary Security Protection   *Most UNIX systems would be rated at C1, although there is no point in getting a C1 rating. The C1 level does not provide enough additional security to justify the cost of getting certified. Also, a system certified at a higher level can be used to fill a slot requiring the C1 level.*

Discretionary security means that each user has control over the objects they own. The user may restrict write access, while permitting read access for all, or make a copy of a restricted file that only the user can read, and then change the permissions on the copy so that anyone can read it. Access privileges are based on three categories—user, group, and other (everyone else).

Users must identify themselves with a login name and a password. This login identification is used to identify the subjects acting on the behalf of the user.

C2 - Controlled Access Protection   *This level adds auditing and increased authentication. Auditing creates records of security-related events, such as those activities performed by an administrator. Auditing can be configured to increase the number of events recorded. Auditing brings with it the necessity for increased authentication because the audit record is meaningless unless the person that initiated an auditable event can be identified. Auditing has the side-effect of using system resources, both the processor and disk subsystems.*

Figure 1-3: Divisions and levels for the trusted computer system evaluation criteria (continued).

*The encrypted passwords must be hidden from unprivileged users. In C1, encrypted passwords appear in the user database file (/**etc/passwd** for UNIX systems). Hiding encrypted passwords helps prevent attempts at cracking passwords.*

B1 - Labeled Security Protection *B1 is the first level that supports multilevel security, for example, both Secret and Top Secret. B1 includes mandatory access controls so that an object under mandatory access control cannot have its permissions changed by the owner of the file. Certification at the B1 level requires an informal proof of the security model.*

Labels add more complete descriptions of the security level and category of subjects and objects. Labels do not replace the permission and ownership of discretionary security, but are used in addition to them. Additional commands exist for the viewing and manipulating of object labels.

B2 - Structured Protection *B2 requires that every object be labeled. Devices, such as disks, tapes, or terminals, may have a single level of security, or multiple levels. Multiple level devices, for example, a tape unit, must be capable of preserving the labels of objects stored there. B2 requires a formal proof of the correctness of the security model. Penetration testing is used to probe possible flaws in the security model.*

B2 includes the beginning of covert channel restrictions. Covert channels are indirect means for communicating between a subject operating at a high level with another process operating at a lower level. Covert channels always imply the inappropriate use of a system capability, like using Venetian blinds to signal in Morse code instead of screening out the afternoon sun. An example of a covert channel would be to signal a process by using up the last free disk block and making it available again to transmit a bit at a time.

B3 - Security Domains *B3 enforces isolation of the security domains with hardware. The security domain may be part of the trusted computing base, for example, a reference monitor. Memory management hardware protects the security domain against access or modification by software operating in other domains.*

B3 systems must provide a trusted path. The trusted path guarantees a user that the terminal used is connected directly to trusted software. The trusted path prevents entering a login name and password to a program masquerading as the **login** *process.*

Figure 1-3: Divisions and levels for the trusted
computer system evaluation criteria (continued).

A1 - Verified Design   *Certification at the A1 level requires a formal mathematical proof of the correctness of the security model. Certification also requires formal analysis of covert channels, a formal top-level specification, and trusted distribution. Trusted distribution means that software and hardware is protected during shipment to prevent tampering with the security mechanisms.*

Very few systems will ever achieve the A1 certification. At the present, only the SCOMP system from Honeywell has been certified at A1. The rating system is open-ended, so that a new certification level, A2, can be added as necessary.

Summary

The UNIX system nearly matches the criteria for C1 level security without modifications. It is unlikely that a NCSC-certified C1 version of the UNIX system will ever be produced because the demand for secure systems starts with C2 systems. Still, the necessary support for good, basic, single level security is present in every UNIX system.

In some ways, the UNIX system has features of the higher Orange Book levels. The UNIX system kernel operates in a physically secure domain, which is defended by hardware. The secure domain protects the kernel and the security mechanisms within it. Because the security mechanisms themselves cannot be thwarted, breaking UNIX system security relies on using legitimate means to illegitimate ends.

To defend against attacks, the ownership and permissions of files and directories must be set correctly. Users must understand the basic rules for choosing passwords, and how to avoid being tricked into sharing their privileges unintentionally. These basic principals form the topic of Chapter 2.

Chapter 2

Basic User Security Practices

This chapter presents the security information that all users of a system need to know. It does not matter if the user is a secretary, marketing or sales representative, a programmer, or a system administrator—*all* users should follow the basic directions described here. The UNIX system, even with the addition of enhanced security features, still requires that all users follow a few, simple security practices:

- Good use of passwords
- Appropriate use of file and directory permissions
- Protecting account privileges
- Being alert for other surprises

There are other principals users must be aware of. For example, the UNIX system can encrypt files, preventing any user from understanding the contents of the encrypted file. But the encryption system does have inherent problems that you need to know about. And every user must be aware of how Trojan Horses can be used to destroy files or give away privileges.

Passwords—The Keys to Your System

Before you can use a UNIX system, you must log in. Have you ever tried using a UNIX system without knowing a login name and password? Facing a screen that presents only a login and password prompt quickly gets frustrating. It is like a gate with a combination lock—you can randomly try combinations for a long time without getting results.

But there are methods for "breaking" the login name-password combinations. These methods only work when the users and administrators on a UNIX system have neglected their first line of security: system protection through passwords.

The UNIX system is cagey about login procedures. The **/etc/passwd** file contains the list of login names and the passwords that accompany these names. If a potential password cracker enters a login name that is not in the **/etc/passwd** file, the **login** process still requests a password, preventing the cracker from determining if the name entered is a valid login name. But if the cracker guesses a login name, then the password must also be guessed—if there is a password. If there is no password, the cracker gets logged in.

Guessing login names is not difficult. Customarily, login names are based on a user's first name, first name and last initial, or first initial and last name. For example, here are three possible login names for Sandy Smith:

- sandy—the first name alone
- sandys—the first name with the last initial
- ssmith—the first initial and last name

An outsider can easily obtain someone's name by calling on the phone and asking for the name of the person who answers. Or asking for the person to talk to for software assistance. Or from a list of sales representatives. Login names are not very secret. Out of a list of 30 common first names, you can expect to find at least one user by that name on every multiuser system. So it is the password that is important, not the login name. And the password is the real problem.

Login names are familiar to people; passwords are alien. The closest thing to a password in use outside of computers are combinations for locks. Simpler combination locks come with predefined combinations, but suitcases and safes have combinations that can be changed. People creating their own combinations tend to choose numbers that they won't forget—like birthdays. Your birthdate works okay for a suitcase, where it is difficult to discover your birthday by examining your suitcase. But not for a password because other people know when your birthday is (and it is certainly in your personnel records).

The best passwords are totally random combinations of letters, digits, numbers, and punctuation. And almost no one can remember this kind of password. Random passwords lead to another problem with passwords—the tendency to write passwords down. If a person cannot remember a complex password, he or she is likely to write the password down in a convenient location. Someone looking for a password need only watch this person logging in. Did the person look in his or her desk drawer? Under the keyboard? In the rolodex or phone number directory? Some people even program their password into their terminal, so that pressing one key sends the password to the system. You might as well leave a key in the ignition of your car, as program your password into your terminal.

People generally don't perform well when it comes to choosing their own passwords. The most common passwords used are names, the login name twice or backwards, or either of these with one digit appended. Words found in dictionaries are also popular. Although the UNIX system stores passwords in an encrypted form, a password cracker encrypts possible passwords and looks for matches with encrypted passwords. (Chapter 3 explains how password crackers work.) So choosing names or words, even with a digit appended, makes password cracking easy.

Choosing Good Passwords

Good passwords are easy to remember, are not names, and are not found in any dictionary. What makes these passwords easy to remember is the use of mnemonic techniques. Mnemonic techniques involve associating a pattern of letters and numbers with funny phrases that stick in your head. For example, one of my 12-year-old son's favorite passwords was "O,I81b4u", or "Oh, I ate one before you." A password cracker has no chance of guessing that one, and it certainly won't be found in any dictionary. Another way to create a mnemonic password is to use the first letter of each word in a phrase, like "IwIh1md." or "I wish I had 1 million dollars." Here are more ideas:

- 88k4Me2
- LeTmEiN!
- LUVdoz9R
- m8kmyDAY
- Hi y'all
- Mi-T tuf

Passwords can be as long as you like, however, only the first eight characters count. You can use upper- or lowercase letters, numbers, most punctuation, and even control keys. The only keys you should avoid are your system's default erase and line kill characters. Many systems recognize and process erase and line kill keys during the entry of the login name and the password. On older UNIX systems, the default backspace character was the pound sign (#), and the line kill character was the at sign (@). Some newer systems recognize the backspace key (control-h) as the erase character and control-x as the line kill key. (The line kill key erases the entire line.) To discover your erase and line kill characters, use the **stty** command (Figure 2-1).

Figure 2-1: Using the **stty** *command without arguments will print out the erase and line kill characters, control-h and control-x in this example.*

```
$ stty
speed 9600 baud; evenp clocal
erase = ^h; kill = ^x
echo echoe echok
$ ▮
```

Avoid erase and line kill characters in your password. Often, the default erase and line kill characters are changed by the shell startup scripts so they will not effect entering a password after you have logged in, but will during login.

Beyond these two or four special characters, the richer the character set used for your password, the better your password is. The only other advice involves the use of a space bar. Although this is a minor point, the space bar sounds different from other keys on the keyboard when it is pressed, and some people feel it should be avoided in passwords.

System V-based UNIX systems force users, other than the superuser, to use a rich character set and a minimum number of characters in their passwords. These restrictions help, but don't prevent someone from creating a password like "sandy2". Enhanced UNIX systems meeting B division *Orange Book* security have *password generators*. Password generators produce random letter combinations based on phonemes, short letter combinations that can be verbalized. Unfortunately, these passwords are not much easier than truly random combinations; worse, they get changed often (every several months), making them even harder to remember.

You do not want to use the same password forever. The best thing you can do is to change your password every month, or every other month. Don't just rotate between two passwords—be creative. If you have accounts on several different systems, don't use the same password on all systems. Otherwise, if your password is compromised on one system, all the systems with your account are now vulnerable. To help you remember multiple passwords, first choose your mnemonic password, then prefix it with a short system identifier, like "X", "Y", or "Z" for three different systems. Then you have one password to remember, and system identifiers for the different systems.

The most important thing is not to write your password down or store it in your terminal. If you absolutely can't remember your password, get a small lockbox with a key. Keep the key in your pocket, not in a purse or desk drawer. The lockbox can contain your written password on a small, folded piece of paper, and you can keep your lockbox in your desk. Don't share your lockbox with anyone else. If your lockbox is stolen, or appears to have been forced open, change your password immediately and notify your system administrator or security officer.

Changing Your Password

You change your password with the **passwd** command. The **passwd** command requests that you enter your old password before it permits you to change your password. This prevents anyone else (who doesn't know your password) from changing your password. If you have forgotten your password, the system administrator can provide you with a temporary password without knowing your old password. Then you can change your password (Figure 2-2).

Figure 2-2: Before you can change your password, you must
enter your old password. Some systems require at least two letters
and a digit, or punctuation or control character in the new password.

```
$ passwd
passwd:  Changing password for sandy
Old password:
New password:
Password must contain at least two alphabetic characters and
at least one numeric or special character.
New password:
Re-enter new password:
$ ▮
```

The UNIX system turns off *echoing*, the display of the characters you type, while you are entering a password. Since you cannot see what you have entered, you must enter the new password twice. In Figure 2-2, Sandy's first attempt to enter a password failed because the character set used was not rich enough. Newer UNIX systems require a minimum of six characters, with at least one digit or special character, and two letters. The special characters are punctuation and control keys (a key pressed while holding the control key down).

UNIX systems based on System V may use *password aging*. The password aging system forces users to change their passwords within a specified maximum time period. Password aging also may prevent users from changing their passwords for a specified minimum time period. If password aging is in force on your system, and your password has expired, you will discover that you must create a new password the next time you log in (Figure 2-3).

Figure 2-3: If your password has expired,
you must create a new one before you can log in.

```
login: sandy
Password:
Your password has expired. Choose a new one
/bin/passwd:  Changing password for sandy
Old password:
New password:
Re-enter new password:
$ ▌
```

A disadvantage of password aging is that you may be taken by surprise. Creating a new password that is both a good password and easy-to-remember takes some thought and consideration. Having to come up with a new password at, for instance, 8 o'clock on a Monday morning is not the easiest thing to do. Password aging may also prevent you from changing your password for a period of weeks, preventing you from immediately switching back to your old password. Unfortunately, this also prevents you from replacing a poorly thought out password with a better one (Figure 2-4).

Figure 2-4: If your system uses password aging, and you try
to change your password before the minimum time period has passed,
the **passwd** *command will prevent you from changing your password.*

```
passwd:  Changing password for rik
Old password:
passwd:  Sorry: < 3 weeks since the last change
$ ▌
```

Your system administrator can elect not to enforce a minimum change time, allowing you to replace your password at any time. If you must change your password and the minimum time has not passed, the administrator can always assist you. Another thing that a system administrator can do is use a program that warns you before your password expires. This program is not part of the UNIX system, but is given later in an Appendix to this book.

Abandoning Your Terminal

By entering your login name and password correctly, you have passed the identification and authentication process of your UNIX system. By means of your user id, you are now accountable for your activities until you log off. Any new files you create will be labeled with your user id, and your access to files will be determined by the same user id. This procedure is unlike entering a secure facility, where you may be challenged to present your physical id at any time. Your logged-in terminal represents your identity.

What do you think happens if you walk away from your logged in terminal? Neither the terminal nor the UNIX system knows you have left. It is like leaving your id card lying out on your desk. Anybody who walks by can use your id simply by using your terminal. The person using your terminal has access to the same files you do, and you will be accountable for any actions the person takes.

The best thing you can do is to log out each time you leave your terminal unattended (even for a minute). However, logging out is inconvenient—you can lose track of whatever you were doing. It would be nice if there was a secure, mechanical method for locking your terminal while you were away. Such a method would also need to include the communication line, so that someone couldn't just unplug your terminal and plug in an unlocked terminal in its place. Self-locking terminals will become common in the future, but are not available today. The next best thing to do is use a **lock** script or program (Figure 2-5).

*Figure 2-5: Never leave your terminal unattended. Either log out or use an approved **lock** program to protect your user id.*

```
$ lock
********* LOCKED **********
Password:
$ ▮
```

A **lock** program either requests a password, or uses the same password you use when logging in, to lock your communication line and terminal. You must enter the correct password to unlock the line and terminal. The **lock** program is not standard on most UNIX systems, and an example is provided in this book. (Sun workstations provide **lockscreen** for protecting the workstation display, however, the **lockscreen** program will not prevent someone from resetting the Sun workstation.) There are dangers in using **lock** programs or scripts, in that a poorly designed or incorrectly installed **lock** program can provide a false sense of security, or even steal passwords (a Trojan Horse **lock** program). Use only approved **lock** programs, and never leave your terminal logged in, unattended and unlocked.

Access Control—Permissions and Ownership

The login procedure provides the first line of defense for your UNIX system. Access control procedures provide the second by determining which users can access which files and what they may do with those files. In the model for physical security, objects to be protected are labeled with their classification and category (like Top Secret, Central America), and may also be associated with a list of persons permitted to view the object. In computer security, the operating system must maintain the label on each object and determine the access permitted by each subject (the user).

The UNIX system's access control model is based on the Multics system. Subjects are divided into three categories: the user (owner of the object), the group, and all others. The types of access are read, write, and execute. (Multics included one additional access type—append, the right to add a file to a directory.) Together, the three categories and three types of access produce nine distinct permissions, which are displayed when using the **ls** command (Figures 2-6 and 2-7).

Figure 2-6: The UNIX system has three subject categories and three access types.

	user	group	others
read	r	r	r
write	w	w	w
execute	x	x	x
	rwx	rwx	rwx

Figure 2-7: The **ls** *command with the long listing
option (-l) displays the permissions, owner, and group.*

```
$ ls -l README notes script
-r--r--r--   1 rik      usr      14977 May 25 01:39 README
-rw-------   1 rik      usr       3485 May 23 01:48 notes
-r-xr-xr-x   1 rik      usr       1067 May  1 11:55 script
$ ▌
```

The UNIX system does not follow the physical security model. Labels on objects and access control lists, appear only in (Orange Book) B level versions of the UNIX system. What is common to all UNIX systems is a discretionary access mechanism, where the owner of an object controls access to the object for the owner, a group, and all others. So there is no classification level or categories associated with objects.

The UNIX system is discretionary because the owner of a file may do anything with it. The access control permissions can be adjusted so that even the owner cannot read a file, or, at the other extreme, so that everybody can read and write to the file. In many versions of the UNIX system, the owner of a file can give the file to some other user. Once the file is given away, the original owner has no control over permissions associated with it.

The group category can be used as a substitute for access control lists. Every user can be a member of multiple groups, and the membership of each group can correspond to users with access to a particular category of information. Although the group access control does not have the degree of control provided by the access control list, it does work in a similar manner. For System V-based UNIX systems, the **newgrp** command is used to change between groups. In BSD versions, users are simultaneously members of all groups in which they are included.

File Permissions

Permissions associated with a file control reading, writing, and executing the file. While these access types seem simple, there are still one or two surprises here. The first surprise has to do with how the UNIX system processes access requests. It is possible, for instance, for the owner of a file to have no access to the file, while members of the group and others are permitted all types of access. The UNIX system follows a simple set of rules for determining which category to check for file access:

- If the user is also the owner of the file, check the owner permissions only.
- If the user is not the owner, but is a member of the group owning the file, check the group permissions only.
- If the user is neither the owner nor the group owner, check the other permissions only.

Although there is no reason to do this, you could remove access privileges for yourself from a file, while leaving privileges for the group or others. Since you own the file, only the user permissions apply when you attempt to access the file—group and other permissions are ignored. You can still change the permissions on the file, so can restore privileges for yourself.

The three access types work somewhat as you might expect:

- Read permission means that the file can be read or copied.
- Write permission allows the file to be modified or truncated.
- Execute permission allows the file to executed as a program or script.

If a file permits reading, but not writing, a user may copy the file and add write permission, permitting modification of the copy. The owner of the copy could also add read privileges to the copy, perhaps permitting others to read a restricted file. The ability of the owner to modify file permissions makes default UNIX system security discretionary.

If a file permits writing, but not reading, the file cannot be edited. However, the file can be appended to (have information added to the end of the file), or have its contents replaced entirely. An empty file could be copied to the writeable file, truncating it (making it have zero length).

Execute permission alone permits the execution of compiled programs. Shell scripts require both read and execute permissions, since the commands in the shell script must be read before they can be executed.

Changing Permissions

Programmers have another name for the permissions on a file—it's called the *mode*. The mode contains information about the type of file and permissions for the file. The type of file is established when the file is created, and may not be changed. The owner of the file can change the permissions of the file using the **chmod** (change mode) command.

The **chmod** command accepts a numeric argument or symbolic arguments for changing permissions on a file. The numeric form changes the mode so that it has exactly the value given by the numeric argument. The symbolic form affects just those portions of the mode included in the symbolic argument.

Numeric arguments consist of three digits, with each digit ranging from zero to seven. Read permission is represented by the value four, write by a two, and execute by a one. To combine permissions, the values are added together (Figure 2-8).

Figure 2-8: The numeric argument for the **chmod** *command can be calculated by adding four for read permission, two for write permission, and one for execute permission.*

```
                  user      group    others
read              r 4       r 4      r 4
write             w 2       w 2      w 2
execute           x 1       x 1      x 1
                 ____      ____     ____
all               7         7        7
                  user      group    others
read              r 4       r 4      r 4
write             - 0       - 0      - 0
execute           x 1       x 1      x 1
read &           ____      ____     ____
execute           5         5        5
                  user      group    others
read              r 4       - 0      - 0
write             w 2       - 0      - 0
execute           - 0       - 0      - 0
read/write____             ____     ____
owner only  6               0        0
EXAMPLE:
$ chmod 777 README
$ chmod 555 script
$ chmod 600 notes
$ ls -l README notes script
-rwxrwxrwx   1 rik      usr       14977 May 25 01:39 README
-rw-------   1 rik      usr        3485 May 23 01:48 notes
-r-xr-xr-x   1 rik      usr        1067 May  1 11:55 script
$ ▊
```

If you are used to thinking in octal, you can use octal numbers to represent the numeric argument. Each permission letter is replaced with a one, and a dash is replaced with a zero, so that rwxr-xr-x is represented by 111101101 or 755 in octal. If octal leaves you cold, just remember the values for read (4), write (2), and execute (1), and add.

The symbolic representation uses letters to indicate the three categories and three types of permissions. The category and type are connected with a plus, minus, or equal sign to indicate whether permission is to be added, removed, or set exactly to the indicated value (Figure 2-9). Categories and types can be combined by using them together without spaces, for example, "ug" for user and group, or "rw" for read and write. Commas can be used to combine multiple patterns, for example "o-rw, g-w" for other minus read-write and group minus write.

Figure 2-9: Using symbolic arguments with **chmod** *permits the relative adjustment of file permissions, without necessarily affecting other permissions.*

```
Categories
u     user
g     group
o     others
a     all (user, group, and others)
Permissions
r     read
w     write
x     execute
Connectors
+     add this permission
-     remove this permission
=     set permission exactly equal to this argument
EXAMPLE:
$ ls -l README notes script
-rwxrwxrwx   1 rik        usr            14977 May 25 01:39 README
-rw-------   1 rik        usr             3485 May 23 01:48 notes
-r-xr-xr-x   1 rik        usr             1067 May  1 11:55 script
$ chmod o-rw README
$ chmod u=rwx notes
$ chmod o-rx,g-x,u+w script
$ ls -l README notes script
-rwxrwx--x   1 rik        usr            14977 May 25 01:39 README
-rwx------   1 rik        usr             3485 May 23 01:48 notes
-rwxr-----   1 rik        usr             1067 May  1 11:55 script
$ ▮
```

If **chmod** and its numeric or symbolic arguments seem like too much trouble to remember, the UNIX system permits the creation of shell scripts to store frequently used commands with their arguments. Figure 2-10 shows four very simple one-line shell scripts for protecting files (by removing access for group and others), sharing files (by permitting read access), making scripts executable (by adding read and execute permissions), and making files writeable by all.

Figure 2-10: Creating simple shell scripts for adjusting permissions with **chmod**.

```
$ cat > protect
chmod ug-rwx $*
<control-d>
$ cat  > share
chmod a+r $*
<control-d>
$ cat  > plusx
chmod a+rx $*
<control-d>
$ cat  > plusw
chmod a+w $*
 <control-d>
$ chmod +rx plusx
$ plusx protect share plusw
$ ls -l
total 32
-rwxr-xr-x   1 rik       usr         19 May 25 14:18 plusw
-rwxr-xr-x   1 rik       usr         20 May 25 14:18 plusx
-rwxr-xr-x   1 rik       usr         16 May 25 14:18 protect
-rwxr-xr-x   1 rik       usr         13 May 25 14:18 share
$ ▮
```

You can create your own scripts, but security scripts with a general utility belong in a directory available to all users, and should be protected against surreptitious modification that would make the scripts less secure. Your system administrator should be the one who creates, or at least checks, and installs scripts used by all users.

Ownership of New Files

In the UNIX system, files are owned by the user who created them. The process that actually creates a file is labeled with the user id for the user who logged in and started the process, and this user id is used to denote ownership of the file. Using the **ls -l** command displays not only file permissions, but also the login name of the file's owner. On UNIX systems running System V, the group owner name also appears, following the login name. BSD (Berkeley Software Distribution) versions do not display the group name by default, but will if the group option is added, **ls -lg**.

In System V-based UNIX systems, the group owner of the file is the same as the group for the process creating the file, and a process may be a member of only one group at a time. In BSD, a user, and any process, can be a member of multiple groups simultaneously, so the problem arises "Which group should own a newly created file?" The solution is to make the group owner of a new file the same as the group owner of the directory where the file is created. Instead of inheriting the process' group, the file inherits the directory's group.

The Sun operating system (SunOS) provides both System V-style group inheritance and BSD-style. Setting the set-group-id bit on the directory's permissions forces the BSD-style group inheritance by the directory's group. If the bit is not set, new files inherit the process' group as it was set from the **/etc/passwd** file.

Users on System V UNIX systems can give away files they own with the **chown** (change owner) command. Only the owner of a file (or the superuser) can give the file away. The ability to give files away is a security problem because it allows users to hide their wrong-doing, lessening accountability. BSD systems do not permit users to give files away. Although not allowing users to change file ownership makes security stronger, the BSD system took away the privilege for another reason. BSD systems can enforce quotas, a method for controlling the amount of disk space each user can utilize. Some users found a way around quotas by giving away files so that those files would not show up in the user's quota. By restricting the **chown** capability to the superuser, BSD systems have improved security and plugged the hole in the disk quota system.

Default File Permissions

The file permissions on new files are controlled by two factors. When a process creates a new file, it must specify the desired default permissions. Editors, wordprocessors, and spreadsheets generally request that new files be made readable and writeable by all. *Linkers*, the programs used to create executable programs, request that all permissions be turned on—read, write, execute for all. You may be thinking this is not so good—new files having all permissions open. The UNIX system deals with default permissions with the second factor, the **umask**.

The **umask**, short for *user mask*, masks off or removes certain permissions from all new files. The **umask** command takes a number as an argument, using the same scheme that **chmod** uses, except by denying permissions. To deny others write permission on newly created files, you use the argument two. To deny the group write permissions, and deny others all permissions, you use the argument 27. Table 2-1 shows setting the **umask** and several common values for it.

*Table 2-1: Some common values for the **umask**.*

umask 0	no restrictions (not secure)
umask 2	no write for others (minimum security)
umask 22	no write for group and others (moderate)
umask 27	no group write, no other permissions (strong)
umask 77	no permissions for group or others (strongest)

The **umask** is not used to deny the user any permissions, so arguments to **umask** are one or two digits, corresponding to other, or group and others. Using **umask** without arguments prints the current value for the **umask** (Figure 2-11).

*Figure 2-11: Entering **umask** alone displays the current value of the **umask**. By increasing the value of the **umask** to 77, new files will not have any permissions granted for group and others.*

```
$ umask
22
$ echo Hi > file1
$ ls -l file1
-rw-r--r--    1 rik      usr          3 May 25 12:40 file1
$ umask 77
$ echo Hi > file2
$ ls -l file2
-rw-------    1 rik      usr          3 May 25 12:41 file2
$ ▊
```

Most UNIX systems have a default **umask** that is fairly permissive, for example, two (deny write for others). To control your own **umask** value, you put the **umask** command into the startup file for your shell program. The **.profile** file is used by the Bourne shell and Korn shell, and the **.login** file used by the C shell. One of these files belongs in your home directory, depending on which shell you use.

You must determine the level of security you need to decide which **umask** value to use. The minimum value you can consider using is two, preventing only writing by others. If you want other members of your group to be able to read and write to your files, a **umask** of two is appropriate. To prevent group members from writing in your files, use **umask 22**. To deny any sort of access to anyone (other than yourself), use **umask 77**, the most restrictive value. With a restrictive **umask**, your files are automatically protected unless you use **chmod** to make them accessible by group or others.

Directory Permissions

So far, we have examined file permissions in the UNIX system. In the UNIX system, directories are also files, with some subtle differences. First, the UNIX system recognizes a directory *file type*, which is represented with the letter d in **ls -l** listings. The second difference is that the data in directories are carefully structured. Essentially, the data in directories consist of lists of filenames and associated numbers. You can display the filenames and associated numbers using the i option of **ls** (Figure 2-12).

*Figure 2-12: The **ls** command with the -i option displays
the filenames and associated inode number in a directory.*

```
$ ls -i
6074 README
8714 notes
4481 script
$ ▮
```

Directories contain the names of files. The actual information about the location of parts of the file, the permissions, ownership, group, and so on are contained in the *inode*, or information node, for the file. The number displayed by using the -i option is the inode number associated with each filename. The UNIX system uses the inode numbers found in directories to access the inode itself, with the filename forming a *link* to the inode. UNIX users, for the most part, do not need to know about the existence of the inode, except that it will help in understanding why directories are different than ordinary files.

Let's explore possible ramifications of using UNIX system directories. Since directories contain filenames and inode number pairs, you might wonder if it is possible for more than one filename to be associated with the same inode number. It turns out that it is not only possible, it is very common for there to be multiple filenames associated with one inode number. These multiple filenames are links to the inode. You create links by using the **ln** command to associate the inode number associated with an existing file to a new filename (Figure 2-13).

*Figure 2-13: The **ln** command makes a link to an inode by using an existing filename to connect a new filename to the associated inode. The number of links to an inode appears after the permissions and before the owner in **ls -l** listings.*

```
$ ln notes notes2
$ ls -la
total 72
drwxr-xr-x   2 rik     usr        96 May 26 12:23 .
drwxr-xr-x   6 rik     usr       704 May 26 12:40 ..
-r--r--r--   1 rik     usr     14977 May 25 08:39 README
-rw-------   2 rik     usr      3485 May 23 08:48 notes
-rw-------   2 rik     usr      3485 May 23 08:48 notes2
-r-xr-xr-x   1 rik     usr      1067 May  1 11:55 script
$ ▮
```

In Figure 2-13, information for the filenames "notes" and "notes2" appears identical, except for the filenames. The digit "2" in front of the owner's name represents two links to the same inode, from which the information for the two filenames was taken. For the sake of security, there are two things you need to be aware of. A file with multiple links has the same ownership and permissions for every link. Someone who is not the owner of a file may make a link to that file, but having the link does not change the permissions on the file.

The second point to watch is when removing files that have multiple links. The **rm** command actually removes the directory entry (the link) to a file, not the file itself. When the last link is removed, the information about the file in the inode is cleared. Before removing a file, check to see if there are multiple links to it. If the link count on a file were two, and you removed your link, the file still exists. Only the superuser (or owner of the file system) can use the **ncheck** command to find the other link to the file. However, if the file is your file, you can empty the file before removing your link to it, preventing use of the file's contents through the other link to the file (Figure 2-14).

*Figure 2-14: When removing a file that has multiple links, the command **echo** filename truncates the file, making the other link to the file useless.*

```
$ ls -l notes notes2
-rw-------   2 rik     usr      3485 May 23 08:48 notes
-rw-------   2 rik     usr      3485 May 23 08:48 notes2
$ echo > notes
$ rm notes
$ ls -l notes2
-rw-------   1 rik     usr         0 May 26 18:00 notes2
$ ▮
```

In Figure 2-13, you should also notice that the directory, ".", has two links to it, and the parent directory, "..", has six links. Every directory has at least two links, the "." entry in the directory and the directory name that appears in the parent directory. Links to directories are made by the UNIX system when the **mkdir** command creates new directories. Only the superuser can use the **ln** command to create additional links to directories, and it is not recommended. In BSD versions, *symbolic* links can be made to directories by using the -s option to the BSD **ln**. Symbolic links are files that contain the pathname of the other files that they are symbolically linked to, unlike direct links. Making a symbolic link does not affect the link count (Figure 2-15).

Figure 2-15: Symbolics links are indicated by the letter "l" in the permissions shown with **ls -l**; *the symbolic link consists of the name of the file it was linked to and does not change the link count.*

```
% echo Hi > notes
% ln -s notes notes2
% ls -l
total 2
-rw-rw-r--  1 rik           3 Jun  4 1839 notes
lrwxrwxrwx  1 rik           5 Jun  4 1839 notes2 -> notes
% echo Ho >> notes2
% ls -l
total 2
-rw-rw-r--  1 rik           6 Jun  4 1840 notes
lrwxrwxrwx  1 rik           5 Jun  4 1839 notes2 -> notes
% ▮
```

Now that the difference between files and filenames in a directory has been described, you are prepared to understand how directory access permissions work differently than ordinary file permissions:

- Read permission on a directory permits listing the filenames in that directory.
- Write and Execute on a directory permits changing or removing filenames in that directory.
- Execute (also called *search* permission) allows access to files which are referenced by filenames in that directory.

Read permission alone on a directory permits listing the directory with **ls**. Listing the directory is equivalent to reading the filenames in the directory. However, if execute permission is absent, performing a long listing with **ls -l** will not be permitted. Creating a long listing requires access to the files, which is not permitted without execute permission.

Write permission permits the use of the **mv** and **rm** commands if execute permission is also present. If a user has write and execute permission on a directory, that user can remove any filename in that directory, *regardless of the permissions and ownership of the file.* If the filename removed is the last link to a file, that file's inode is cleared. This is very important. Because filenames and the files themselves are different entities in the UNIX system, a filename may be removed by anyone with write and execute permission in the directory containing the filename (Figure 2-16).

Figure 2-16: If a user has write and execute permission in a directory,
that user may remove filenames even if he or she has no access to the file.

```
$ chmod 700 script
$ chown sandy script
$ ls -l
total 40
-r--r--r--   1 rik     usr        14977 May 25 01:39 README
-rwx------   1 sandy   usr         1067 May  1 11:55 script
$ ls -ld
drwxrwxr-x   2 rik     usr          128 May 26 18:26 .
$ rm script
script: 700 mode ? y
$ ▌
```

In Figure 2-16, the user rik changes the access permissions on the file "script" so that only the owner of the file has access. Then, rik gives the file away with **chown**. But since rik still has write and execute permission in the directory, rik can remove the filename "script". The **rm** command does warn rik with the question "script: 700 mode ?", but rik ignores the warning by responding with "y". The warning indicates that the permissions on the file do not permit rik to modify the file; but it is only a polite warning, and does not prevent rik from removing the file.

Write and execute permission also permit renaming filenames and creating new files in a directory. Together, these privileges allow setting up Trojan Horses for unsuspecting users who have not set their directory permissions accordingly. This type of Trojan Horse is described later in this chapter.

Execute permission is also called *search* permission. Search permission permits access to the files linked by the filenames in a directory. Without search permission, directories can be listed, but filenames cannot be changed or removed, or the files referenced by the filenames accessed. Figure 2-17 shows how search permission affects files in a directory.

Figure 2-17: Removing execute (search) permission from "dir1" with **chmod -x** *makes the file "hidden" inaccessible even to its owner.*

```
$ mkdir dir1
$ echo Hidden file > dir1/hidden
$ ls dir1
hidden
$ cat dir1/hidden
Hidden file
$ chmod -x dir1
$ ls -ld dir1
drw-rw-r--   2 rik     usr            48 May 26 19:04 dir1
$ ls dir1
hidden
$ cat dir1/hidden
cat: cannot open dir1/hidden
$ rm dir1/hidden
rm: dir1/hidden non-existent
$ █
```

Removing execute permission for others, or group and others, on a directory makes files and subdirectories listed in that directory unaccessible by others, or group and others. Removing execute permission also prevents the renaming of removing of filenames. While this might seem an ideal way to protect files and subdirectories, there is another approach that you can use (Figure 2-18).

Figure 2-18: Directories without read access prevent listing the directory without preventing access to files within that directory.

```
$ chmod 111 dir1
$ ls -ld dir1
d--x--x--x   2 rik     usr            48 May 26 19:04 dir1
$ cat dir1/hidden
Hidden file
$ ls dir1
can not access directory dir1
$ █
```

Removing read access to a directory prevents listing the contents of that directory. If a user does not know the exact name of a file, then that file cannot be accessed. Wildcards will not work since the shell, which expands wildcards (like *) into filenames, must read the directory in order to do the expansion. The advantage of permitting execution instead of reading (as in Figure 2-17) is programs that operate using the other access category, like **uucp**, **lp**, or **lpr**, can still access files. Suggestions for adjusting file and directory permissions are given later in this chapter.

Startup Files

Many UNIX commands look for startup files. Startup files contain configuration information used to customize the environment to the user's satisfaction. You use your startup files to establish a secure working environment. You must protect your startup files from modification by others, who could make you do anything by slipping commands into your startup files.

The most commonly used UNIX shells, the Bourne, Korn, or C shells, always check for startup files in the user's home directory. Shell startup files are used to set the PATH, the **umask**, terminal type, other variables, and to define shell functions or aliases. Startup files for the shells function in the same manner as do shell scripts. The commands found in shell startup files get executed when the shell is launched at login time, or, in the case of the C shell, each time a new shell starts.

The Bourne shell only looks at startup files during the login process. A system-wide startup file, **/etc/profile**, is executed first. The system administrator can place commands in the **/etc/profile** that will become part of all Bourne shell users' environments. The **/etc/profile** provides an excellent mechanism for providing good default values for users (Figure 2-19).

*Figure 2-19: The **/etc/profile** performs setup functions for all users of the Bourne shell. It is the place to establish a good default **umask** and PATH.*

```
$ cat /etc/profile
cat /etc/motd           # display the message of the day
. /etc/TIMEZONE         # set the TZ (timezone) variable
umask 27                # establish a default umask
PATH=/bin:/usr/bin:/usr/bin/X11:/usr/lbin:.
export PATH             # establish a safe PATH
$ ▮
```

Each user may also have a personal version of **/etc/profile** kept in the home directory and named **.profile**. The **.profile** gets executed after the commands in **/etc/profile**, so that each user may override the definitions made in the system-wide file. While this approach permits maximum flexibility, it has a downfall of allowing users to change things they would be better off leaving alone.

A Good PATH

The first thing *not* to do is to reset your **umask** to a less secure value. The **umask** and its purpose were described previously. The second is to use a safe PATH. The PATH defines the directories searched for commands entered to the shell. These directories are searched in order, so the first directory in the PATH is the first searched, and so on. For many years, UNIX systems came delivered with a very unsafe PATH, that included the current directory, ".", first. Having the current directory first is very convenient for UNIX system programmers who may be testing new versions of commands in the current directory. It is a disaster for everybody else.

> *Wrong* `PATH=:/bin:/usr/bin:/usr/bin/lbin`

Having the wrong PATH permits a "bad guy" to insert a version of a Trojan Horse in your search PATH. A Trojan Horse is an instruction within a program that allows the program to function normally, but also perform illegal functions. For example, a script named **ls** could be created in the **/tmp** directory, which is writeable by all. Then, any user with the wrong PATH who tried to execute **ls** while in the **/tmp** directory would get a nasty surprise (Figure 2-20).

In Figure 2-20, I created the Trojan Horse, then fell prey to it. In real life, you would be unaware that a Trojan Horse existed, perhaps even after being caught by one. Changing the permissions on someone's home directory is very mild, and not very subtle. Trojan Horse scripts can be more vicious, for example, removing all of a user's files, or much more subtle, by adjusting permissions on a single file or directory. The Trojan Horse could also be a program, or be designed so that it removed itself after doing damage.

Figure 2-20: A relatively benign example of what can happen when the wrong PATH is used. Instead of executing the real **ls***, in* **/bin***, the script named* **ls** *gets executed, removing all permissions for the user's home directory, before executing* **/bin/ls***.*

```
$ cd /tmp
$ echo $PATH
:/bin:/usr/bin:/usr/bin/X11:/usr/lbin
$ cat > ls
chmod 000 $HOME
/bin/ls $*
<control-D>
$ chmod +x ls
$ ls
Ex00316
Rx00316
$ cd
Permission denied
$ ▮
```

Besides the current directory, a directory containing locally added commands is a good place for inserting Trojan Horses. Some system administrators permit any user to add new programs to the local command directory, such as **/usr/lbin** or **/usr/local/bin**. These directories must be treated like system directories, and the system administrator should check out new additions and install them personally.

Good   `PATH=/bin:/usr/bin:/usr/lbin:`

A good PATH places the system directories where most commands are found early in the PATH. System directories, like **/bin** and **/usr/bin** must precede both local directories and the current directory. Note that a leading or trailing colon, or two colons together (::) represent the current directory in the PATH variable.

The C shell uses slightly different syntax for setting the PATH. The **setenv** shell command sets the PATH variable and exports the PATH into the environment. In the C shell, the PATH variable is set using all lowercase letters, *path*, unlike the Bourne shell.

`setenv path=(/bin /usr/bin /usr/bin/X11 /usr/lbin .)`

Spaces separate components of the PATH, and a dot indicates the current directory. The entire path must be enclosed in parentheses.

The important thing to remember is to arrange to use a good PATH by setting your PATH with your **.profile** or **.login**. Always put the system directories containing commands before your current directory and local directories containing commands. If you want to execute a command in the current directory, all you need to do is precede the command name with two characters, **./**. For example, if I am testing a program named **wc**, I don't want to invoke the version of **wc** in the **/usr/bin** directory. I can ensure that I invoke the correct version by specifying all or part of the pathname to my **wc** command, for example, **./wc**, or **../mybin/wc**. Typing two or more extra characters is a small price to pay to avoid being caught by a Trojan Horse.

Protecting Startup Files

Your startup files contain instructions crucial to setting up a secure environment. However, if your startup files are writeable by group or others, anyone can alter your startup information. An unfriendly user could change your PATH, or set your **umask** to 0 so that it leaves your new files unprotected.

However, the trickier "bad guys" will do something else. They can insert instructions that they would like you to execute into your startup file. The next time you log in, the added instructions are executed *by you*. The added instructions may do something obvious, like log you out immediately. More likely, the new commands will perform a more subtle task.

As an example, let's suppose you are responsible for determining who will receive Christmas bonuses, and how large each employee's bonus will be. You are keeping the information in a file named *bonuses* that is readable and writeable by the owner only. If someone else discovers that your startup file is writeable, they could add a single line to the startup file,

```
mail toni < bonuses
```

When you log in the next time, a copy of the bonuses file will be mailed to toni. The **mail** command will complete without any messages as usual, so you will not notice anything different while you are logging in. The slight delay caused by the extra command will either be unnoticeable, or easily explained away by thinking that the system is busier than usual.

So now you have removed write permission for group and others on your startup file. However, let's suppose you have allowed write for a group on your home directory. This permits a member of your group, bobby, to try the approach in Figure 2-21.

Figure 2-21: A member of your group takes advantage of write
permission on your HOME directory by moving the original **.profile**
to **.oprofile**, *and creating a new version with additional commands.*

```
$ cd yourhome
$ mv .profile .oprofile
$ cp .oprofile .profile
$ cat >> .profile
mail bobby < bonuses
. .oprofile
mv -f .oprofile .profile
<control-d>
$ [cursor]
```

The new version of the your **.profile** contains a command to mail the bonuses file to bobby. The line ". .oprofile" executes the original **.profile** script. Then, the new **.profile** renames the old version. This removes the new version of **.profile** and replaces the original version. Once again, all you would notice is a slightly longer execution time. The only trace left by this approach is that the modify time on your HOME directory will be changed by the move.

Other UNIX commands look for startup files. Some look only in your HOME directory, while others will look both in your current directory and then in your HOME directory. The **vi** editor is a good example of the latter. The **vi** looks for the file **.exrc** first in your current directory, and next in your HOME directory, but only if the startup file wasn't found in your current directory. The **.exrc** file can contain commands for setting built-in variables in **vi** (or **ex** and **view**), defining abbreviations, and mapping key sequences. The **.exrc** startup file can also contain shell escapes, permitting the execution of commands while **vi** starts up (Figure 2-22).

If you start **vi** and there is a shell escape in the startup file, your only warning will be an exclamation point that appears briefly before the screen is cleared. In Figure 2-22, the exclamation point appears after the command **ex** was invoked, and remains visible since **ex** is a line editor.

*Figure 2-22: An example of an **.exrc** file written in a public directory.*
*Starting **ex**, **vi**, or **view** in the **/tmp** directory executes the command*
chmod +rw $HOME/.profile, *making your **.profile** readable and writeable by anyone.*

```
$ cat /tmp/.exrc
!chmod +rw $HOME/.profile
:se wrapmargin=15 showmatch
$ ls -l .profile
-rw-------   1 rik     usr          112 Apr 26 15:58 .profile
$ cd /tmp
$ ex temp
!
No lines in the buffer
"temp" [New file]
:q
$ ls -l $HOME/.profile
-rw-rw-rw-   1 rik     usr          112 Apr 26 15:58 .profile
$ ▊
```

BSD versions of UNIX have made the **.exrc** startup files safer by ignoring **.exrc** files that are not owned by the user. In System V, Release 4, **vi** will only execute the **.exrc** in your HOME directory, unless you set a variable permitting it to do otherwise. If you are using versions of System V before Release 4, do not start **vi** or the related commands **ex** and **view** in publicly writeable directories, unless you check for **.exrc** first. You must also protect the versions of **.exrc** in your own directory tree.

Other UNIX commands use startup files. For example, the **Mail** or **mailx** program (two names for the same program) reads the **.mailrc** file in your $HOME directory for configuration, and will also execute commands using a shell, much like **vi**. Interactive commands, such as editors, wordprocessors, and debuggers, are the type of programs that look for startup files. If you are uncertain if a particular program looks for a startup file, check in the manual entry for the program. The *FILES* section lists files that are used by the command. Startup files often begin with a dot (so they do not appear in **ls** listings by default) and end in *rc*.

Correcting Permissions

I hope you are convinced that there is danger in not correcting permissions in your HOME directory tree. Not protecting your files and directories guarantees that someone with only a basic understanding of UNIX commands can read or modify your files, or remove files and directories. Through the use of Trojan

Horse programs, another user can make use of your access privileges to compromise any data to which you have access. Or, a Trojan Horse version of the **su** program can steal the superuser password, and gain total access to your system.

There are certain files (your startup files) that you must protect unequivocably, along with your HOME directory. Beyond that, you have to make some decisions. Do you want to permit your group to write to files or modify directories without your explicit permission? The choice is to either remove write permission from group or to permit it. The safer approach is to remove write permission. If you wish to permit writing in a file, you can adjust (**chmod**) permissions for that file. And if someone wishes to give you a copy of a file, the user can either mail you a copy, or tell you where to find the file and permit you to make your own copy. This method insures that you never need to grant write for group in any of your directories.

You should also decide if you want members of your group even reading your files. Remember that if someone can read a file, they can copy it and do whatever they want to with the copy. You can make files that you want to share readable by the group or others. No read or write for group and others is the most secure option. In the following example, I assume that you will permit members of your group to read your files and list your directories.

Figure 2-23: Command to correct permissions. On systems without the **xargs** *command, use the second version of the* **find** *command, (or* **chmod -R 751**, *the recursive option to the BSD-version of* **chmod***).*

```
$ find . -print | xargs chmod 751
find: cannot chdir ./noperms
chmod: can't change ./.exrc
$ ▮
(Or, for BSD systems without xargs)

% find . -exec chmod 751 {} \;
find: cannot chdir ./noperms
chmod: can't change ./.exrc
% ▮
```

If you do not want members of your group reading your files or listing your directories, change your permissions to 711 instead of 751. In Figure 2-23, you can use the **xargs** command if you are working on a System V-based UNIX system, or a Sun workstation running Sun OS 4.0 or later. BSD-based UNIX systems do not provide **xargs**, which expands arguments and speeds up command execution by executing **chmod** once for many files.

Also in Figure 2-23, there were two error messages. The **find** command could not change directory to the *./noperms* directory. The permissions on *./noperms* directory do not permit the user to search it. The file *././exrc* is owned by another user, and **chmod** cannot be used on files owned by other users (Figure 2-24).

Figure 2-24: Fixing the problems from Figure 2-23. The noperms directory does not include search (execute) permission, but using **chmod** *fixes it. The .exrc file belonged to another user; after checking its contents, you can make a copy of it and remove the version owned by another user.*

```
$ ls -l ./.exrc ./noperms
drw-r-----   2 rik    usr          32 Jun  1 12:46 ./noperms
-rwxr-x--x   1 jon    usr          20 May 28 12:51 .exrc
$ chmod +x noperms
$ find noperms -print | xargs chmod 751
$ mv .exrc jons.exrc
$ cat jons.exrc
:set wrapmargin=15
$ cp jons.exrc .exrc
$ chmod 751 .exrc
$ rm jons.exrc
jons.exrc: 751 mode ? y
$ ▮
```

In Figure 2-24, the **ls** command displays the permissions and ownership of the problem files, which were discovered while correcting permissions. The *noperms* directory lacked search permission, which I restored using **chmod +x**. After restoring search permission, the permission changing **find** command must be run a second time, since **find** could not check the *./noperms* directory previously.

The *.exrc* file was owned by the user jon—this is not good. Perhaps jon copied his own **.exrc** file to my HOME directory so I could use it. But, if jon owns this startup file, he can edit it later, perhaps introducing a Trojan Horse.

To change the ownership of the *.exrc* file, I first renamed it using **mv**, then listed its contents with **cat**. Jon's *.exrc* does not contain any suspicious commands, so I created my own copy of it with **cp** and removed Jon's copy. My copy of *.exrc* is owned by me, and I corrected permissions on the file with **chmod 751 .exrc**.

If the permission correcting **find** command (in Figure 2-23) uncovers directories owned by others, you might need the help of your system administrator. Examine the contents of these directories using **ls -l**, and try to determine why you have these directories in your HOME directory tree. If the contents appear benign, and are owned by a user you know, you can ask that user to give you ownership of these directories. If you are uncertain as to the purpose of these directories, or they are owned by users unknown to you, bring the problem to the attention of your system or security administrator.

Keeping Your HOME Safe

Once you have corrected permissions and ownership in your HOME directory tree, keep it that way. You can do so by using a good password, and by setting up your startup files correctly. The elements necessary in secure startup files are a safe PATH and a secure **umask**. We have already discussed these topics, but before showing you example startup files, I'd like to mention two other ideas that you can use.

The first idea is to have your last login time presented each time you log in. BSD versions of UNIX do this for you, but System V-based versions do not. To create your own display, you use a file named *.login_time* as a time stamp, and list the *inode change* time. The inode change time gets updated whenever a file is modified, or the inode is changed, for example, by changing permissions. The inode contains two other time stamps, the *access* time (last time the file was read, and the *modify* time (last time the file was written). The modify time gets displayed by default when you use the **ls -l** command. To display the inode change time, you use **ls -lc**.

You can add three lines to your **.profile** file. The first line collects the inode change date by using the Bourne shell's **set** command. Backquotes surround the **ls** command so that its output becomes the arguments to the **set** command. The next line uses **echo** to display the time stamp, and the third line updates the time stamp with **touch** (Figure 2-25). (If your version of the **ls** command does not display the group owner by default, you will need to replace the arguments "$6 $7 $8" with "$5 $6 $7".)

Figure 2-25: The **set** *command places the output of the* **ls -lc** *command into the shell's number arguments, and* **echo** *prints the sixth, seventh, and eighth arguments. The* **touch** *command updates the time stamp.*

```
$ cd
$ set - 'ls -lc .login_time'
$ echo "Last login time was $6 $7 $8."
Last login time was Jun 12 10:52.
$ touch .login_time
$ ▮
```

Each time you log in, you should notice the last login time displayed. If the time displayed does not correspond to your last login time, someone else has logged into your account. Change your password immediately and tell your system or security administrator that your account may have been broken into, and give him or her the date displayed by the last login message.

There is one other problem brought to you courtesy of new terminal technology. Some of the most popular terminals include the ability to store information in the terminal's memory, and play it back. A clever system breaker decided that this was a neat way to write a Trojan Horse. The Trojan Horse sends the smart terminal the codes that tell it to load local memory. The Trojan Horse sends the commands it wants executed to the terminal, which saves the commands in local memory. Finally, the Trojan Horse sends the codes that replay the terminal's local memory. The local memory is sent back to whatever shell or program that the logged-in person is currently using, so that shell executes the commands as if the person had entered them.

It is easy to disable this threat, by using the command **mesg n**. The **mesg** command removes write permission for group and others on your login port. The side-effect of **mesg n** is that other users can no longer **write** or **talk** to you. The **write** command allows other logged-in users to send characters to your terminal, which is what the terminal Trojan Horse does. Wyse terminals, and terminals that emulate Wyse terminals, are among the smart terminals that fall prey to this Trojan Horse. If you are certain that your terminal does not have some local memory (or buffer) that can be downloaded from the UNIX system and uploaded again, you can permit writing to your terminal. If you are not sure, ask your system or security administrator, or look in the terminal's manual in the table of special escape codes for commands that load local memory or buffers.

Figures 2-26 and 2-27 provide minimal startup files for the Bourne shell and the C shell. If you are using the Korn shell, you can use the **.profile**. file, as the Korn shell works like the Bourne shell. Your startup files should contain at least these four security elements:

- Setting a correct PATH
- Setting a restrictive **umask**
- Prevent writing to your terminal
- Display your last login time

Most BSD-based UNIX systems will display your last login time without you having to add anything to your startup file. If you don't see your last login time when you login, modify your startup file.

Figure 2-26: An example Bourne shell startup file,
.profile*, containing the elements necessary to maintain security.*

```
$ cat .profile
PATH=/bin:/usr/bin:/usr/lbin:/usr/bin/X11:.
export PATH
umask 27
mesg n
set - 'ls -lc .login_time'
echo "Last login time was $6 $7 $8."
touch .login_time
$ ▉
```

Figure 2-27: An example C shell startup file, **.login***, containing necessary security commands. Notice that the C shell's* **set** *command works differently than the Bourne shell's.*

```
% cat .login
set path=(/bin /usr/bin /usr/lbin /usr/bin/X11 .)
umask 27
mesg n
set arg=('ls -lc .login_time')
echo Last login time was $arg[6] $arg[7] $arg[8].
touch .login_time
% ▉
```

File Encryption

Even if you have set the file protection mode so that only you can read your files and directories, there are other users who can still read your files. Every UNIX system has special accounts used for administering to the system, for example, by performing routine backups of all files. Without the privileged accounts, each user would be responsible for backing up his or her own files, which is not desirable. However, the ability to backup files implies the ability to read files, and indeed, the account used for file backup also permits reading any file, regardless of the permissions.

Your UNIX system may include commands with encryption capabilities. According to Federal law, only domestic UNIX systems may be equipped with the DES encryption scheme, so systems destined for foreign distribution will be lacking these facilities. Unfortunately, many manufacturers do not include the encryption commands, so they do not have to maintain distinct foreign and domestic versions of the UNIX system. If your system lacks an encryption command, a simple encryption program is provided in an Appendix.

Although there are some problems with encrypting files, encryption does provide you with a greater measure of privacy, and to a lesser extent, security. There are four problems with UNIX encryption, with the first three problems common to any encryption scheme:

- The encryption is based on a password, which must be a good password or the data can easily be decrypted
- If unencrypted and encrypted versions of a file exist, the password can be discovered and other files decrypted
- Encrypting files changes their contents from ASCII to data, possibly drawing attention to the files
- Techniques for decrypting files using the UNIX encryption scheme without knowing the password are known

It is important that you realize that these problems exist, so you do not rely on encryption to protect your secrets. Let's examine the UNIX **crypt** command to better understand what these problems are.

The **crypt** command reads information redirected to it, encrypts the information, and writes it to a redirected file. The **crypt** command either reads a password from the command line, or requests a password after it is invoked. The output file will be the same size of the input file (Figure 2-28).

Figure 2-28: Using **crypt** *to encrypt the file named "in" using the*
password WasteNOT. Using **crypt** *with the same password decrypts the file.*

```
$ cat > in
This is a private message!
<control-D>
$ crypt WasteNOT < in > out
$ ls -l in out
-rw-r-----    1 rik        usr            27 Jun 13 22:23 in
-rw-r-----    1 rik        usr            27 Jun 13 22:23 out
$ rm in
$ cat out
 s3h1B*ijq#!mn>f|o]X
$ crypt <out
Enter key:
This is a private message!
$ ▮
```

When encrypting files, the output files will all have exactly the same size.
However, the files will not appear the same length if displayed because the encrypted file contains non-printing characters. In Figure 2-28, the password was
entered on the command line during the first invocation of **crypt**. In the second
invocation, **crypt** prompted for a password. The password is not echoed when
crypt prompts for one, which prevents others from learning the password by
watching your screen.

The same password must be used when encrypting or decrypting a file. The
password is used to build the encryption tables that **crypt** utilizes to encrypt or
decrypt files. Because the **crypt** program must rely on passwords, everything that
was previously said about passwords applies to ones used with **crypt**. If you
don't use good passwords, it will be easy for someone else to decrypt your encrypted files.

Even though your password gets displayed when it appears on the command line, there is one advantage to entering the password that way. Unlike the
passwd command, **crypt** doesn't require you to enter the same password twice
before proceeding. (If you don't include a password with the command, **crypt**
will prompt you to enter a "key".) If you mistyped the password you are using,
crypt will encrypt your file with a password nobody knows—including you!
Since you must remove the unencrypted copy of your file after encryption, it is
possible to lose your file because you don't know the password. Also, if you forget your password you will be unable to decrypt your file.

Once you encrypt a file, it appears to be data to someone who might be browsing through your directory. The browsing intruder can use the **file** command to determine the likely types of files in your directories (if the intruder can read your files). A few data files in a directory containing wordprocessing files may serve to draw attention to the encrypted files. So, even if you encrypt files, it is important to prevent reading whenever possible.

Some editors incorporate the standard UNIX encryption mechanism, permitting you to edit encrypted files without creating a decrypted copy. The **vi** family of editors and **emacs** will request a password if you invoke them with the **-x** flag (Figure 2-29).

*Figure 2-29: The **vi** family of editors permits the editing of encrypted files. To print an encrypted file, decrypt the file and pipe the output to the line printing spooler program.*

```
$ ex -x out
"out", 1 line, 27 characters
key:
:1p
This is a private message!
:q
$ cat out
 s3h1B*ijq#!mn>f|o]X
$ crypt WasteNOT < out | lpr
$ 
```

As mentioned previously, the method used by **crypt** is breakable. A set of crypt-breaking tools exists in the public domain, and a paper was published describing weaknesses in **crypt** in 1984. Decrypting files relies on traditional **crypt** analysis routines, such as letter frequencies. You can make your encryption more secure by packing or compressing your files before encrypting them.

The **pack** program on System V systems and **compress** on BSD-based systems both perform data compression on files. These programs work by building tables of frequently repeated patterns, and replacing these patterns with an index into the table. The table gets stored with the compressed file, which typically gets shortened anywhere from 20% to 70%, depending on the patterns found in the file. Compression won't work on shorter files, when the compressed version would be longer than the uncompressed version, and **pack** and **compress** will quit without doing anything (Figure 2-30).

*Figure 2-30: Packing a file before encrypting destroys the patterns used
to break the encryption. Packing or compression only works on larger files.*

```
$ ls -l large small
-rwxr-x--x   1 rik     usr        36359 May 24 11:19 large
-rw-r-----   1 rik     usr         1478 Jun 13 15:01 small
$ pack small
pack: small: no saving - file unchanged
$ pack large
pack: large: 40.1% Compression
$ crypt < large.z > large.out
Enter key:
$ rm large.z
$ █
```

To get an encrypted and packed file back, first decrypt the file, and then use
unpack or **decompress** to restore the file. The **pack** command replaces the name
of the packed file with the filename followed by **.z**, and **compress** puts a **.Z** at the
end of a compressed file. Both commands remove the original version of the file
after compression. Before either will unpack a packed file, it must have the
proper suffix, either .z or .Z, so create files by these names when decrypting with
crypt (Figure 2-31).

*Figure 2-31: To get back a packed and encrypted file, first decrypt the file using the same
key and creating a file with the proper suffix, then* **unpack** *the file.*

```
$ crypt < large.out > large.z
Enter key:
$ unpack large
unpack: large: unpacked
$ █
```

Conclusion

This chapter covers the basic security topics that every user must know. By following the examples, you can help keep your system secure. But your job doesn't
end here. You must remain alert for unusual files that you may find in your directories, files owned by other users, and unusual events. If you have taken the
time to read this book, you are probably serious about security. Don't let possible
security violations slip by. Report your suspicions to your system or security administrator. And remember these basic points:

- Use a good password; one that is easy to remember, not a name or in any dictionary; nonsense phrases are best.
- Never leave a logged-in terminal or workstation unattended; either log out or use a safe **lock** program.
- Protect all your files and directories from writing by group and others.
- Use a restrictive **umask** (27) that removes all permissions for others and write for group on all new files and directories.
- Use a safe PATH, with system directories, like **/bin** and **/usr/bin** *before* the current directory.
- Watch for your last login time as you login; if you don't see one displayed, edit your startup files.
- Check the permissions of your startup files, and watch out for startup files in publicly writeable directories (like **/tmp**).
- Prevent group and others from writing to your terminal if it has the capability to upload and download local memory.

Chapter 3

Security for System Administrators

System and Security Administrators

Every user of a UNIX system is responsible for security, but some users have additional responsibilities. These are users who have been selected to administer to the whole system, and have special access privileges to help them with their work. A *system administrator* is a user who knows the root password and is responsible for maintaining one or more UNIX systems. A *security administrator* has the more narrowly defined focus of maintaining system security, performing security audits, and examining audit trails. Only UNIX systems operating at the higher *Orange Book* levels (C2 and B) will have security administrators.

The system administrator has, through the root's *superuser* privileges, the ability to access any file or directory, regardless of the file's ownership and permissions. Unlike an ordinary user, whose responsibilities ends outside his or her HOME directory tree, the superuser must manage all the files in all file systems. If a user is not managing permissions or startup files correctly, the system administrator must help and educate this user. The system administrator must also manage communications security.

The system administrator can also, in most UNIX systems, completely hide all traces of wrongdoing, if that person is so motivated. One of the requirements of *Orange Book* level B systems is to prevent any user from performing security related activities that cannot be audited. In non-secure versions of the UNIX system, an expert system administrator can cover *every* trace of any activity. Although completely hiding evidence is difficult, the expert who remembers all details can certainly do so by using the tools and programs provided by the UNIX system.

If you expect to have a secure UNIX system, the system administrator must be trustworthy and competent. The expertise to break system security and hide the evidence is not limited to system administrators—programmers are even more likely to break system security in subtle ways. Even not-so-subtle break-ins can be difficult to track down, even for a good system administrator. Since not every system administrator can be an expert, it is a good idea to provide expert consulting services for your secure systems.

If you are a system administrator, you are a special target for would-be system breakers. Your special privilege, becoming the superuser, attracts system breakers like flies to honey. The security principles for users, explained in Chapter 2, become even more important for system administrators. A single chink in your armor is enough for a clever intruder or cracker, and your privilege makes your files, directories, and password targets for close scrutiny. Become a paragon of good security practices.

Security administrators, in the systems that have them, must practice the same caution as system administrators. Although the security administrator will not have the same privileges as the system administrator, the privileges involved are important to the more sophisticated security breaker—the ability to cover up evidence. Practice good user security.

System Administrator Security Duties

Besides maintaining the security of their ordinary user accounts, the system administrators have other duties. The system administrator has the responsibility for tracking the passwords for all users. The password file itself is a target for system crackers, and the system administrator can do much to improve security by watching over the password file. The ownership and permissions of every file, but in particular those files owned by system accounts, are also the responsibility of the system administrator.

Of the system's files, there are special files for devices that may appear harmless, but can be the source of much trouble. Some programs have special privileges associated with them that involve the set-user-id principle, and these files deserve special attention. Finally, the system administrator is responsible for communications, which will be the subject of Chapter 4, and detecting attacks, which is covered in Chapter 5. Techniques for increased awareness of activity and discovering traces of past events are also topics for Chapter 5.

The Password File

Passwords are the keys to your UNIX system, and the **/etc/passwd** file contains these keys. The **/etc/passwd** file is the system's user database, and includes information about every user account. The **/etc/passwd** file also describes special accounts, the *system* accounts, which are used for administration purposes, or to denote ownership of files.

Subtle mistakes in the **/etc/passwd** file can make your UNIX system unusable. Although most UNIX systems have a command for checking the **/etc/passwd** file, it is seldom used. Small changes in an ordinary user's account can give that user special privileges, since the **/etc/passwd** file is the source that establishes system privileges. In this area, the **/etc/group** file has a role which will also be discussed.

The **/etc/passwd** file also holds users' passwords in encrypted form. Although the encryption used is unbreakable; that is, encrypted passwords cannot be decrypted, there are well-known techniques for guessing passwords. There is much you can do as a system administrator to make guessing passwords more difficult. System V versions of UNIX also incorporate a mechanism for aging passwords, which forces users to change their passwords at reasonable intervals.

Structure of the Password File

The **/etc/passwd** file has a very inflexible structure for each line. Each line, or *account entry*, has seven fields separated by colons (:). If an account entry is missing a field, that account *and all accounts that follow it* will be ignored by the UNIX system. Figure 3-1 shows the seven fields.

Figure 3-1: Each account entry in the
/etc/passwd *file must have seven colon-separated fields.*

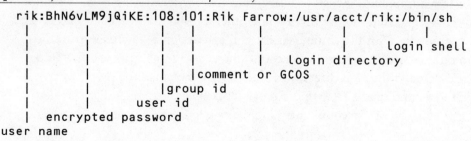

```
rik:BhN6vLM9jQiKE:108:101:Rik Farrow:/usr/acct/rik:/bin/sh
 |       |          |   |       |             |          |
 |       |          |   |       |             |       login shell
 |       |          |   |       |         login directory
 |       |          |   |    comment or GCOS
 |       |          |  group id
 |       |        user id
 |   encrypted password
user name
```

User Name   The first field contains the *user name*. The user name is used as part of the authentication procedure during login. The login name can be up to eight characters long, and should consist entirely of lowercase letters. Certain UNIX commands, such as **ls**, **find**, and **chown**, use the **/etc/passwd** file to convert between a user name and the user id number that labels files.

As mentioned in Chapter 2, user names are not difficult to guess. Instead of using first or last names and initials, some sites use the first, middle, and last name's initial, or combine two initials with four digits. Such user names are more difficult to guess (the first and last name are easy to come by, but not the middle initial or randomly assigned digits). For example, I would be rrf (three initials) or rf4019 (two initials with four digits). Although converting user names is likely to encounter user resistance, instituting a better naming convention at a new installation would be easier and can help improve the user authentication process.

Password   The second field contains the encrypted password. I will cover the encrypted password in detail later in this chapter, while discussing the process of encrypting passwords. The second field can also include optional password aging information, four letters or digits that follow a comma in the second field. In systems with a shadowed password file, the encrypted password has been replaced with some other character, for example, an exclamation point or pound sign.

User Id   The third field holds the *user id* number. The user id number uniquely identifies every user and is used to label processes started by the particular user and files owned by this user. The user id does not uniquely identify a user if any other account entry in the **/etc/passwd** file uses the same user id number. If two (or more) users have the same user id, only the user name from the account entry where the user id first appears will be shown by the **ls -l** command. While it appears that only the first account owns any files, every account with the same user id has equal access to all files labeled with that user id (Figure 3-2).

The system administrator assigns user id numbers when adding new account entries to the **/etc/passwd** file. If you or some other administrator has mistakenly added two accounts with the same user id, you can assign a new user id to the second account. After changing the account entry, you must also use the **find** command to descend through directories and **chown** to change the ownership of the files in the second user's HOME directory tree, since they will still be labeled with the user id of the first account entry, and belong to the first user.

Figure 3-2: Although the user pat should own the files in his home directory,
they are also owned by the user steve because both users share the same user id.

```
$ grep 110 /etc/passwd
  steve:bHN7vLM9jQiKE:110:100::/usr/steve:/bin/sh
pat:mCbmwKXwt8Kq2:110:100::/usr/pat:/bin/sh
$ cd /usr/pat
$ ls -la
total 40
drwxr-x--x   3 steve  usr         96 May 13 21:23 .
drwxr-xr-x   5 root   rootgrp     96 May  1 11:02 ..
-rw-------   1 steve  usr        157 May  2 11:47 .profile
-rw-------   1 steve  usr          0 May 13 21:22 .last_login
$ ▮
```

You can do two things to avoid assigning duplicate user ids. If you add account entries manually, use your editor to search for the user id to discover if it appears in another account entry. You can also make your life easier by sorting the **/etc/passwd** file, using the user id as the sorting key (Figure 3-3).

Figure 3-3: Using the **sort** *command to produce a copy of the*
/etc/passwd *file sorted by the third colon-separated field, the user id.*

```
# sort -t: +2n -3 /etc/passwd
root:xD7vejWLM2wtC:0:1::/:
daemon:*no login*:1:1::/:
  sys:*no login*:2:2::/usr/src:
bin:*no login*:3:3::/:
adm:*no login*:4:4::/usr/adm:
uucp:*no login*:6:6:uucp administrative login:/usr/lib/uucp:
sync:*no login*:8:2::/:/bin/sync
lp:*no login*:71:71::/usr/lib:/bin/sh
rik:BhN6vLM9jQiKE,21fE:100:100::/usr/acct/rik:/bin/sh
canyon:mCbmwKXwt8Kq2:101:100::/usr/acct/canyon:/bin/sj
rose:dXqaynD1GLn3I:107:100::/usr/acct/rose:/bin/sh
# sort -t: +2n -3 /etc/passwd > /tmp/passwd
# mv /etc/passwd /etc/opasswd
# mv /tmp/passwd /etc/passwd
# chmod 444 /etc/passwd
# ▮
```

In Figure 3-3, the output of the **sort** command was sent to the terminal. Once you have tried sorting the password file, you can redirect the output of the command to a temporary file, move the original to a backup file, and move the sorted version into position.

There is only one special user id. The user id of zero signifies that this account has superuser privileges. Only the *root* account entry must have a user id of zero. Some systems provide other accounts with zero user ids, for example, the System V Release 2 (and later) *sysadm* accounts. These accounts execute the restricted Bourne shell, and follow scripts to provide help in administering to UNIX systems. In earlier versions, the accounts are a security hole.

The sysadm accounts permit non-superusers to perform activities requiring root's access privileges. By logging into a sysadm account, for example, "mountfsys", any user that knows the password for this account can mount a file system. The sysadm system allows less expert users to participate in system administration. But, prior to Release 3.2, it is also a problem (Figure 3-4).

Figure 3-4: Using the **su** *command (switch user) to run the*
"mountfsys" sysadm script instead provides a restricted root owned shell.

```
$ su mountfsys
Password:
# ▮
```

Although the shell provided by using **su** is a restricted one, the restrictions imposed are very minimal, essentially preventing the changing of directories and file output redirection. An innovative user quickly surpasses these small aggravations, and can take full advantage of having superuser privileges. You must check your system if you have any sysadm accounts. If you are not using these accounts (they have impossible passwords), then you will not have problems with them. If these accounts have passwords, try the test in Figure 3-4. If you get a root prompt by entering the correct password, you should only permit fully qualified and trusted users to know the passwords for these accounts. To change the password, use **passwd accountname** as the root, or edit the password file and replace the passwords for these accounts with "no*login".

One way that system breakers get superuser privileges is by adding a new account entry with a user id of zero. This account entry can occur anywhere in the password file, and will most likely be disguised so that it appears to be a legitimate account. You can list all the accounts with a user id of zero with the command in Figure 3-5.

Figure 3-5: Listing all account entries that have a user id of zero.

```
$ grep '^[^:]*:[^:]*:0*' /etc/passwd
root:hIxhM35DmKcDg:0:1::/:
$ ▮
```

A craftier user might instead choose to use the same user id as an administrative account, such as **bin** or **adm**. Although the administrative accounts do not possess the same privilege as the user id of zero, they can be used to obtain superuser privileges, or perhaps simply to obtain whatever information the system breaker is after. By sorting the password file, you can look for duplicate user ids in administrative accounts. Typically, administrative accounts have user ids less than 100, although this is only a convention. Sometimes, accounts used by the UUCP system will share the same user id. Sharing the same user id for UUCP accounts is a problem, and will be covered in Chapter 4.

Group Id   The fourth field in an **/etc/passwd** file account entry contains the *group id* number. Unlike the user id, the group id can be shared with other users, and usually is shared. The group id in an account entry labels the user's processes for group access to files. In System V the group id is also used to label newly created files. The group id should correspond to an entry in the **/etc/group** file which provides a group name. In BSD 4.x versions, each user's processes are also labeled with all the group ids which the user name appears in the **/etc/group** file (Figure 3-6). Because the user rik appears in the user lists for "sys" and "user", rik would be a member of both groups under BSD.

*Figure 3-6: The **/etc/group** file maps group ids appearing in the **/etc/passwd** file to group names, and also permits users to be members of multiple groups.*

```
# cat /etc/group
rootgrp::1:root
sys::2:root,bin,sys,adm,rik
bin::3:bin
adm::4:root,adm,daemon
uucp::6:uucp
mail::7:root
daemon::9:root,daemon
lp::71:lp
usr::100:canyon,rik,rose
# ▮
```

Membership in groups confers the access privileges of those groups. In Figure 3-6, the user rik is a member of both the "usr" group and the "sys" group. In a System V version of the UNIX system, the **newgrp** command is used to switch between groups. When the user rik uses the command **newgrp sys**, he gives up the access privileges of the group "usr" and gains the privileges of "sys", an administrative group. An unscrupulous user can use group access privileges to gain access to files or directories, and through this access become the superuser or obtain or modify privileged information. Ordinary users should not be members of administrative groups.

In BSD 4.x, the **wheel** group is the administrative group. Only users who are members of this group can use **su** to become the superuser. So, membership in the **wheel** group is mandatory (and appropriate) in BSD systems for system administrators.

Although it is possible to add passwords to the second field in the **/etc/group** file, it is not recommended. The password is intended to permit users knowing the password to use **newgrp** to change to a group where the user does not belong. The problem with this approach is that shared passwords are just too easy to share—they invite lax security. Don't use passwords in the group file.

Comment Field   The fifth field in an account entry is the *comment field*. Although this field may be empty, it most commonly contains identifying information about the account. The fifth field commonly includes the full name of the user, and possibly a phone number or location. The **finger** command on BSD systems uses this information. This field historically contained the GECOS information, used for providing accounting information to non-UNIX systems.

The comment field, in particular the user's full name, can be used to supply clues to the user's password. Password crackers use variations based on the user's full name as possible passwords. If you have educated your users in the selection of passwords, the comment field does not pose any danger. Other than password cracking, the comment field has no security-related implications.

Home Directory   The sixth field holds the account entry's *HOME* directory. The **login** program sets the HOME environment variable to this field, and attempts to change directory to it. If this directory does not exist, or the permissions do not allow the user to change directory to it, one of two things will happen. In System V systems, the user will be prevented from logging in, and in BSD systems, the user will be warned and then placed in the root (/) directory. The establishment of a HOME directory does not provide any special access privileges; the permissions and ownership of the HOME directory control the user's access, exactly the same way that directory access works for any other directory.

Login Shell   The final field contains the login shell. As its last act, the **login** program executes the program found in this field. If the field is empty, the default shell, the Bourne shell, will be executed. Though some systems permit it, it is usually not possible to execute shell scripts as login shells. The login shell can be replaced with a special purpose program that does not provide the full freedom of the shell and restricts the user's activities. The use of restricted environments is discussed in Chapter 4. If the login program does not exist, login will not succeed, but will warn the user with a message like *no shell*.

Sharing Accounts

Every non-restricted user of a UNIX system must have an individual account. If users are permitted to share accounts, then *accountability*, the ability to determine who did what, is lost. The account entry provides the user identification information while that user is logged in. When a user becomes the superuser, through the **su** command, a record identifying that user is also kept. Each command executed by the user is identified if process accounting has been enabled. The user and group ids determine file and directory access for each user.

Inactive Accounts

When a user leaves on a vacation or sabbatical of some sort, their account becomes inactive. The UNIX system does not recognize this condition, although it can be detected by looking through accounting records. If you run System V system accounting, the daily report includes last login times for all users. If your users make use of the **.lastlogin** file, you can check the dates on these files.

Inactive accounts are often used by system crackers. The directories belonging to these accounts are unlikely to be searched by anyone, making them good places for a system cracker to work. Logging in here as an authorized user is less likely to arouse suspicion. You can temporarily deactivate inactive accounts by installing an impossible password.

If an account becomes inactive because an employee has quit or been fired, deactivate the account immediately. If possible, have management inform you *before* they inform an employee that is to be fired so you can change that user's password. (In secure or sensitive computer operations, such as banks, the employee is escorted out by security guards at termination, or the moment after the resignation is turned in.) When a user leaves, files and directories belonging to that user may still have some value, so they are generally not removed immediately. Keeping the account entry identifies the ownership of these files and directories—just make certain the password is changed.

Passwords for Every Account

By this point, you should thoroughly understand the importance of good passwords. Without good passwords, there is no first line of defense against unauthorized use. There is a time when your system might not have passwords, and that is during installation. You may also be tempted to create new account entries without passwords, but there is no reason for doing so.

Only the system accounts will be present in the **/etc/passwd** file when a new system or a new release of the UNIX system is installed, and these accounts will probably not have passwords. (The Sun386i is an example of a system that comes with a root password installed. The password is the host id and is displayed by requesting login help.) Some vendors have included installation routines that force the installer to add passwords to system accounts during installation. Other vendors provide the option to add passwords, while some make no mention of passwords at all. If you are given the option, I suggest that you *do* add passwords at installation time.

Since you will need to come up with anywhere from two to a dozen passwords during installation, and these are important passwords, I suggest that you write them down. Use the technique explained in Chapter 2; that is, use a lockbox with a key to store the written passwords, and keep the lockbox and the key in secure locations. The ideal lockbox for system passwords requires two keys, with the security administrators keeping one key, and system administrators copies of the other. Like a safe deposit box, both keys must be used before the box can be opened.

Older versions of the UNIX system came without passwords for any accounts. The system administrator was supposed to either provide passwords, or fill in the password field with an "impossible" password. An impossible password includes characters never present in passwords, such as spaces, the asterisk, and dashes, for example, *no login*. Impossible passwords must contain characters not found in encrypted passwords, since an encrypted password could match a string with legal characters, such as "no.login.here". As the UNIX system made the transition from limited distribution to commercial distribution, the tradition of not providing passwords survived. Figure 3-7 shows how system accounts should appear.

*Figure 3-7: The beginning of an /**etc/passwd** file, with
either a password or an impossible password for each account.*

```
$ sed -n '1,10p' /etc/passwd
root:Mt1cag7v7N.tH:0:1::/:
daemon:*no login*:1:1::/:
sys:*no login*:2:2::/usr/src:
bin:*no login*:3:3::/:
adm:*no login*:4:4::/usr/adm:
listen::37:4:Network Admin:/usr/net/nls:
uucp:EK1Jj6Cte6sAd:6:6:uucp administrative login:/usr/lib/uucp:
sync:*no login*:8:2::/:/bin/sync
lp:*no login*:71:71::/usr/lib:/bin/sh
$ 
```

In Figure 3-6, only the uucp and root accounts have passwords. The other accounts have impossible passwords that prevent anyone from logging into or **su**'ing into these accounts.

Notice that there is an account with the user name "sync" that has the command **/bin/sync** as the login shell. Many systems come with a **sync** account that has no password. In itself, the **sync** account is harmless—it can only run the command **/bin/sync**, which copies in-memory images of disk files to the disks. The ability to quickly execute the **sync** command was especially important to older minicomputers running variants of the UNIX system, since they would often crash after a couple of weeks. Experienced users could recognize the symptoms of the crash as it was happening and **sync** (synchronize) the file systems.

Today, UNIX systems have become more reliable, and the slow motion crashes of yesteryear less common. What the password-less **sync** account provides is a subtle service to system breakers who work through communication lines. The **sync** command is unique to UNIX systems, and if a stranger can execute **sync** without logging in, the stranger knows he or she is dealing with a UNIX system. Another popular password-less account is **tty**, which identifies the port from which the command is run. System administrators use the **tty** account to quickly determine which port a terminal is connected to. Not using a password on the **tty** account is convenient. However, this information, how to determine if a system runs the UNIX OS, has appeared on bulletin boards dedicated to breaking into computers. Use passwords on all accounts.

Although system accounts like **bin**, **daemon**, **adm**, **lp**, and **sys**, are rarely logged into, these accounts *can* be logged into and must be protected by passwords or impossible passwords. Several years ago it was commonplace to find that system accounts had no passwords. This omission happened because it never occurred to the system administrator to protect these accounts since he or she never used them. The primary purpose for these accounts is to identify the owner of system files, directories, and devices. Use passwords or impossible passwords to protect all accounts.

Finally, there is the matter of the **guest** account. Some system administrators set up guest accounts for occasional users. These accounts may be restricted in some way, or simply accounts in a group with no other members (which I do not recommend). Guest accounts must also have passwords. The best guest accounts use the **chroot** environment (covered in Chapter 4) and have passwords that are changed frequently. The system breaker will try logging in as guest on an unfamiliar system (after trying other well-known accounts, such as root.) You don't want uninvited guests in your system, no matter how secure you have made it.

Checking the Password File

The **/etc/passwd** file is so important to UNIX system security, that it should be checked routinely. The checks include:

- The ownership and permissions of the **/etc/passwd** file
- The correctness of the fields in each entry
- The existence of a password for each account
- The user id of zero

The **/etc/passwd** file must be owned by the root account, and have read-only permissions for all. The **ls -l** command can be used to list the ownership and permissions. Each account entry must be correct, that is, have seven colon-separated fields. The **pwck** or **pwdck** command processes the **/etc/passwd** file for correctness. The **pwck** command not only checks for the appropriate fields, but also checks for the existence of the login directory and login shell. All accounts must have passwords, which can be checked by using the **grep** command. And only administrative accounts can have a user id of zero, also checked using the **grep** command (Figure 3-8).

*Figure 3-8: The commands used to make the four checks on the /**etc/passwd** file.*

```
# ls -l /etc/passwd
-r--r--r--   1 root     sys            675 Jun 16 15:26 /etc/passwd
# pwck

sys:*no login*:2:2::/usr/src:
         Login directory not found

sandy:nCbmwKXwt8Kq9:213:200:/u2/sandy:/bin/sh
         Too many/few fields
# grep '^[^:]*::' /etc/passwd
sync::8:2::/:/bin/sync
# grep '^[^:]*:[^:]*:0' /etc/passwd
root:fMLPVeemziQfK:0:1::/:
# ▊
```

In Figure 3-8, the **ls** command shows that the permissions and ownership of the /**etc/passwd** file are correct. The /**etc/passwd** file must be readable by all and owned by the root account. The root can still write to the /**etc/passwd** file since the root can write to any file, regardless of permissions. (If you try writing to the /**etc/passwd** file with **vi**, it will not succeed unless you follow the command to write with an exclamation point, as in ":w!".) The file must be readable by all, or commands like **ls** and **find** will not work correctly.

The **pwck** command will produce some output for almost any password file. Warnings about missing login directories about system accounts are just that—warnings. The second error message, *Too many/few fields*, is critical—this account entry *and all that follow it* are invalid, and will not be recognized by the **login** or **su** programs. In Figure 3-8, the entry for sandy has only six fields (the comment field is missing). It is difficult to notice by just looking at the entry that anything is wrong; that is why it is a good idea to run **pwck** after editing the /**etc/passwd** file. On Xenix and AIX systems, **pwck** is named **pwdck**.

The last two checks are performed by using the **grep** command and two different patterns. The first pattern matches two colons that follow any number of characters that are not colons. The second pattern matches a leading zero in the user id field. The commands in Figure 3-9 can be combined in a simple shell script that can be run automatically or interactively.

Figure 3-9: The **passwdck** *script combines the four checks in Figure 3-8.*

```
# cat /etc/security/passwdck
#!/bin/sh
PATH=/bin:/usr/bin:/etc
export PATH
# Set and export a good PATH
IFS='
'                        # Establish safe Input Field Separator
DIR=/etc/security        # Directory where database files reside
OUT=$DIR/out$$  # Temporary output file
SA=root          # Recipient of mail if non-interactive
trap "/bin/rm -f $DIR/pwck$$ $DIR/suid$$ $OUT; \
   exit 1" 0 1 2 3  # Cleanup if interrupted
# Capture permissions and ownership, and test
set - 'ls -lc /etc/passwd'
if [ "$1" != "-r--r--r--" -o "$3" != "root" ] ; then
    echo "Warning! Permission or ownership problem." >>$OUT
    echo $* >> $OUT
    echo "Correcting mode and owner of /etc/passwd." >>$OUT
    chmod 444 /etc/passwd
    chown root /etc/passwd
fi
# Run pwck and capture the standard error.
pwck > $DIR/pwck$$ 2>&1
# If the database file pwck.out does not exist, create it.
if [ ! -f $DIR/pwck.out ] ; then
    echo "$DIR/pwck.out did not exist; created." >>$OUT
else  # Compare pwck with past pwck, and warn if different
    diff $DIR/pwck$$ $DIR/pwck.out >> $OUT || \
        echo "New problems detected by pwck." >> $OUT
fi
# Search for passwordless accounts
grep '^[^:]*::' /etc/passwd >> $OUT && \
    echo; echo "Add passwords to these accounts!!" >> $OUT
# Search for accounts with user id of 0
grep '^[^:]*:[^:]*:0' /etc/passwd > $DIR/suid$$
# If the database file pwck.out does not exist, create it.
if [ ! -f $DIR/suid.out ] ; then
    echo "$DIR/suid.out did not exist ; created." >> $OUT
else  # Compare output with past, and warn if different
    diff $DIR/suid$$ $DIR/suid.out >> $OUT || \
        echo "New accounts with 0 uid detected." >> $OUT
fi
/bin/mv -f $DIR/suid$$ $DIR/suid.out  # Save current output
/bin/mv -f $DIR/pwck$$ $DIR/pwck.out
if [ -s $OUT ] ; then
```

*Figure 3-9: The **passwdck** script combines the four checks in Figure 3-8 (continued).*

```
# If there was any output,
   if [ -t 1 ] ; then
# and standard out is a tty,
      cat $OUT
  # display the output file
  else
      mail $SA < $OUT  # else, mail it to $SA
  fi                         # And always append it to the log.
  date >> $DIR/passwdck.log
  cat $OUT >> $DIR/passwdck.log
fi
/bin/rm -f $OUT
exit 0
# ▊
```

The **passwdck** script only sends messages if there are problems with the **/etc/passwd** file or either of the two database files does not exist. The two database are "pwck.out", which contains the output of the **pwck** command, and "suid.out", which contains a list of accounts with user ids of zero. The **diff** command compares the contents of these files with the current output of the **pwck** command and the **grep** command that checks for accounts with zero user ids. If the script completes normally, the current output of **pwck** command and the **grep** commands are used to update the database files. Any output generated by the script is appended, along with the date, in the "passwdck.log" file.

The **passwdck** script can be run interactively, or by the **cron** daemon. The output of the command, if any, is mailed to the user specified by the variable SA (root in the example). The **/etc/security** directory was created for use with this script. You may choose to locate your security directory elsewhere in the file systems; just use a system account-owned directory that is not readable or writeable by group and others.

I will introduce several other scripts for managing system security, and all these scripts share a common failing. Any script kept on-line is subject to modification. A clever intruder looks for and modifies the scripts to hide any evidence. Thus, scripts kept on-line can provide a false sense of security, since a modified script wouldn't sound the alarm. The solution is to keep copies of the scripts and database files off-line, and periodically restore these files and run the scripts. Alternatively, you can restore these files, or mount them on a physically removable device (such as a WORM laser disk), and compare the scripts and database files to off-line copies.

Encrypted Passwords

The UNIX system encrypts passwords using a method that *cannot* be reversed. Once a password has been encrypted, it is impossible to decrypt it. The algorithm used is the Data Encryption Standard (DES) that has been modified in 4,096 different ways. The modification to the UNIX encryption scheme makes it impossible to use encryption hardware (designed for encrypting communications) to encrypt passwords. All UNIX systems use the same encryption algorithm.

Passwords were originally developed as a method for authenticating people on multi-user systems. These easily systems did not encrypt passwords, but merely hid them from most users. However, knowledgeable users could locate the passwords, making the system not very secure. Surprisingly, some proprietary systems still maintain databases containing clear text (not encrypted) passwords.

Passwords on most UNIX systems are kept in the open, but in encrypted form, within the **/etc/passwd** file. Since there is no way to decrypt these passwords, there appears to be little danger in letting users see the encrypted passwords. The problem with leaving passwords visible is related to what happens when you enter your password during the login process. Obviously, the UNIX system must do something to check the password you enter against the one stored in encrypted form in the **/etc/passwd** file. What the UNIX system does is encrypt the password you enter and compare it to the encrypted password.

Encrypted passwords in the UNIX system are 13 characters long, and have two parts. The characters are upper- and lowercase letters in the alphabet, the digits 0 through 9, the period, and the slash. The first part of an encrypted password is called the *seed*, and is two characters long. The seed is calculated when a password is encrypted using the **passwd** command, and is based on the current time and the process id of the **passwd** command. The last 11 characters are the result of the encryption.

The UNIX system provides a user command for creating encrypted passwords. **/usr/lib/makekey** reads eight characters from the standard input, followed by a two-character seed, and sends the encrypted result to the standard output. To demonstrate this, suppose that the user sandy uses the password "ILuvBuns". Figure 3-10 shows how sandy's password appears in the **/etc/passwd** and how to re-encrypt "ILuvBuns", along with the two-character seed, "v3".

Figure 3-10: The **/usr/lib/makekey** *command uses the identical password encryption that* **login** *uses. The letters "v3" form the seed.*

```
$ grep sandy /etc/passwd
sandy:v3iiDXuMFyM4o:213:200:/u2/sandy:/bin/sh:
$ /usr/lib/makekey
ILuvBunsv3
v3iiDXuMFyM4o$
```

The **/usr/lib/makekey** command reads eight characters from the standard input, then two characters for the seed. It sends the encrypted password to the standard output, without a newline character, so that the prompt appears directly after the encrypted password. If the password to be encrypted is less than eight characters long, follow the password with an end-of-file character (usually control-d) and the two characters of seed.

Passwords generated with **/usr/lib/makekey** can be used in the **/etc/passwd** file. The same encrypted passwords can also be used on other UNIX systems, including XENIX, ULTRIX, AIX, BSD, SunOS, System III, System V, Version 7, etc. This is where the real danger lies. Anyone who can get a copy of an **/etc/passwd** file containing encrypted passwords can use any UNIX system to try to guess passwords.

What password cracking programs do is guess passwords. The encrypted passwords are truly impossible to decrypt, so the cracker functions by selecting likely passwords, encrypting the passwords, and looking for matches. The seed makes this process more difficult, since a single password has a different encryption for each of the 4,096 possible seeds. If two users have the exact same password, their seed will be different and the encrypted passwords will also be different.

The DES encryption algorithm was designed to take a significant amount of computer time to complete. But what took a computer of the 1970s much time can now be done very quickly, even by personal computers. So the performance improvements in computers have made the UNIX encryption algorithm less secure. Still, standard UNIX encryption does take some time. A 16-bit microprocessor running at 10 million cycles per second takes several seconds to encrypt a password, but 32-bit RISC-based processor running at 33 million cycles per second takes less than two tenths of a second.

Making matters worse, techniques for speeding up the UNIX encryption have been published. The Morris worm took advantage of some of these techniques, and improved the encryption algorithm by a factor of nine. The password cracking portion of the Morris worm has become a standard tool for security at some of the sites infected by the worm. Even so, password cracking takes time.

The UNIX encryption mechanism receives eight characters, each containing seven bits, for a total of 56 bits to encrypt. There could be 2 to the 56th power passwords, or approximately 72 followed by 15 zeros (in decimal) potential passwords. If a computer can encrypt 10 passwords each second, it could encrypt 315,360,000 passwords in a year, and would take 2.28 billion years to encrypt all possible 56-bit combinations. These calculations ignore the salt, which means that each combination must be done 4,096 times. Looking at UNIX encryption from this perspective, things appear quite fine.

Reality is very different from this scenario. People tend to use less than half of the 128 characters potentially possible in passwords, using only the upper- and lowercase letters, and 10 digits for a total of 62. This impoverished pool of characters cuts the potential number of passwords in half. Much more dramatic, however, is that most passwords are names or words found in a dictionary. Often, these words or names will have a single digit appended, so if a list of 10,000 words and names are used, each with a 1-digit appended, encrypting these 100,000 passwords would take the ten-password-per-second computer a little more than one day. This one-day figure ignores the salt, which, if included, means there are 409,600,000 salt and password combinations, bringing the total time up to a little more than a year.

Still, I am being generous by using a 10,000 word list. A study by Grampp and Morris published in 1984 attempted to crack passwords on 200 systems using a list of 20 common women's names. To each name, they appended one digit, for a total of 200 passwords. And they were able to guess at least one password on every one of the 200 systems. The Morris worm's password cracker used a 432 name/word list, plus information gleaned by reading the **/etc/passwd** file.

Most password cracking programs follow the same pattern as the Morris worm. The password cracker first tries permutations of the user name, permutations of the information in the comment field, then a list of favorite passwords. Favorite passwords are "secret", "password", "wizard", "unix", "mary", and so on.

The words in Morris' list represented past successes at cracking passwords on many systems. It is likely that the favorite word lists posted on cracker bulletin boards are based on having successfully guessed a password at least once.

There are several things that you can do to prevent people from guessing passwords. Although you cannot make the **/etc/passwd** file unreadable, newer versions of the UNIX system support a *shadow* password file. The shadow password file contains the encrypted password for each user, along with other security information for each account. The **/etc/passwd** file still exists, but the password fields do not contain encrypted passwords. An administrative command is used to convert a regular **/etc/passwd** file to a shadow password file. For example, SunOS 4.x uses the **C2conv** script to convert the **/etc/passwd** file to the secure format, with encrypted passwords listed in **/etc/security/passwd.adjunct**. IBM's AIX uses **pwdck -y ALL** and **mkpasswd** to perform the conversion, keeping the shadowed version in **/etc/security/passwd**. System V Release 3.2 actually names the shadow file **/etc/shadow**.

The second thing you can do is teach your users to choose good passwords. You can do this by stressing the importance of good passwords, not writing down passwords, and techniques for creating good passwords. When explaining passwords to users, I usually say something like "choose a password that uses six or more letters, digits, and punctuation, that is not a name or found in any dictionary. Good passwords are nonsense phrases, like vanity license plates." Then give some examples.

Many UNIX systems enforce using good passwords by rejecting passwords that do not contain both letters and digits, or that are a permutation of the user's login name. You can discover if this is true for your UNIX system by checking the manual page for the **passwd** command. You can also try to enter bad passwords, such as your own user name twice, and see if the **passwd** command accepts them. The superuser is not restricted in the choice of passwords, and will not be prevented from entering poor passwords.

Finally, you can do what the administrators of many large UNIX sites did after the invasion of the Morris worm. You can run a password cracker yourself. The worm included a sophisticated encryption mechanism, methods for concocting likely passwords, and a list of "popular" passwords. Even though the worm had been stopped, the technology it carried was left in the hands of many people. So, the administrators used the portion of the worm that included the password cracker to discover unsafe passwords in their systems. I cannot share with you the secrets of the worms encryption techniques, but I will explain how to use a password cracker to search for bad passwords.

I have already explained how to guess passwords using the **/usr/lib/makekey** command. Unfortunately, **makekey** does not fit very well into shell scripts because of the way it reads the password guess and seed from the standard input. The **makekey** command works well when the password is eight characters log, but requires an embedded end-of-file between shorter passwords and the two characters of seed. To replace **makekey**, I was forced to create a short C program. While this is not a problem for users of larger UNIX systems and workstations, small UNIX systems that run SCO, Interactive, or Intel versions of the UNIX system often come without C compilers. The bright side to this picture is that small systems generally run on Intel CPU's, and have binary code compatibility—the ability to compile and link code on one system and use it on another.

Password crackers can also be purchased commercially, along with instructions and shell scripts to drive them. Lachman Associates (now owned by Interactive Systems) sells an expensive package that includes on-site installation and a check for security problems. Less costly packages that include password crackers are available from Unisolutions Associates (Usecure) and Lawrence and Associates (Security Administrator's Workbench). These packages also contain scripts and programs much like the ones in this chapter.

Password crackers can be broken into two components: the encryption routine and the possible password generator. It is the encryption routine that must be replaced with a C program. Figure 3-11 contains a simple C program that takes an encrypted password on the command line, and reads possible passwords from the standard input.

The checker.c program requires the encrypted password on the command line. This password is copied to a local array, password. The **while** loop reads the standard input until the end-of-file is reached. The **if** statement contains a comparison of the account entry's password and the encrypted password returned by the **crypt()** function. If the comparison returns 0, the two passwords are equivalent, and the program exits with the return value of zero. For shell scripts, a return code of zero is true; all other return codes are false or failure.

Figure 3-11: The checker.c program reads guesses, encrypts
them using the original seed, and returns a true exit code on success.

```
$ cat checker.c
#include <stdio.h>
main (argc, argv)
    int argc;
    char * argv[];
{
    char password[18], guess[24];
    if (argc != 2) {
        fprintf(stderr, "Usage: %s password\n", argv[0]);
        exit(2);
    }
    strcpy(password, argv[1]);
    while (fscanf(stdin, "%s", guess) != EOF)
        if (!strncmp(password, crypt(guess, password), 13))
            exit(0);
    exit(1);
}
$ cc checker.c -o checker
$ ▮
```

The checker.c program could be modified by replacing the **while** loop that reads the standard input with program logic that creates and tests possible passwords. Since this is not a C programming text, I will use a Bourne shell script as an example password generator. Note that the **crypt()** function is the key to password cracking. The **crypt()** function takes a password guess and the seed and returns a pointer to an encrypted password. This function works like **makekey**, and is not the same as the **crypt** command discussed in Chapter 2.

The checker program can be used interactively by executing the program and entering possible passwords, one at a time. However, it is much easier to let a script perform the repetitive work. The real art to password cracking is coming up with a good list of possible passwords. We really are not interested in cracking good passwords—which should be impossible anyway. What we want to do is search for bad passwords, and create a list of users that have bad passwords.

The shell script in Figure 3-12 first checks to see if a previous operation has been interrupted. The file "PWUSER" contains the user id being tested during a previously interrupted invocation of pwguess. The **awk** command scans the **/etc/passwd** file and passes the user name, encrypted password, user id, and comment field to the **while** loop. The encrypted password gets passed to the checker program. The user name is tried as a possible password, with both pre-fixed and trailing digits. Information in the comment field is also tried, along with trailing digits. Next, the shell script looks for a file containing personal in-formation about each user. This file contains the names of the user's friends, fam-ily, pets, car, favorite athletes, technical terms familiar to the user, and so on. Obviously, you must know something about the user to create this file, although personnel information could provide some data. Finally, a local dictionary of password guesses is checked. The local dictionary should contain generally pop-ular passwords ("wizard", "unix", etc.), locally favorite technical terms ("quark", "blackhole", "acctspay", "acctsrcv", "apple", etc.).

Figure 3-12: A shell script that searches for bad passwords. If the shell script is interrupted, the last user checked is contained in the file PWUSER.

```
#!/bin/sh
# pwguess - shell script that calls checker with bad or weak
# passwords; current user saved in PWUSER; only user accounts
# (after FIRST_USER) are checked. The personal directory
# contains files named after users containing possible passwords
# for each user. Dictionary (dict1) contains list of bad passwords.
PATH=/bin:/usr/bin; export PATH
FIRST_USER=100
DIR=/etc/secure.
LOG=$DIR/pwlogfile
trap "/bin/rm -f LIST$$" 1 2 3
# Check for previously incompleted operation
if [ -f $DIR/PWUSER ] ; then
    FIRST_USER='cat $DIR/PWUSER'
fi
# Filter information from password file
awk -F: '$3 > '$FIRST_USER' { print $1, $2, $3, $5 }' /etc/passwd |
# Now process each user
while read LINE
do
    set $LINE
    USER=$1
    PASS=$2
    UID=$3
    COMMENT1=$4
    COMMENT2=$5
    echo $UID > $DIR/PWUSER
# First try some user name combinations
    echo ${USER} ${USER}${USER} > LIST$$
    for i in 0 1 2 3 4 5 6 7 8 9
```

*Figure 3-12: A shell script that searches for bad passwords. If the shell
script is interrupted, the last user checked is contained in the file PWUSER (continued).*

```
do
      echo ${USER}$i $i${USER} >> LIST$$
done
# Try comment field combinations
echo ${COMMENT1} ${COMMENT1}${COMMENT2} ${COMMENT2} >> LIST$$
for i in 0 1 2 3 4 5 6 7 8 9
do
      echo ${COMMENT1}$i $i${COMMENT1} >> LIST$$
      echo ${COMMENT2}$i $i${COMMENT2} >> LIST$$
done # Look for file with personal information
PERS=
if [ -f $DIR/$user ] ; then
      PERS=$DIR/$user
  fi
# Pass list to the checker program
if cat LIST$$ $PERS $DIR/dict1 | checker $PASS
then
      echo "$USER has a weak password" >> $LOG
  fi
done
rm -f $DIR/PWUSER LIST$$
```

The possible passwords used by the pwguess script assume that the system
being examined is based upon System V. The System V **passwd** command forces
users to use at least six characters and one digit in the first eight characters of the
password. Without this constraint, possible passwords with leading or trailing
digits are not as common, and the two **for** loops that append or prepend the digits zero to nine could be removed.

The dictionary file for System V must also consider the same constraints if it
is to be successful. In other words, each possible password must contain at least
one digit, and be a total of six characters long. After preparing a list of popular
passwords, based on Morris' research, I used a program named "fix.c" to filter
out too short passwords and to append or prepend digits. My dictionary of bad
passwords and the "fix.c" program appear in an Appendix. If your **passwd** command does not make constraints on password selections, your dictionary does
not need to adhere to these constraints either. Systems which do not make constraints permit just hitting the RETURN key as a password (which will be encrypted and look okay), single letters or digits, the user name, and other awful
passwords.

I ran pwguess on the password files of systems that I administer, and found that systems that placed constraints on passwords had few bad passwords. I was both surprised (and pleased) that people had paid attention to my admonishments about using good passwords. Without the password cracker, I had no way of knowing how secure those systems were. Although I have not eliminated the possibility of password cracking by someone using a more extensive list, I have determined that the most common weak passwords are not in use on those systems.

Password Aging

Password aging is another feature of the System V **passwd** command. The password aging mechanism forces users to change their passwords after a set period of time has passed since their passwords were last changed. The aging mechanism can also prevent users from changing back to the old password immediately. That is good news, because passwords should be changed routinely, and aging automates the process. Chapter 2 showed how password aging appears to end users (see Figure 2-3). The bad news is that there are some problems with password aging.

Password aging uses an unusual base-64 numbering system for storing date, maximum age, and minimum time before the password can be changed. The date the password was last changed is stored as two base-64 characters, and is the number of weeks since Jan 1, 1970. For example, the week of July 4, 1990 is represented by the characters "hE". Converting the number of weeks since New Year's Day in 1970 is difficult enough (except for computers), but the base-64 numbering scheme takes the cake. Neither users nor administrators can examine the aging date and determine what it means without a C program. Something else unusual about the base-64 numbering scheme is that the rightmost character is most significant, unlike most familiar numbering schemes. For example, 13 follows 12 in decimal or hexadecimal, but "iE' follows "hE" in base-64.

Some versions of the **passwd** command (after System V Release 3.2), for example, have added capabilities that permit users to display the date in humanly understandable terms, and the superuser to administer the aging information without using base-64. The Xenix system provides **pwadmin** for administering to password aging. Some shadow password files include separate fields for password aging. Administrators of earlier System V systems must learn something about the base-64 scheme.

The other big problem with most password aging schemes is the element of surprise. Imagine that it's Monday morning after a great weekend, and you show up at work somewhat tired. As soon as you login, you find your password has expired. Monday morning is not the best time to create a new password, especially one that *you cannot change for several weeks*. The same minimum time before the password can be changed prevents improving the password without the assistance of the system administrator. And the aging date, using weeks, almost guarantees that the change will occur Monday morning. Users need to be warned in advance, so they can think about a new password and change it before Monday morning rolls around. System V Release 4 does warn users automatically.

Password aging is added to an account by using an editor, and appending a comma and the aging information after the encrypted password. For example, Figure 3-13 shows an account both before and after password aging has been added.

*Figure 3-13: An /etc/passwd account entry
before and after password aging has been added.*

```
canyon:w1dLLkC2yuu8Y:101:100:Canyon Moon:/u/canyon:/bin/sh
canyon:w1dLLkC2yuu8Y,21:101:100:Canyon Moon:/u/canyon:/bin/sh
```

The first digit after the comma is the number of weeks before the password expires. The second digit is the number of weeks before the user can change the password. The next time that the user canyon logs in, he or she will be told his password has expired, and to choose a new password. After choosing a new password, the date code is added after the maximum and minimum dates. If canyon had changed the password on July 5, 1990, the password aging information would become ",21hE".

The base-64 numbering system uses the period, slash, digits zero through nine, the letters a through Z, and a through z. Table 3-1 presents the values in decimal for this unusual numbering scheme.

Table 3-1: Base-64 numbering scheme used by password aging.

.	/	0	1	2	3	4	5	6	7	8	9	A	B	C	D
0	1	2	3	4	5	6	7	8	9	10	11	12	13	14	15
E	F	G	H	I	J	K	L	M	N	O	P	Q	R	S	T
16	17	18	19	20	21	22	23	24	25	26	27	28	29	30	31
U	V	W	X	Y	Z	a	b	c	d	e	f	g	h	i	j
32	33	34	35	36	37	38	39	40	41	42	43	44	45	46	47
k	l	m	n	o	p	q	r	s	t	u	v	w	x	y	z
48	49	50	51	52	53	54	55	56	57	58	59	60	61	62	63

Password aging can be introduced to an account by adding just a comma and the number of weeks before the password expires after the encrypted password. The comma and maximum dates can be placed in an empty password field, forcing the new user to provide a password during the first login. Since this account is not initially password protected, I do not recommend this. If you do not provide a minimum time before the password can be changed, **passwd** will supply a period, representing one week before the password can be changed.

You can also force users to change their passwords just once by appending ",." (comma period) to their encrypted passwords. The next time they login, they must change their passwords, and the **passwd** command will remove the aging information.

The period of time before a password should expire depends upon how secure your system must be. Very secure systems, or sensitive accounts, will have rapidly (weekly) changing passwords. More commonly, passwords for users should expire after two weeks to two months for relatively secure systems, and from six months to a year for other systems. To prevent surprising your users on a Monday morning, you can invoke the **pwage** program, (a C program described in an Appendix), as part of the login process and inform users how many weeks they have before their password expires.

For systems without password aging, there is no reliable method for forcing users to change their passwords. Although you could make a copy of the password file, tell users to change their passwords, and use **diff** to compare the **/etc/passwd** file with the copy, even if all the passwords appear changed, users are not prevented from reusing their old passwords. Even with password aging, some users switch to temporary passwords, and return to their regular passwords after the minimum time has passed.

System Owned Files and Directories

Users are responsible for the files that they own. The system administrator is responsible for everything else. This is a large territory, and encompasses the UNIX system's commands, device files, configuration files, scripts, libraries, and databases. Yet there are just a few simple rules to follow to make a system more secure:

- System files and directories are owned by system accounts and system groups

- No write for others on system-owned directories with the exception of temporary directories
- No write for others on system-owned files
- No read for others on a few critical files
- Correct ownership and permissions for device files
- Make routine checks on permissions, ownership, and checksums of critical files

System Ownership and Groups

The system accounts are administrative accounts in the **/etc/passwd** file like **root**, **bin**, **adm**, **system**, **uucp**, **daemon**, and **lp**. Most of these accounts exist for the express purpose of showing ownership of a group of related files and directories. The system files and directories include everything except those files and directories within users' HOME directory trees. No non-administrative user should own any file or directory outside of his or her own tree (with the exception of mail and other temporary files). Finding a file or directory owned by an ordinary user account indicates that system security has been violated by that user. The ownership should be corrected, permissions corrected, and the security infraction investigated if necessary.

Figure 3-14: Long listing of a system directory, the root. There appear to be problems with group ownership and permissions in this example.

```
$ ls -l /
total 8078
drwxr-xr-x    2 root     sys          512 Jun 29 11:52 admin
lrwxrwxrwx    1 root     other          7 Jun 29 09:12 bin -> usr/bin
drwxr-xr-x    8 root     root        5632 Jul  9 10:22 dev
-rwxr-xr-x    2 root     other    1488794 Jul  3 10:07 dgux
-rwxr-xr-x    2 root     other    1488794 Jul  3 10:07 dgux.raven
-rwxr-xr-x    1 root     sys      1134082 May 11 13:23 dgux.starter
drwxrwxr-x   19 root     sys         4096 Jul  9 14:59 etc
lrwxrwxrwx    1 root     other          7 Jun 29 09:12 lib -> usr/lib
drwxrwxr-x    2 root     sys            0 Apr 18 12:50 local
drwxr-xr-x    2 root     root         512 Jul  3 08:40 lost+found
drwxr-xr-x    3 bin      bin          512 May  4  1989 sbin
drwxr-xr-x    7 bin      bin          512 Jun 29 12:13 srv
drwxr-xr-x    2 bin      bin            0 Apr 18 12:50 tftpboot
drwxrwxrwx    3 root     sys          512 Jul  9 20:20 tmp
drwxr-xr-x    5 root     root         512 Jul  3 08:25 u
drwxr-xr-x   18 bin      bin          512 Jun  4 13:01 usr
drwxr-xr-x   14 bin      bin          512 Apr 20 07:23 var
$ 
```

Figure 3-14 shows a long listing of the root directory on a newly installed Data General workstation. The ownership of the kernel file **dgux** is root, but the group owner is "other", which appears to be a problem. Is "other" a system group, or a catchall user group? Looking at the **/etc/group** and **/etc/passwd** file provides the answers (Figure 3-15).

Figure 3-15: The "other" group has the group id of one, and
account entries belonging to the "other" group are for system accounts.

```
$ grep other /etc/group
other::1:
$ grep :1:/etc/passwd
root:3Z4pZFTjHV.bZ:0:1:Special Admin login:/:/sbin/sh
daemon:*:1:1:Daemon Login:/:/sbin/sh
uucp:*:5:1:UUCP Admin Login :/usr/lib/uucp:/sbin/sh
mail:*:8:1:Sendmail Login:/usr/mail:/usr/bin/mail
$ ▊
```

On the Data General workstation, the "other" group is a system group. Only system accounts, (root, daemon, uucp, and mail) belong to the "other" group. The ownership of the files and directories in the root directory are either root or bin, (both are system accounts), so there are no problems there.

Symbolic Links   There are two symbolic links in Figure 3-16: **/bin** is symbolically linked to **/usr/bin**, and **/lib** is symbolically linked to **/usr/lib**. The leading letter l in the long listing indicates a symbolic link. The permissions appear to allow writing for all, which would be a problem, especially for the **/bin** directory, a great place to put Trojan Horses. However, symbolic links are akin to hard links. The symbolic link permits ordinary users to make links to directories, and also permits linking across file systems. A file of type link contains only the path to the linked file. The permissions on the link itself cannot be changed, and always appear to be read, write, and execute for all. Executing **chmod** on the link affects the file or directory connected by the link. Removing or renaming the symbolic link requires write and execute permission on the directory where the link is listed.

Symbolic links in the root directory are used in Data General's DGUX OS (and SunOS 4.x and System V, Release 4) to preserve the traditional structure of the UNIX root directory. Symbolic links are not found in System V releases before Release 4. The important thing to remember is that symbolic links are similar to hard links—the ownership and permissions on the real file control access. The difference is that symbolic links can span file systems and do not affect the link count of the file or directory referenced.

Figure 3-16: Symbolic links appear to have permissions for all;
however, the permissions on the linked directory apply. Any user
may make a link to any directory that the user can read and execute.

```
$ ls -l /bin
lrwxrwxrwx  1 root    other    7 Jun 29 09:12 /bin -> usr/bin
$ rm /bin/cat
rm: /bin/cat not removed.
Permission denied
$ ls -ld /usr/bin
drwxr-xr-x  2 bin     bin    5632 Jun 29 14:04 /usr/bin
$ cd
$ ln -s /usr/bin bin
$ ls -l bin/cat
-rwxr-xr-x  1 bin     bin   34536 Apr 18 12:53 bin/cat
$ ▌
```

Write Permission on System Directories

Allowing others to write in system directories is a serious security problem. Although people often think that the permissions on the files in the directories protect those files, they do *not*. In Chapter 2, I showed how someone could replace a user's startup file with only write permissions on the user's HOME directory (see Figure 2-20). Write permissions for others in the root directory would permit any user to replace the startup files for the root account.

System directories contain much more vital information than just root's startup files. Write permission on a command directory permits substitution of commands with look-alike Trojan Horses. Even a shell script could be used for the Trojan Horse (Figure 3-17).

The Trojan Horse in Figure 3-17 will add write permission for others to **/etc** only when executed by the root. Although this horse is written as a shell script, it could also be written as a program, making it difficult to detect after it was installed. The preventive measure is to forbid writing in command directories.

Figure 3-17: Write permission on a commands directory
permits the installation of simple shell script Trojan Horses.

```
$ ls -ld /bin
drwxrwxrwx  2 bin      bin          5632 Jul 10 09:30 /bin
$ cd /bin
$ mv cat ocat
$ ocat > cat
:
if id | grep root > /dev/null ; then chmod +w /etc ; fi
exec /bin/ocat $*
<Control-D>
$ ▮
```

If the Trojan Horse in Figure 3-17 succeeds, write permission for all will be added to the **/etc** directory. Write permission on the **/etc/** directory permits users to edit the **/etc/passwd** file, even though it is unwriteable. The password file is readable, and the system breaker can make a copy of the file, edit it, and **mv** it into place (Figure 3-18).

*Figure 3-18: Becoming a superuser when the **/etc/** directory is writeable.*

```
$ ls -ld /etc
drwxrwxrwx 19 root     sys          4096 Jul 10 08:17 /etc
$ cp passwd ptmp
$ cat >> ptmp
bob::0:0:Super Bob:/:
<Control-D>
$ mv ptmp passwd
mv: passwd: 444 mode? y
$ su bob
# ▮
```

The same technique used to replace a startup file in a user's write-enabled HOME directory can be used to replace the **/etc/passwd** file. Although the password file is the keystone, other UNIX configuration files are nearly as sensitive. There are other ways of gaining superuser privileges that do not involve having a personal superuser account. And system security may be broken just by the ability to read or modify secure files, which does not necessarily require superuser privileges.

The easiest way to fix the write-for-others problem is to remove write permission for others on all system directories. This approach would work if there weren't several system directories that must be writeable by others. These directories are used as repositories for temporary files, and are known to commands and utilities that need to create temporary files. These directories are:

- **/tmp** directory, used by the **vi** editor and other programs
- **/usr/tmp** directory, used by the C compiler and the linker
- **/usr/spool/uucppublic** directory, the public directory used for file transfer between systems via **uucp**

The other thing you want to avoid is changing the permissions on every file and directory. Although it wouldn't hurt (much) to remove write for others everywhere, experience has taught me to be careful about changing permissions. What I recommend is waiting until you bring your system to single user mode. Single user mode prevents other users from working and also will typically unmount all file systems. You especially want to make sure that remotely mounted file systems are unmounted. Then, mount **/usr** if it is not already mounted, and use **find** to collect a list of writeable directories (Figure 3-19).

Figure 3-19: Collecting a list of writeable directories in single-user mode. This could also be done in multi-user mode. (System V type shutdown is shown.)

```
# shutdown -is -y
Shutdown message from rik: Log off now or risk file damage!!
[shutdown messages]
INIT: SINGLE USER
# mount
/dev/dsk/root on /
/dev/dsk/usr on /usr
# find / -type d -perm -2 -print > /tmp/writeable
# ▮
```

There are other options to the **find** command that can help you collect a list of writeable system directories. The BSD version of **find** includes the **-prune** option to prevent descending into a directory. Some System V versions of **find** recognize the options **-mount**, restricting the search to one file system, and **-local**, preventing going out over the network to remotely mounted file systems.

The reason for not immediately changing the permissions of all directories is that the writeable directories which are found may have been manipulated by some system breaker (Figure 3-20). After all, if you can find these directories, so can a system breaker.

Figure 3-20: The list of writeable system directories contains some surprises.

```
# cd /tmp
# ls -l writeable
-rw-r-----  1 root     other          263 Jul 10 20:03 writeable
# cat writeable
/tmp
/tmp/.X11-unix
/usr/opt/X11
/var/tmp
/var/mail/.locks
/var/spool/bftp
/var/spool/uucppublic
/var/preserve
/var/reelexchange
/var/reelexchange/Adn
/var/reelexchange/dev
/var/reelexchange/Dlibrary
# ls -l /usr/tmp /usr/preserve /usr/spool
lrwxrwxrwx  1 root   other   15 Jun 29 09:18 /usr/preserve -> ../var/preserve
lrwxrwxrwx  1 root   other   12 Jun 29 09:18 /usr/spool -> ../var/spool
lrwxrwxrwx  1 root   other   10 Jun 29 09:18 /usr/tmp -> ../var/tmp
# ▮
```

Instead of finding just three writeable system directories, I found 12 in a newly installed System V-based workstation. This is where the detective work must begin, because I have to decide which (if any) of the additional directories requires write permission for others. The general rule is temporary directories must only be writeable by others.

The first clue comes from trying **ls -l** on **/usr/tmp**. The **/usr/tmp** directory wasn't in the list of writeable directories, although I expected to find it there. This System V-based UNIX system models System V, Release 4. The **/usr** file system does not have to be a writeable file system; this permits mounting the **/usr** file system as read-only, and prevents the modification of the files and directories found there—a real boon for security. However, certain writeable directories are traditionally found in **/usr**. The solution has been to use symbolic links to sub-directories of **/var**, typically part of the root file system. The **ls -l** command in Figure 3-20 shows that there are symbolic links to these directories in **/var**.

But what about some of these other directories? The **/usr/preserve** directory is linked to **/var/preserve**, and is used by **vi** to preserve editing sessions that are interrupted. The **/usr/lib/expreserve** program actually performs this work, and was previously a privileged program and a security hole. In this system,

/usr/lib/expreserve is not a privileged program, so **/usr/preserve** must be write-able by all. This type of information can be gleaned from the FILES section of the manual page entry for **expreserve**. You can use **grep** to search through on-line manual pages for the names of mysterious files. On-line manual pages are found in subdirectories of **/usr/man** or **/usr/catman** (preformatted).

The two directories referencing X11 were harder to figure out. The **/usr/opt/X11** directory is part of an optional (opt) installation package, and should not require write permissions. The **/tmp/.X11-dir** appears to have something to do with the windowing system; since it gets recreated each time the system is restarted, changing its permissions will have no long-term effect. Neither are mentioned in system documentation, but **/usr/opt/X11** is definitely not a temporary directory.

The **/var/mail/.locks** directory has a group owner by the **mail** group, and both mailer programs have group mail privileges, so it appears that this directory does not require write for others. Since I am not sure, I can either try removing write permission and see what happens, or leave this directory alone. It is currently empty, and with a name like *locks*, is probably used for temporary lock files, so I will let it be.

The name **/var/spool/bftp** suggests a spooling directory for boot ftp (file transfer protocol), that could be used by networked devices (like X terminals). It is also currently empty and appears to be a temporary directory, so I will leave it alone.

The **reelexchange** directories all contain data files or subdirectories with data files. I have never seen anything about **reelexchange** before, and cannot not find it in the documentation for this system. Because it does contain data and is therefore not a temporary directory, I will remove write permissions for others from these directories.

The next step is to edit the list of writeable directories to create a new list. This list contains the names of writeable directories that I intend to fix by removing write permissions. If problems using the system show up later, I can refer to this list and restore write permissions to these directories in an attempt to fix the problem that appears related to these directories. Then, using this list write permissions are removed (Figure 3-21).

Figure 3-21: The edited list of writeable directories
and the **chmod** *command that removes write for others.*

```
# cat writeable
/usr/opt/X11
/var/reelexchange
/var/reelexchange/Adn
/var/reelexchange/dev
# chmod o-w `cat writeable`
# mv writeable /etc/security
# ▮
```

If the list of writeable directories is very long (greater than 5,120 characters), you cannot use the command shown in Figure 3-21. You can either split the list into smaller lists, or pipe the list using **cat** into **xargs chmod o-w**.

The Sticky Bit and Directories   The *sticky* bit makes executable files either remain in memory or swap space after their execution has completed (they stick in memory). This stickiness helps system performance because the program starts up faster the next time it is invoked. Care must be taken when making files sticky, because overuse of the sticky bit fills up memory and swap space.

In earlier versions of the UNIX system, the sticky bit had no meaning when it came to directories. Directories are not executable, and are only read into memory while being listed or searched. A meaning for the sticky bit and directories was defined in SunOS 4.x and System V Release 3—a sticky directory prevents a user from moving or removing files not owned by that user. Since **/tmp**, for example, has write and execute permissions for all, anyone can remove any file that is in **/tmp**. By making **/tmp** sticky, only the owner of a file and the superuser can remove or move files in **/tmp**. Figure 3-22 shows how to set the sticky bit.

Figure 3-22: Setting the sticky bit on temporary directories
prevents others from moving or removing files in these directories.

```
# chmod +t /tmp /var/tmp /var/preserve
# ▮
```

In Figure 3-22, I made three temporary directories sticky. Only the superuser can set the sticky bit. If your system does not have the sticky bit set for these directories, you can try setting it, but only later versions of the UNIX system will recognize this bit on directories.

Write Permission for System Files

There are few system-owned files that must be writeable by others. Offhand, I cannot think of any, but let's make a sweep of a UNIX system (see Figure 3-23) and see what has been left write-enabled for all.

Figure 3-23: The **find** *command created a list of files writeable by others (***-perm -2***). Only* **/var/spell/spellhist** *needs to be in this list.*

```
# find / -type f -perm -2 -print > write_files
# cat write_files
/admin/.profile.proto
/etc/log/fsck.log
/etc/log/old.fsck.log
/etc/log/nfsfs.log
/etc/log/old.nfsfs.log
/etc/sysadm/cmdlist
/etc/fstab
/etc/netinit.script
/etc/syslog.pid
/etc/state
/etc/rmtab
/var/spell/spellhist
/var/Build/system.raven
/var/Build/system.raven.config
/var/Build/conf.c
/var/Build/system.raven.build
/var/Build/ld_script
/var/Build/conf.o
/var/spool/lp/interface/ln03.orig
/var/reelexchange/Adn/drive1
/var/reelexchange/default.adn
/var/reelexchange/tapecap
/.profile.proto
/srv/admin/releases/PRIMARY
/srv/admin/clients/MY_HOST,PRIMARY
/srv/admin/clients/MY_HOST
# █
```

Typically, you will find that newer UNIX systems have fairly good default file permissions. The problems often show up where the vendor has made their own additions to the base UNIX system, and there are several examples in the list in Figure 3-23. The **.profile.proto** files are used while configuring the system—

the actual **.profile** files in these directories have identical contents, but the correct permissions and ownership.

The **/etc/log** files are created by scripts in the **/etc/init.d** directory of this system (fairly common for System V-based systems). Simply changing permissions on these files will be ineffective since they get recreated every time the system changes into a multi-user state (every reboot, for example). These scripts can be edited, and a **umask** of 22 can be added. Also, the scripts are invoked from a script started by the **init** process. By adding the **umask 22** to this script, the scripts invoked in **/etc/init.d** use the same **umask**. The **/etc/state**, **/etc/rmtab**, and **/etc/syslog.pid** are also created during the transition to multi-user state, and permissions on these files can be corrected by adding the **umask** command to the shell scripts that create these files.

So far, the writeable files that have been found are not dangerous. The ability to modify a log file will not provide a system breaker with any real advantage, although changing some files, like **/etc/syslog.pid**, could affect an orderly shutdown. The configuration files and scripts are more important. If the **/etc/fstab** file is modified, it can prevent the system from mounting file systems correctly. The **/etc/netinit.script**, while not a shell script, does permit the execution of programs listed within it. By adding a program or script to this file, a system breaker can gain root privilege when the system is rebooted.

The **/etc/sysadm/cmdlist** contains the names of shell scripts run by the **sysadm** command. Although the ability to change this file would not automatically permit a system breaker to gain some system privilege (the system administrator would have to be tricked into cooperating), there is no reason to permit writing here. The **sysadm** script itself is responsible for several files in Figure 3-23's list. On this system, the **sysadm** script sets the **umask** to zero, granting maximum permissions to all newly created files and directories. This means that newly mounted file systems have writeable root directories and that newly configured kernels (such as **dgux.raven)** are writeable; in fact, any files created through the **sysadm** shell script and not intentionally modified with **chmod** will be writeable by all. The solution here involves changing the **umask** command in **sysadm** to **umask 02** and correcting permissions for these files.

The **/var/reelexchange** directories were writeable, and so are some files in these directories. The **/srv/admin** directories contain files created during the installation of networking utilities by **sysadm**, and need to be corrected.

The only file in this entire list that can writeable by others is **/var/spell/spellhist**, a log file containing information obtained by running the **spell** script. You may find other log files maintained by programs or shell scripts that include useful, but not critical information. Some games keep log files containing previous high scores which must be writeable by others, but this system doesn't have any (yet). The **spellhist** file was removed from the **write_files** list and permissions were removed (Figure 3-24).

Figure 3-24: Write permission for others was removed from the
files in "write_files" after removing **/var/spell/spellhist** *from the list.*

```
# cat write_files | xargs chmod o-w
# █
```

Remember that in many cases, write for others will reoccur unless you edit the scripts that are creating the writeable files. System startup scripts were a big culprit in this system, as was **sysadm**. BSD-based systems do not have **sysadm** but do have startup scripts, typically **/etc/rc** and **/etc/rc.local** which may potentially create files with incorrect permissions. Also, in System V, Release 4, the **sysadm** script has become a program and cannot be edited.

Writeable System Scripts and Programs   In Figure 3-23, the **find** command discovered only one script, the **/etc/netinit.script**. If you discover any writeable scripts while searching for writeable system files, you must check the script for possible modifications. The easiest thing to do is to recover the original of the script from the installation tape or disk. If this is not possible, you have a difficult task ahead of you.

System shell scripts are executed by the superuser, and confer superuser privileges upon all commands contained in the scripts. If a system cracker can insinuate commands into such a shell script, these commands will have superuser privileges too. Reading shell scripts is not that easy, but I will tell you what I generally look for. I look for commands that create new files, including through redirection, commands that change permissions (with **chmod**) and ownership (**chown**), and commands that modify files (**sed** and **ed**, for example). Making life more difficult, these commands can be hidden in shell scripts called by the system script. All shell scripts called by system shell scripts are potential problems. System shell scripts include not only startup scripts, but also scripts executed via cron, atrun, sysadm, and locally written scripts (that perform backups or file restore, for example).

Of course, a clever system breaker would remove write permission after modifying a shell script, so not finding write for others on shell scripts is no guarantee that the shell script has not been modified. When teaching security, one of my favorite tricks is to modify a startup file so that it creates a security hole each time the system is rebooted. Thus, even if the security hole is discovered and repaired, rebooting recreates it.

I suggest that you spend some time checking the system scripts. Once you feel you have uncovered and corrected any problems, make backup copies of these scripts. Then, if you suspect changes in these scripts, you have clean replacements ready (offline). To help you find these scripts, I suggest looking in these places:

- The **/etc/inittab** file contains commands executed during system startup and changes run levels for System V-based UNIX systems.
- BSD-based systems use the **/etc/rc*** shell scripts.
- The shell scripts executed by the **cron** daemon in **/usr/spool/cron/crontabs** directories (System V.2) or **/usr/spool/cron** older UNIX systems.
- Other system administration scripts, such as **/etc/shutdown** (System V), **/etc/mvdir** (System V), and any locally written scripts.

Writeable programs present a different challenge. If you find programs that are writeable, they may have been modified in a subtle fashion by a programmer (or virus), or less subtly by replacing the program with a shell script. Some of the commands in **/usr/bin** are shell scripts, and are subject to editing and modification. If the system breaker can copy a program, it is possible to write a simple shell script Trojan Horse that calls the original program and does something for the perpetrator (see Figure 3-17). The simplest solution is to replace writeable programs from the installation tapes or disks. Chapter 5 has more to say about detecting changes in programs.

Read Permission and System Files

Many sensitive system files require read permission for all. The **/etc/passwd** file is a good example. If **/etc/passwd** is not readable, then commands that display (or accept as arguments) user names will not work. On the other hand, the ability to read the encrypted passwords permits password cracking. There are other files that must be readable by all, so simply removing read for others from all but a few system files is not practical.

There is one system file that must *not* be readable by anyone except the root. The **Systems** or **L.sys** file contains information used by **uucp** to connect remote systems, including unencrypted passwords and the phone numbers for these systems. Although the passwords are for logging into accounts that run the **uucico** daemon instead of a shell, the phone numbers alone are dangerous. And **uucp** can be abused by having it copy password files between systems. Chapter 4 covers **uucp** communications in detail.

Another important file to protect is the **/usr/adm/sulog** (or **/var/adm/sulog**). The **sulog** contains the user names of people who know the root password and have used the System V **su** command. For strangers, this provides information they might not otherwise be able to get. System administrators should also watch this file, because it reveals who has learned the superuser password. On BSD systems, the **/usr/adm/messages** file contains messages sent to the console after boot, including messages from **su** about who has used the command.

There are other files you can make unreadable by others. The scripts run during startup, scripts run by the **cron** daemon, and any script run by the superuser or administrative accounts do not need to be readable by others. Leaving these scripts readable lets potential system crackers look for problems in these scripts, for example, ways to trick the script into doing something extra. One thing to remember is that security may only be a parttime job for you, but for many system crackers it is a full-time occupation. Much patience and ingenuity is wasted by system crackers on their self-ordained quest to break-into other people's computers. The more you can do to make their "job" harder, the less likely your system will be broken. Removing read permission from system scripts, such as the "rc" scripts, makes your system less vulnerable.

The publicly executable UNIX commands are usually readable by all. Executable programs do not require read permission, because the *kernel* (the heart of the UNIX operating system) has all privileges and handles the invocation of executable programs. Scripts, however, are executed by users' shell programs and cannot be executed without read permission. You could remove read permission from publicly executable programs, for example in the **/usr/bin** directory, but not from the scripts found there. You would use the **file** command to discover which commands are executable programs and which are command scripts. The reasons for removing read permission are that executable files do not require read permission and read permission enables users to examine program code with debuggers looking for possible holes. These are not the strongest reasons for spending the time removing read permission from executable programs. It would be better if UNIX systems were distributed without read permissions for these commands.

Device Files

In the UNIX systems, devices, such as terminals and disks, are accessed through special files. These special files have permissions, owners, and groups, just like other files, but they are different in that special files connect, through the kernel, to devices. The files themselves contain no data, only the reference to the device (which is stored in the inode). Yet, these special files are important to system security.

There are two types of special files. The *block* device files are indicated by the letter "b" in the **ls -l** listings. Block devices are hard disks, optical disks, and sometimes tape devices. Block refers to the organization on the device, where information is stored and retrieved as a block of data, for example, a 512-byte sector of a disk. The *character* devices are marked with the letter "c" in long listings. Character devices have no constraints on number of characters read or written to the device, such as terminals, printers, and modems.

Figure 3-25: Block devices are distinguished by the letter "b", and character devices by the letter "c".

```
$ ls -l /dev/dsk/usr /dev/kmem
brw------- 1 root     root     4,  2 Jul 18 08:04 /dev/dsk/usr
crw------- 1 root     root     3,  1 Jul 18 08:04 /dev/kmem
$ ▮
```

Instead of a size, the **ls -l** listing shows the device numbers for each file. The **major** device number (3 for **/dev/kmem** in Figure 3-25) specifies which device driver the kernel will be using. The **minor** device number (2 for **/dev/dsk/usr**) is used to pass information to the kernel, in this case, which disk partition to use. The major and minor device numbers are the real hooks into the UNIX kernel. Any device file with the same major and minor device numbers and same type (block or character) accesses the same device.

Users connect to the UNIX system through character devices with names that usually begin with **/dev/tty** (see Figure 3-26). For example, **/dev/tty01** would be the second terminal device. Terminal devices are owned by the user logged in through them until the session ends. On newer UNIX systems, ownership of terminal ports reverts to the root after logout in order to prevent some other user from using the port. In the past, a user could run a program or script known as a *spoof*, which presents a phony login prompt on an unused port, and collects a password from an unsuspecting user. Secure versions of the UNIX system provide a mechanism, called a *safe path*, that closes and reopens the terminal port before a login can take place, disconnecting any spoofing program.

Figure 3-26: The /dev/tty file is owned by the root, but readable and writeable by all. Other /dev/ttyNN ports are owned by the user currently logged in.

```
$ ls -l /dev/tty /dev/tty01
crw-rw-rw- 1 root    root      2,  0 Jul 18 08:04 /dev/tty
crw------- 1 rik     editing  11,  1 Jul 18 08:04 /dev/tty01
$ ▮
```

The character file **/dev/tty** (not followed by any digits) represents any user's current terminal. The **/dev/tty** file is owned by the root, but must be readable and writeable by all. This file is used by the **login** program to read passwords, and if it is not writeable by all, users cannot log in.

Systems that permit shell layers or windows also have pseudo-ttys, with names like **/dev/ttyp01** or **/dev/ttyq01**. These files follow the same scheme as the terminal port devices, and are owned by the user during a login or window session.

Although disks are considered block devices, UNIX systems also will have character interfaces to the disk devices. The character interface to a disk is used while making or checking file systems, and for fast file system copies. Most UNIX systems follow a naming convention where the letter "r" is added in the name of the character, or *raw*, device file for disks. So the names of the block and character device files will usually be similar. The major and minor device numbers may be different for the different types of interfaces. Section 7 (Devices) of the UNIX documentation has information about device naming conventions for your system. Not all vendors bother to update this section, so it may reflect some other vendor's devices.

Disk device files, both block and character, must be owned by a system account, and readable and writeable by the owner only. A disk device that is readable can be read directly by a program that mimics the actions of the kernel but ignores access controls. This program reads the disk device like a file, interprets inode and directory information, and reads files. If there is write permission on the disk device, the program can also modify files, or change the permissions, owner, and group of any inode regardless of the permission or ownership.

Direct access to file systems is dangerous. Mounting makes file systems accessible to users. If users can directly access disk devices, they can read or write directly, or even destroy the entire file system. As an example, Figure 3-27 shows how a writeable file system can be destroyed by a naive user attempting to redirect some output and "save" it to a disk.

Figure 3-27: Any user can destroy a file system that is writeable
by redirecting output (or otherwise writing directly) to a disk device.

```
$ ls -l /dev/dsk/c1d0s5
brw-rw-rw 1 root    root    3,  5 Jul 14 12:05 /dev/dsk/c1d0s5
$ cat chapter1 > /dev/dsk/c1d0s5
$ ▮
```

The mistake made in Figure 3-27 (presuming it was a mistake) could also be done through the character device, which would be **/dev/rdsk/c1d0s5**. It is important to check all your disk device files and correct ownership and permissions if necessary. Old UNIX systems and BSD-based UNIX systems tend to keep all their device files in the **/dev** directory. System V-based systems have added several subdirectories to **/dev**: **/dev/dsk** for block disk files, **/dev/rdsk** for character (raw) disk files, and **/dev/rmt** for raw magnetic tape files.

Tape devices (and floppy disk drives) are often readable and writeable by all users. Providing access to these devices is a convenience to the system administrator, but not necessarily a good idea. After a backup has completed, anyone who can read the tape (or floppy disk) device file can also read everything on the tape, regardless of permissions. If you plan to backup any sensitive information on a tape or floppy drive, the drive must be owned by an administrative account and readable and writeable by the owner only.

The **/dev/kmem** and **/dev/mem** character device files provide interfaces to kernel memory and general physical memory. The **/dev/kmem** file is used by the **ps** command to read information in the kernel's process table. If either of these files is readable by others, users can fish through memory for any information currently in disk or character buffers (such as recently entered passwords). If these files are writeable, a user could "patch" the kernel or, much easier, crash the system. Both these files must be owned by an administrative account (generally the same as the owner of the **ps** command), and readable and writeable by owner *only*.

Stray Device Files   There is nothing sacred about the **/dev** directory. Device files are created by the superuser with the **mknod** command. Anyone who has super-user privileges can make a device file anywhere in the UNIX file system. The device file could even be on a floppy disk containing a file system. The kernel is not concerned with where in the directory hierarchy the device file exists. If a user can read and write the device file, that user has direct access to the device specified by the major and minor device numbers given in the device file. Figure 3-28 shows a command line that is used for uncovering device files not in the **/dev** directory.

Figure 3-28: The **find** *command ferrets out all block or character device files, and* **grep** *eliminates all those in the* **dev** *directory.*

```
# find / \( -type b -o -type c \) -print | grep -v '^/dev'
/u/rik/Prog/fsys
# ls -l /u/rik/Prog/fsys
brw------- 1 rik    editing  4,  2 Jul 14 18:34 /dev/dsk/usr
# rm /u/rik/Prog/fsys
#
```

If a user owned or accessible device file is found using the **find** command, it should be removed. Users do not need to have their own "private" access to files. The "best" use for such private access would be to violate system security.

Setting Up a System File Database

Once you have removed write permission from system files and directories, and examined system-owned scripts, you are ready to create a database of system files. This database contains the permissions, owner, and group of every file and directory that you wish to monitor. At a minimum, you need to watch the files and subdirectories of **/etc**, the commands in **/bin**, **/usr/bin**, **/usr/lib**, and possibly **/usr/etc**. Files in the root directory, such as the kernel and root's startup files bear watching. Or you can collect information on every system file and directory.

You may also want to keep tabs on the startup files that belong to individual users, such as **.profile** or **.cshrc**. Putting these startup files and users' HOME directories in your database will help you later.

The first step to building your database is to generate the list of files and directories to watch. If you are going to watch every system file and directory, you can use a **find** command starting at the root (/) directory, or you can use **find** with a list of directories to watch (Figure 3-29).

Figure 3-29: Collecting a minimal list of files for the database.

```
# find /etc /bin /usr/bin /usr/lib /usr/lib/uucp  \
/usr/etc /sbin -print  watchfiles
# cat >> watchfiles
/vmunix
/vmunix.old
<control-D>
# awk -F: '{ printf "%s\n%s/.profile\n", $6, $6 }'  \
/etc/passwd | sort -u >> watchfiles
# ▮
```

Figure 3-29 shows how to use **find** to create your lists of files, use **cat** to add the kernel file, and **awk** to add users' HOME directories and the **.profile** startup files. For example, C shell users will have **.login** and **.cshrc**, and Korn shell users will have **.kshrc**. I describe this as the minimal list for your database. The more inclusive list is all the system files and directories, users' HOME directories, and user startup files. Remember that users may have other startup files than **.profile**—you want to add these to your list too.

With your list prepared, you are ready for the next step. The permset script collects information for the database. The script uses the file **permfile** by default, but permits changing the output file by including the name of a file as the second argument (Figure 3-30).

The permset script can take two arguments. The first argument is the name of the file containing the list of files and directories to collect, for example, watchfiles. The second optional argument can be the name of the output file. If there are no arguments, the standard input is read for the names of files and directories, and the database is written to **permfile**.

The database will contain the permissions, owner, group, and pathname of all files. Additionally, files that are executable programs or scripts will be checksummed, and the size and checksum will be included. The checksum is important for discovering if executable files have been manipulated. The database can contain comments by beginning a line with the pound sign (#).

Figure 3-30: The permset script creates the file and directory database.

```
# cat permset
#!/bin/sh # permset - setup a permissions database from a
# list of files; for every file, get permissions,
# owner, group, and for executable  programs or
# scripts get size and checksum, too.
PATH=/bin:/usr/bin; export PATH
PERMS=./permfile
case $# in
 0 ) LIST="" ;;
 1 ) if [ -f "$1" ] ; then
          LIST=$1
        else
          echo Cannot open $1 1>&2; exit 1
      fi ;;
 2 ) PERMS=$2 ;;
 [3-9] ) echo Usage: $0 [listfile [outfile]] 1>&2; exit 3 ;;
esac
# preserve old permissions file, if it exists
if [ -f $PERMS ] ; then mv $PERMS $PERMS.old ; fi
# write out a column heading comment, and protect file
echo \#Mode\\t\\tOwner\\tGroup\\tSize\\tChecksum\\tFilename > $PERMS
chmod 600 $PERMS
# read from LIST, or the standard input
cat $LIST |
while read FILE
do
 set -- `ls -ldc $FILE`
 PERM=$1
 UID=$3
 GID=$4
 SIZE=$5
# if the file is executable and a program or script, run sum
 if test -x $FILE && file $FILE |
    egrep 'commands|executable' > /dev/null
 then
   set `sum $FILE`
   SUM=$1
   echo $PERM\\t$UID\\t$GID\\t$SIZE\\t$SUM\\t$FILE >> $PERMS
 else
   echo $PERM\\t$UID\\t$GID\\t\"\"\\t\"\"\\t$FILE >> $PERMS
 fi
done
# ▮
```

Running the database on a list of over 8,000 files and directories took 35 minutes on a fairly fast workstation. The database was 400,000 bytes long when completed. The 8,000 files include a fairly complete UNIX system, with X Window and on-line manual pages, and is a complete list of all system files and directories, and user HOMES. This database provides a snapshot of presumably good permissions, ownership, group, and program integrity, since the collection was done after checking system security.

If you wish to update the database at a later date, create a list of files to add or update, and use a different name for the output file. Then edit the original database, removing outdated entries and appending the new database file.

Checking the System Against the Database

The system checking script, **permck**, is based on a program I encountered many years ago. The **vchk** (version check) program was added by UniSoft, a VAR for System V UNIX system software. The **vchk** program could generate a database or check a system against the database. Its purpose was to check that the proper files and directories would be shipped with a new UNIX system. If permissions, ownership, or group were different, the program would write a script to fix them. And if executable files were modified or out of date, they could be downloaded from another system.

The permck script is not as fancy as the **vchk** program, but retains many of the same features. It does create a script that will fix permissions, ownership, and group. (The **sed** script that converts permissions into octal was found in Kochan and Wood.) It also creates a list of files that have been modified and should be restored from backups. One thing the script does not do that the **vchk** program did was report on new files in the system. This would be useful, since a new file could be a Trojan Horse or other security problem. You can add this functionality by writing a script that creates your list of database files, rerunning the script, and using **comm** or **diff** to compare your two lists. The permck script shown in Figure 3-31 will detect files or directories that have disappeared since the database was created.

Figure 3-31: The permck script compares
information in the database with current information.

```
# cat permck
#!/bin/sh # permck - check files against a permissions database;
# for every file, get permissions, owner, group, and for
# executable programs or scripts get size and checksum, too.
# A script to fix problems is contained in $FIX, and a list of
# files to restore from backups are in $RESTORE - rf
PATH=/bin:/usr/bin; export PATH
umask 77
FIX=./fixes
RESTORE=./restore
CDIR=x
case $# in
 0 ) PERMS=./permfile ;;
 1 ) PERMS=$1 ;;
 [2-9] ) echo Usage: $0 [permfile] 2>&1 ; exit 1 ;;
esac
# preserve previous fix and restore files, if any
if [ -f $FIX ] ; then
 mv $FIX $FIX.old
fi
if [ -f $RESTORE ] ; then
 mv $RESTORE $RESTORE.old
fi
# put the starting date in the fix file.
echo \# permck run on `date`. > $FIX
# read PERMS, using sed to strip out comment lines
cat $PERMS | sed '/^#/d' |
while LINE=`line`
do
 set -- $LINE
 PERM=$1
 UID=$2
 GID=$3
 SIZE=$4
 SUM=$5
 FILE=$6
 DIR=`dirname $FILE`
# report on the current directory if run interactively
 if [ -t 1 -a $CDIR != $DIR ] ; then
   echo Working in $DIR
   CDIR=$DIR
 fi
# if cannot find the file, put a comment in FIX and
# the name in RESTORE
```

Figure 3-31: The permck script compares
information in the database with current information (continued).

```
if [ ! -r $FILE ] ; then
  echo \# $FILE: Not found, restore? >> $FIX
  echo $FILE >> $RESTORE
  continue
fi
set -- `ls -ldc $FILE`
CPERM=$1
CUID=$3
CGID=$4
CSIZE=$5
# set flag to "No problem"
problem=no
if test -x $FILE && file $FILE |
   egrep 'commands|executable' > /dev/null
then
  set `sum $FILE`
  CSUM=$1
  if [ $PERM\\t$UID\\t$GID\\t$SIZE\\t$SUM != \
  $CPERM\\t$CUID\\t$CGID\\t$CSIZE\\t$CSUM ] ; then
# something does not match, so there is a problem.
    problem=yes
# if the size or checksum changed, replace the file
    if [ $SIZE != $CSIZE -o $SUM != $CSUM ] ; then

      echo \# $FILE: size and/or checksum have changed. >> $FIX
      echo $FILE >> $RESTORE
      echo \# Replace $FILE from backups. >> $FIX
    fi
  fi
else
  if [ $PERM\\t$UID\\t$GID != $CPERM\\t$CUID\\t$CGID ]
  then
    problem=yes
  fi
fi
if [ $problem = "yes" ] ; then
# if permissions changed, put chmod in fix script
  if [ $PERM != $CPERM ] ; then
    echo \# $FILE: mode changed from $PERM to $CPERM >> $FIX
    MODE=`echo $PERM | sed "
    s/^.//
    s/\(..[sS]..[sS]..[tT]\)/7\1/
```

Figure 3-31: The permck script compares
information in the database with current information (continued).

```
      s/\(..[sS]..[sS]..[^tT]\)/6\1/
      s/\(..[sS]..[^sS]..[tT]\)/5\1/
      s/\(..[sS]..[^sS]..[^tT]\)/4\1/
      s/\(..[^sS]..[sS]..[tT]\)/3\1/
      s/\(..[^sS]..[sS]..[^tT]\)/2\1/
      s/\(..[^sS]..[^sS]..[tT]\)/1\1/
      s/S/-/g; s/s/x/g; s/t/x/; s/T/-/; s/--x/1/g
      s/-w-/2/g; s/-wx/3/g; s/r--/4/g; s/r-x/5/g
      s/rw-/6/g; s/rwx/7/g; s/---/0/g"`
      echo chmod $MODE $FILE >> $FIX
    fi # if ownership changed, put chown in fix script
    if [ $UID != $CUID ] ; then
      echo \# $FILE: owner changed from $UID to $CUID >> $FIX
      echo chown $UID $FILE >> $FIX
    fi
# if group changed, put chgrp in fix script
    if [ $GID != $CGID ] ; then
      echo \# $FILE: group changed from $GID to $CGID >> $FIX
      echo chgrp $GID $FILE >> $FIX
    fi
fi
done
# ▌
```

The permck script accepts only a single argument—the name of an alternative database file. If no arguments are given, the default name is used. The permck script always creates a FIX file, containing a least a comment and the start date. The FIX file, "fixes" by default, will also contain commands to fix permissions, ownership, and group. A second file, RESTORE ("restore" by default), contains a list of files to be replaced from backup—see Figure 3-32 for an example of permck's output in these two files.

The permck script took about twice as long to run as the permset script. If the script is run interactively, it will output the directory name each time the directory changes as a way of reporting progress. The script could also be run by **cron** late at night, since it does use considerable system resources on smaller systems. The script does not require interaction, but creates action reports.

The permck script is not infallible. In Figure 3-32, the "fixes" file shows that the **/etc/fstab** file had read and write privileges for all when the database was written, but the **/etc/fstab** file currently has read-only for all and write by owner only. These permissions are correct, and the database needs changing. Had the permissions been incorrect, the "fixes" file could be executed as a shell script. The point is that you cannot follow the dictates of security scripts without checking them first yourself.

Figure 3-32: Some example output from permck in the "fixes" and "restore" files.

```
# cat fixes
# permck run on Sun Jul 15 13:31:54 PDT 1990.
# /etc/fstab: permissions changed from -rw-rw-rw- to rw-r--r--
chmod 666 /etc/fstab
# /usr/bin/sysadm: size and/or checksum have changed.
# Replace /usr/bin/sysadm from backups.
# cat restore
/usr/bin/sysadm
# ▌
```

The second problem uncovered by permck was a discrepancy in the size or checksum of the **/usr/bin/sysadm** script. In this case, I had modified **sysadm** between the time that the database was created and the permck script was run. Had this not been true, I would have first examined the inode change time on **sysadm** to determine when it had last been modified, then replaced it with a backup copy. The time it was modified can help uncover who modified the **sysadm** script. Details on uncovering security violators are covered in Chapter 5.

Since the database created incorrect results when compared with current system by permck, the database needs to be edited. The correct permissions for **/etc/fstab** need to be inserted, and the correct size and checksum for **/usr/bin/sysadm**. The database file may be edited, and the corrections added. If there are many corrections to make, remember that permset can take a list of the files to be modified and a filename, and put the corrections in a new file. The old lines can be deleted from the database, and the new file appended, updating the database with the corrections.

Storing the Database File   There is nothing magic or difficult to understand about the database file used for monitoring permissions, ownership, group, sizes, and checksums. It is an ASCII file that can be viewed with **more** or **pg** and edited with any programming editor. And that's just the problem. If you leave the database file on-line, someone else can modify it.

Although not all system crackers are that clever, the more sophisticated will look for signs of monitoring. In the *Cuckoo's Egg* (by Clifford Stoll), the elusive intruder would logoff immediately at the slightest suspicion of any monitoring of his activities. An in-house system breaker who becomes the root can examine *or modify* any file in your system, and any routine security checks will be high on the list.

Ideally, you would like to run at least a scaled-down version of a system security check nightly. This check requires that the necessary database files and scripts be kept on-line, so that **cron** can run the checks. Since these files are accessible, the system cracker can modify the database files to cover up the effects of any wrongdoings. So these files are vulnerable.

What you can do to protect your system is to keep off-line copies of your database files and security scripts. Every week you should restore these files to a secure directory and compare them with the on-line copies. If your on-line copies haven't changed, you can feel relatively safe. But only relatively, since the system cracker may have caught on to your routine checks, and just as routinely restores the files to their previous state. A system cracker can be as clever as you are, and often has more time to waste.

For your complete database and full-scale checks, keep them off-line, as tape backups, and restore them before running checks. A further check would be to run checksums on your files and compare the checksums with hardcopy values. If this approach seems too paranoid, I can't blame you. But remember, to a system cracker, it's all a game to see who can be the cleverest.

Set User and Set Group Property

Once upon a time, the alchemists believed in the existence of a "Philosophers Stone" which would have the magical property of turning lead into gold. While the UNIX system does not possess this stone, it does have the set user and group property. This property permits any user to temporarily obtain the privileges of other users or groups. This lesser transmutation is still potent, since the ability to be the superuser, even momentarily, bestows enormous power on the invoker.

Perhaps for this reason, the set user and group property has become a focal point for both system crackers and UNIX security. While this property poses a security problem, it is only one of many. Let's take a look at it, see how it works, and what it is good for.

Bestowing User Privileges

To understand the set user and group property, it helps to take a deeper look at what happens when a user starts a UNIX command. First off, the user already has been given two sets of ids. Each set contains a user id and a group id. The first set is called the *real user id*, and represents the user and group id established during the login process. The second set represents the *effective user id*, which may be changed during the course of a login session by the set user and group property.

Access privileges depend on the effective user or group id rather than the real user or group id. The reason for this will become clear in a moment. Both sets of ids are normally inherited by an child process of a user's login shell (Figure 3-33).

Figure 3-33: The real and effective user and group ids normally remain the same when a new process, in this case /bin/date, is invoked.

```
process           /bin/sh --->   /bin/date
real user         rik            rik
real group        editing        editing
effective user    rik            rik
effective group   editing        editing
```

Something different happens when the user invokes a command with the set-user-id bit set. Instead of inheriting the effective user id of the parent process, the newly invoked process inherits the user id of the *owner* of the invoked command. For example, when a user invokes the **passwd** command, he or she can now change the **/etc/passwd** file, *even though it can only be written to by the superuser!* (Figure 3-34).

*Figure 3-34: The effective user id while using the **passwd** command is root.*

```
process           /bin/sh --->   /bin/passwd
real user         rik            rik
real group        editing        editing
effective user    rik     --->   root
effective group   editing        editing
```

The set user and group property is very useful. It permits ordinary users to change their own passwords, to display free disk space (with **df**), to send mail to other users, to use **uucp**, and to display the contents of the kernel's process table (**ps**). These are familiar examples of how this property gets used in the UNIX system. Essentially, the set user and group property permits access to files that would normally be denied.

Well, there's no problem here. This property is very important to the UNIX system, since it permits many actions that would be impossible, or require special support from the kernel, to do. The set user and group property prevents having to rewrite the kernel every time it is necessary to temporarily share access to protected files.

The Problem

The problem with the set user and group property only occurs when the access to protected files is uncontrolled. Commands, such as **passwd** or **ps** control our access to protected files. The only thing you can do with the **passwd** command is change a password. You cannot add new accounts, change the comment field, modify the user id of your account, or anything else. The **ps** command (see Figure 3-35) only displays process status—it won't modify anything.

Figure 3-35: The set user-id bit is indicated by a letter s (or
capital S) in place of the user or group x for execute in long listings.

```
$ ls -l /bin/passwd /bin/ps
-rwsr-sr-x 1 root    sys      161864 Apr 18 12:59 /bin/passwd
-rwxr-sr-x 1 bin     sys      104472 Apr 18 12:59 /bin/ps
$ ▋
```

The **mailx** command (known as **Mail** on BSD systems) uses set group property to permit writing to other users' mail files. The **mailx** command does permit executing any command through the use of shell escapes. Before the shell escape does anything, however, the user's effective group id is changed back to their real group id (see Figure 3-36).

In Figure 3-36, the **id** command shows the effective user and group ids of the user rik. Even after invoking a new shell via the **mailx** shell escape, the effective user and group ids have remained the same. What has happened is that the **mailx** program is well-behaved, and restores my effective group id before giving me an unrestricted shell to play with.

Figure 3-36: The shell escape in **mailx** *restores the user's*
effective group before giving the user access to the shell.

```
$ ls -l /usr/bin/mailx
-rwxr-sr-x 1 bin     mail      192616 Apr 18 12:58 /usr/bin/mailx
$ mailx
mailx version 3.03 01/18/88  Type ? for help.
"/usr/mail/rik": 1 message 1 new
>N   1 rik                Mon Jul 16 21:16      4/51
? sh
$ id
uid=100(rik) gid=100(editing)
$ ^D
? d1
? q
$ id
uid=100(rik) gid=100(editing)
$ ▮
```

Programs with the set user or group id property have been designed with this property in mind. There are a limited number of such programs in every UNIX system, and as we have seen, these programs are essential to normal use of the system. Even ordinary users can write programs and make them set user id to their own accounts if they wish.

The set user or group id property is turned on or off through the **chmod** command (and associated system call). Only the owner of a file, or the superuser, can set or unset these bits. Symbolically, the set user and group bits are represented by the letter s. If using the numeric arguments to **chmod** (see Figure 3-37), the number 4000 sets the set user id bit, and 2000 sets the set group id bit.

Figure 3-37: Two commands executed as root
can give any user lasting superuser privileges.

```
# cp /bin/sh /u/bob/.sh
# chmod 4777 /u/bob/.sh
# ▮
```

The two commands shown in Figure 3-37 create a set-user-id shell, a favorite tool for system crackers. It only takes a couple of seconds as the superuser to execute these two commands. Of course, these commands can be hidden in a startup file, and executed with root privileges during system startup or during root's login. The perpetrator could also use some other command, such as the C or

Korn shell, or even an editor, as the file to copy. Making the file writeable by all is unnecessary, but it must be executable by others if it is to work.

The person who invokes a root-owned set-user-id shell is using a shell program with an effective user id of root. Through this program, the user can read, write, or remove any file. Only programs that look at the real user id will be unaffected by this ruse. Changing the root password won't affect this user's access. Of course, any user that finds this set-user-id shell can execute and use it.

System V, Release 4 will remove some of this problem by making the shell check to see if it was invoked from a set-user-id file. If the set-user-id bit was set, the shell will exit. Although this is a good start, there are ways around this fix, since other programs can be used besides the Bourne shell.

The Solution

The most obvious solution is not to let anyone create a root-owned set-user-id file. You have only never to abandon a root owned shell, never execute a Trojan Horse while root, never permit the modification of startup scripts or programs run by root, and never execute as root any locally contributed software. I haven't made this seem difficult—it is difficult to prevent something that is so easy to do, and fairly general knowledge besides.

The next best solution would be to forbid the set user or group property. A C2 version of the UNIX system actually did remove set user and group property from the kernel. To replace the affected commands, the vendor produced daemons that were started during the transition to multi-user run level and ran with root privileges. These daemons listened to sockets (which are somewhat like the shell's pipes) and serviced requests, for example, to change a user's password or display process status. Only one vendor chose this approach.

The best approach for most of us is eternal vigilance. If someone succeeds in creating a root-owned set-user-id shell, they must have managed to temporarily have root privileges. However, if the file is discovered quickly enough, the perpetrator won't have as much of an opportunity to use it. Discovering the file quickly also makes it simpler to catch the perpetrator and fix any other damage or modifications made by the system breaker.

You start out by collecting a list of the files which currently have either the set-user-id or set-group-id bit set. This **find** command should be run as root with all file systems mounted (Figure 3-38).

Figure 3-38: The command to create a list of all set user or group property files.

```
# find / \( -perm -4000 -o -perm -2000 \) -print > setfiles
# ▮
```

The next step is more difficult. You must go through the list of "setfiles" and determine if each of these files is a legitimate set user or group program. Lists of these programs, taken from System V and SunOS 4.x systems are presented in an Appendix. However, no two UNIX systems are exactly alike, and you can almost count on your system being different. Also, third-party software often includes set user or group files.

Legitimate set user or group files will be clustered in several system directories. A set user or group program in a directory containing only data files is cause for suspicion. A system-owned set user or group program anywhere in a user's HOME directory tree is definitely illegitimate. While users can set the set user or group bits on their own program, they should own these files—not a system account. Remember that it is the *owner* of the file (or the group) that sets the effective user or group id. A user owned set-user-id file bestows the same access privileges as the owner on anyone who can execute the program. Writing set user or group programs is not a simple task because of the dangers implicit in making a programming mistake. An Appendix provides some simple rules for writing safe set user or group programs.

A good way to pick out legitimate set user or group files is to look up these files in system documentation. UNIX manual entries do not tell you that a program should be set user or group—but it will tell you that at least the people who wrote your system documentation knew about the program. You can ask yourself the question "Does this command require special access privileges to do its job?" The FILES section of the manual page can help you answer this questions, since FILES should tell what files must be accessed. For example, **ps** accesses **/dev/kmem**, and **/bin/passwd** accesses /etc/passwd.

One reason for using the manuals is to make sure that someone has not hidden a wolf among the sheep. The best disguise for a illegitimate set-user-id program is to appear to be a UNIX system command or utility. About half of the illegitimate set-user-id programs that I have found were disguised as system files; the remainder were "hidden" in users' own directories.

Some of the hardest files to justify will be those that come with third-party applications, such as office automation software. These won't be included in your

UNIX documentation, and may not be explained in the application's documentation either. You can try calling the vendor and asking the support staff about suspicious programs. I wouldn't put it past vendors to include their own personal "back-doors", via root-owned set-user-id programs, with their software.

If you find what you think are illegitimate set user or group files, you need to do several things. First is to investigate the file by examining its inode change time (see Figure 3-39). The inode change time provides the only clue as to when the file was created or changed. Chapter 5 goes into methods for investigating security violations and tracking down the perpetrators. Next, you want to record your actions. If you have made a mistake, and the file is legitimate, you want to be able to restore permissions and ownership properly. Finally, you must remove either the file itself, the set user or group property, or change the ownership of the program. If you are not certain about the illegitimacy of a file, don't remove it; just change the permissions or ownership.

Figure 3-39: Listing and saving the inode change time of a
suspicious set-user-id file before removing the set-user-id file. Less
obvious files would have the set user property removed with **chmod u-s**.

```
# ls -lc /usr/lib/libcsh.a
-rwsr-xr-x 1 root    other   281040 Jul 15 13:38 /usr/lib/libcsh.a
# ar -t /usr/lib/libcsh.a
ar: /usr/lib/libcsh.a not in archive format
# ls -l /usr/bin/csh
-rwxr-xr-x 1 bin     bin     281040 Apr 18 12:54 /usr/bin/csh
# ls -lc /usr/lib/libcsh.a >> /etc/security/bad_SUID_files
# rm /usr/lib/libcsh.a
# ▮
```

In Figure 3-37, the program generating the suspicion has been disguised as a library archive file. Further investigation showed that it was exactly the same size as the C shell, and was not a library archive at all. At this point, the program could be removed. However, replacing a program like this with a simple set-user-id program could be better. This program, which I call a "catcher", writes both sets of user ids to a secure file, along with the time, and exits. Thus, someone who thinks he or she is running the root-privileged shell will actually be incriminating his or her self by writing a record in a secure file. This program is included with the Appendix on writing safe set user or group programs.

Once you have edited your list, and are as certain as you can be that you have eliminated all illegitimate files, you now have a master "setfiles" list. You can keep this list in your on-line security directory, but also copy it quickly to a safe backup. After this much work, you don't want to lose this list, or have someone modify it. The "setfiles" list can be used with a simple script to report on new programs with the set user or group property (Figure 3-40).

Figure 3-40: Once the "setfiles" list has been established, piping the output of the **find** *command through* **comm** *picks out only those set user or group files that are new.*

```
# find / \( -perm -4000 -o -perm -2000 \) -print | \
comm -13 setfiles -
# ▉
```

Summary

This chapter has presented a two-pronged approach to controlling access to UNIX systems. The first method is to prevent unauthorized entry into your system through the use of good passwords. The **/etc/passwd** file must be correct for your system to function, and privileged accounts protected with passwords or impossible passwords. Unused accounts should be disabled (through impossible passwords) and later removed. The integrity of the password file should be checked often.

The second approach is to clean permissions, ownership, and groups of all system files and directories. The most difficult parts of this task are to check scripts that may include Trojan Horse commands and the list of set user or group programs. Once your system has been cleaned up, routine checks can help keep it clean.

This chapter also presented a number of shell scripts to help maintain a secure system. These shell scripts can be used in two ways. They can be run automatically, at least weekly, and they can be run interactively. Besides suggesting that you keep these scripts and database both in a secure directory and off-line, I made no suggestions about how to automate the process or collect these scripts into a single suite. Rather than write a cookbook, I think that it is better that each system administrator be innovative and use the ideas presented here. If a cookbook approach were spelled out, system crackers would look for the cookbook files on every system. Choose your own names for your scripts and database files. Hide your database files and don't make security a predictable routine. The more unpredictable you can be, the more likely you are to catch possible system crackers. And the better job you do at maintaining your system's security, the less likely its is that you will ever have your system cracked.

Chapter 4

Communication and Network Security

Extending Access

Communication and networking extend the usefulness of computers. This extension also increases the access to any computer on the network, providing both a means to log in remotely and a mechanism to copy data between computers.

In secure computer installations, communication and networks do not extend beyond a physically secured area. Traditionally, this has meant enclosing the computer, disks, tapes, printers, and terminals in a vault. The vault is lined with a copper screen that prevents electronic emissions from escaping. Only authorized individuals can enter the vault, and they cannot carry in or out software or data on magnetic media without going through lengthy procedures. For example, to get a new release of software into a defense contractor's site required two weeks for inspection and paperwork.

Currently, there is no way to have a secure computer on a network that is connected to other, non-secure, computers. A single, untrusted computer can listen in on conversations between trusted (secure) computers, making the entire network unsecure. In the case of large distributed networks, such as the Internet, there is no way that communications across the network, or computers connected directly to the Internet, can be considered secure. The security of individual computers can be improved, but these computers cannot be considered completely secure because of their network connections.

Modems attached to computers create a problem. Anyone with a home computer can probe the telephone network for modems. Once a modem is discovered, the cracker has the same access to the computer as someone who is sitting at an unlogged-in terminal. And data can be copied over the modem as easily, albeit slower, than across a network.

This chapter discusses the problems with communication and security. Modems are covered first, along with suggestions for improving modem security. The use of the UUCP system is covered next, with emphasis on security configuration. Network security, mainly for NFS and TCP/IP networks, follows. Finally, the use of restricted accounts is explained.

Modem Insecurity

Connecting a modem to a computer automatically makes the system less secure. The modem represents an extension of the computer, much the same way that a terminal is an extension of a computer. The problem with the modem is that anyone who can learn the phone number connected to the modem, has access to the computer.

Getting the phone number is not difficult. The easiest way is to ask someone for it. People share modem numbers with friends (so they can play games or do homework). Even if you trust your friends, do you trust their friends? Phone numbers may also be acquired by calling in on a voice line and tricking someone into giving away the modem phone number.

The second way is almost as easy. During the eighties, computer software was developed that permitted inexpensive home computers to call every number in an exchange and listen for the answer tone generated by a modem, a process known as *sweeps*. The computer commands the modem to dial a number, listens for a modem, and records whatever information is available. For example, which baud rate was used, and which characters (if any) were transmitted by the answering system. The cracker can examine the output of the sweep later, and pick out targets based on the information collected.

Once a cracker has chosen targets, he or she can next assign the computer to make a *run*. During a run, the computer dials into the modem, and tries a predetermined sequence of login names and passwords. The attack may also be manual, with a live cracker sitting at a keyboard trying possible login-password sequences.

The defense against runs and attacks is to require the use of passwords for every account, and to use good passwords. If your doors are securely locked, having someone attacking through your modem becomes more of a nuisance. However, the attacker is denying the use of the modem to authorized users. And, the cracker may get lucky, and guess a poorly chosen password. Chapter 5 explains what to do if you discover someone trying to break into your system through a modem.

Modems can also be tapped. The knowledge necessary to tap a telephone line is widely known, and not really complicated. A tap allows someone to record everything that passes on the line, including valid login names and passwords. Of course, the tap itself might be sufficient for collecting the desired information.

There are several ways to improve modem security. The best way is not to use them at all. Although this is unpleasant, many site managers have taken this course to eliminate the threat caused by modem access.

The first step is to correctly configure your modem ports. The modem port should log out users if they get disconnected. The following methods help improve security when modems are used. Dialup passwords add an additional password to selected ports. Special hardware and/or software can be used to call back users, request additional passwords, or encrypt communications. You can also use a restricted environment to help minimize the access of modem users.

Modem Port Configuration

Connecting modems to your system is not the same as connecting terminals. Modems require a remote connection to another modem in order to function correctly. While this remote connection exists, the modem sends a signal out of its port called *carrier detect*. If the remote connection is lost, the carrier detect signal changes.

The carrier detect signal is crucial to modem security. If the carrier detect signal is not passed by the cable to the computer's port, or the kernel does not watch for changes in carrier detect, then the modem is incorrectly installed and *should not be used*.

When someone logs in through a modem, that user owns both the port and the shell process attached to that port. When the user logs out, the login shell is terminated and the ownership of the port reverts to **root**. However, if the modem user hangs up, or gets disconnected, the system must treat the disconnection like a log out. The system sends a HANGUP signal to the login shell process, the port is closed, and the ownership of the port changed.

Your computer can only detect a disconnection if the port and kernel are properly configured. If not, when a user gets disconnected, or hangs up without logging out, *the next user to call in gets the previous user's login shell.* This is the equivalent of walking up to an abandoned terminal, only that anyone calling into the modem gets to use the shell that is waiting there.

You can check for proper configuration of modem, cable, port, and kernel with a simple test. Log into the modem as an ordinary user and hang up. Immediately call back, and see if you get a log in prompt, or your previous shell. If it is your previous shell, you won't see a prompt until you hit a return. (Note that a safer way to do this test is to set up a restricted account first.)

If your system does not log out users when they hang up, you need to check several things.

- The cable that connects the modem to the computer must carry the signal from pin 8 (carrier detect) to the computer's pin 8.
- The port used must be capable of detecting changes in carrier detect. Some systems have two versions of each port, for example, **/dev/tty01** and **/dev/tty129** (the high bit set). Use the correct port device for modems. Some kernels must be rebuilt to attend to carrier detect. SunOS requires that certain flag bits be set before carrier detect is watched.
- The HUPCLS flag should be set on this port. The Hang-UP on Close flag forces the kernel to send a hang up signal when the modem disconnects.
- Logging out should drop data terminal ready (pin 20), forcing the modem to hangup.

The details on configuring kernels vary widely, as do the conventions for determining if a particular device name must be used with carrier detect. Check your UNIX system documentation for serial devices, usually in section 4, *Special Files and Devices.* You may also be able to learn more by reading the system-specific documentation for reconfiguring your kernel.

On systems that use terminal servers connected to modems, the terminal server must be configured to pass along the carrier detect information. If you are using a terminal server connected to a bank of modems and phone lines, simply calling in is not a sufficient test. You might not get the same modem and port the next time you dial in. Instead, you can determine the process id number of the shell, and check to see that it was killed after hanging up. You can simply send the hangup signal to the process; if it dies, you won't get a message, and you have a problem. If the process had already exited, you will see an error message—"No such process".

Dialup Passwords

Since the release of AT&T System V, the **login** program of UNIX systems (not based on BSD) has had the ability to force users to supply *two* passwords. With the release of SunOS 5.0, Sun systems will also have this capability. Setting up the second password, called the *dialup password*, relies on two configuration files.

The first file, **/etc/dialups**, contains a list of ports for which a dialup password will be required. Each line in this file has the full name of a port connected to a modem (or other login port to which you want to add protection).

The second file contains two colon-separated fields. The first field holds the name of a login program, for example, **/bin/sh**. The second field holds the encrypted password, which will be used with this login program. Figure 4-1 shows an example of each of these two files.

Figure 4-1: Example contents of two files that
control dialup passwords for System V-based systems.

```
# cat /etc/dialups
/dev/tty129
/dev/tty130
/dev/tty137
# cat /etc/d_passwd
/bin/ksh:H4fFsWOjoDw2D:
/bin/sh:f3OkDC4Fge5Jf:
/usr/lib/uucp/uucico::
# ▮
```

In Figure 4-1, only three ports, **/dev/tty129**, **/dev/tty130**, and **/dev/tty137**, will require users to enter a dialup password at login. If the user's account has **/bin/ksh** as the last field in the **/etc/passwd** entry (login program), he or she must enter the first password. If the account uses **/bin/sh**, the user must enter the second password. Systems logging into **uucp** accounts and using **uucico** will not be required to enter a dialup password.

When the **/etc/d_passwd** file has only a single entry, all users are required to enter the dialup password, regardless of the login program. In multiple line **/etc/d_passwd** files, users whose login programs do not match any login program fields in the **/etc/d_passwd** file will not be allowed to log in. Figure 4-2 depicts an **etc/d_passwd** file that only permits **uucico** users to log in.

*Figure 4-2: Using **/etc/d_passwd** to allow only **uucp** logins.*

```
# cat /etc/d_passwd
/bin/sh:NO LOGIN:
/usr/lib/uucp/uucico::
# ▌
```

The **login** program reads the **/etc/dialups** and **/etc/d_passwd** files, if they are present. The **login** program runs with superuser privilege, so both of these files should be root owned, and readable and writeable by owner only.

If your UNIX system is a hybrid of BSD and System V, you can try running the **strings** command on the **/bin/login** program. Look for the names of the two dialup password files, **/etc/dialups** and **/etc/d_passwd**. Note that you may not find anything about dialup passwords in your documentation, as this feature has existed undocumented for years.

Special Modem Hardware

This section explores several methods that attempt to solve the modem security problem using additional hardware and some software. These solutions all share a common feature—they add cost to supporting modems. On the positive side, each does provide real additional protection to systems with modem access.

- Dialback systems
- Challenge-response systems
- Encryption devices

Dialback systems have both incoming and outgoing modems. To use the system, a user logs into the incoming modem, which acknowledges the login and then hangs up. While the user was logged in, if the user's account occurs in a file (or the device's memory), the outgoing modem is given the phone number of the the user's modem to dial. When the user's modem answers the call, the user is again presented with a login prompt.

The advantage to dialback systems is that it prevents unauthorized users from dialing in. Only users in the callback file can use modems. There are also several disadvantages. If a user is in the callback file, but calls from some other location, the outgoing modem still calls the only number it knows. Maintenance of the callback list is considered a problem. Plus, the site pays for all modem class, since most traffic is outgoing.

Callback systems can be done entirely in software, requiring only external modems to complete the system. Instead of running the **getty** program on ports, the callback program is run on the incoming port. Although a callback system using only a single modem can be created, a warning is necessary. All telephone systems in the US permit the called party to hang up briefly, and pick up the phone again. This gives the called party time to move to another phone without being disconnected. The time varies, and is between two and ten seconds. System crackers have discovered this feature, and if they call a modem on a call back system, the cracker simply holds the line open while the callback programs attempts to call back. (Modems usually do not detect dial tones, so cannot detect that dialing has failed.) To prevent this problem, either use two modems, or pause 20 seconds between the incoming call and the outgoing call.

Some hardware callback systems use touch tone signals to enter the caller's identification. These systems also use a computer-generated voice single to respond to the caller. Such a system has the advantage of not being recognized by a "sweep" program looking for modems.

Challenge-response systems require special hardware at the system end, and for each user permitted to use the modem. The system end hardware sits between the modem and the system, and prevents access until a challenge has been responded to correctly. After the modem answers, the challenge device requests a login name. The device looks up the login name, and issues a one-time challenge to the user.

The challenge is based on a unique code built into the user's response device and the current time. The user enters the challenge into his or her response device, then types the key presented by the response device. If the key matches, the user is permitted to access the system, and begin the real login process.

The advantage to challenge-response systems is that each response is used only once. Responses change every minute, so capturing a response by tapping, or watching someone else enter a response will not work (unless it is used immediately). The disadvantage is that every user allowed to use modems must carry the response device, and each modem port must also be outfitted with the challenge device.

Encryption devices add two types of security to modems. If a line has been tapped, the encryption device makes using the collected information more difficult. Also, logging in or using a modem that passes through an encryption device is not possible without the matching encryption. Once again, each user (and port) must have an encryption device that uses the same key, so hardware cost and maintenance of keys are the disadvantages. On the positive side, the cost of encryption devices has fallen considerably in the late eighties, making encryption technology more affordable.

UUCP Security

The UUCP (Unix-to-Unix Copy) system has been the mainstay of inter-Unix system communication for many years. The UUCP system provides for transmission of both ASCII files (such as mail) and binary files between different systems. The only requirement is that both systems possess compatible **uucico** programs and be configured correctly. Versions of the UUCP system have also been produced for non-UNIX systems.

The original UUCP system was written by Mike Lesk of AT&T Bell Labs in 1976. A second version, known as Version 2 UUCP, was distributed with Version 7 UNIX systems, the precursor to System III, and later System V. In 1983, a new version of UUCP was written by Peter Honeyman (Princeton University), David Nowitz (AT&T Bell Labs), and Brian Redman (Bell Communications Research). The new version was called HoneyDanBer, after its authors. AT&T prefers to call it the "Basic Networking Utilities." The two versions of UUCP will talk to each other without problems.

One reason that HoneyDanBer UUCP was written was to address serious security problems with the old Version 2 UUCP. These problems are severe enough that you should not run Version 2 UUCP if you can use HoneyDanBer, or want to run a secure system. The HoneyDanBer system is more secure and easier to administer than the older system. HoneyDanBer UUCP does have a security problem, but can be fixed with a simple program.

Both versions of UUCP share some security problems in common. Systems connect to each other by logging in, so both user names and passwords get in the act. Almost every UNIX system I've ever seen comes with an **uucp** account, for example. This user name is well known, and you should *not* use it. And make certain that every account has a good password, just like all your other accounts. Even though UUCP accounts run the **uucico** program as the login program (a type of restricted account), you still need passwords for these accounts. Figure 4-3 shows several sample UCP accounts.

Figure 4-3: Some example UUCP accounts in the /etc/passwd file.

```
# grep uucp /etc/passwd
uucp:NO LOGIN:5:1:UUCP Admin Login:/usr/lib/uucp:
nuucp:NO LOGIN:23:9:default:/usr/spool/uucp:/usr/lib/uucp/uucico
uusun:mfpeFd. xjOWFI:24:9:Sun:/usr/spool/uucp:/usr/lib/uucp/uucico
uunet:rF4pRezyDent. :25:9:UUNET:/usr/spool/uucp:/usr/lib/uucp/uucico
# ▮
```

The first account shown in Figure 4-3 is the UUCP administrative account. The user id of 5 owns the UUCP files, directories, and programs. Other UUCP accounts, those used by remote systems, should *not* share the UUCP user id or group id. In this example, remote systems have user id's in the range 23 through 25, and a group id of 9. These are not special user id's, but they do serve to further identify the systems calling in. Sharing the UUCP administrative user id, five in this example, potentially allows remote sites to read or overwrite local UUCP configuration files (not a good idea).

As mentioned, the **nuucp** account has an impossible password, and could even be removed from the **/etc/passwd** file. The **uusun** and **uunet** accounts have **/usr/spool/uucp** as their home directory, and **/usr/lib/uucp/uucico** as their login programs. All accounts for remote sites should use this home directory, and must use the **uucico** program.

Version 2 Security

Version 2 UUCP has several security problems. Most serious is that the **uucico** program has a flaw in it that makes it less secure. Although I do not recommend you keep anything that must be secure on a system with modems, using Version 2 **uucico** makes the system ever less secure. You can tell whether you have a Version 2 UUCP system by examining the **/usr/lib/uucp** directory for the file **L.sys**. The **L.sys** file has been replaced with the file **Systems** in the HoneyDanBer version.

The other problems with Version 2 have to do with the security administration files. The **USERFILE** controls where in the file system files may be read and **L.cmds** determines which commands can be executed. Both of these configuration files are contained within the **/usr/lib/uucp** directory. These files provide a frequently misunderstood means of controlling access to your system via UUCP.

Accessible Directories, USERFILE   The **USERFILE** consists of single-line entries with two or three space-separated fields. The first field contains a login name-system name pair. These two names are separated by a comma. The second field is optional, and may either be missing or contain the letter c (for *callback*). The third field consists of a list of one or more directories.

```
login-name,system-name [c] directories
```

The login name is used to find a matching entry in the **USERFILE** when a remote system logs in using that user name. The login name field can also be used to control the directories on the local system from which users can copy files using **uucp**. The **USERFILE** is searched from the top for a matching login name, or the first entry with a blank login name (an entry beginning with a comma). Put wildcard entries (those starting with a blank followed by a comma) last.

Figure 4-4: An example **USERFILE.**

```
# cat /usr/lib/uucp/USERFILE
uusun,sun c /usr/spool/uucppublic
uunet,uunet /usr/spool/uucppublic
uworld,uworld /usr/spool/uucppublic /usr/spool/uucp/uworld
,snoopy /usr/spool/uucppublic
rikf,      /usr/spool/uucppublic /u/rik/tmp
# ▊
```

When a login name is combined with a system name, both names must match. In Figure 4-4, only the system named **sun** will be permitted to use **uucico** when logged in as **uusun**. Likewise, if a system logs into the **uunet** account, it must present the system name **uunet**. The combination of login names and system names in each entry provides the best way to define access for remote systems.

For systems that never call you, and thus never login, the login name is not used. Instead, a comma followed by the system name is used. In Figure 4-4, *snoopy* is a system that is polled (called by the local system), and never logs in.

If a login name or system name not appearing in the USERFILE is encountered by **uucico**, the connection to the remote system is terminated. Of course, wildcard entries prevent this mechanism from working.

The final entry in Figure 4-4 represents an example entry for a local user. The user logged in as **rikf** can copy files from **/usr/spool/uucppublic** or **/u/rik/tmp**. Default entries for all users on the local system could be created by using, *hostname*, where *hostname* is the system name for the local system.

If a lone comma forms the first field of a **USERFILE** entry, any login name from any system not matching the preceding entries will match this line. This wildcard entry exists in the **USERFILE**s delivered with many UNIX systems (Figure 4-5).

Figure 4-5: The default **USERFILE** *delivered with many UNIX systems. Do not use!*

```
# cat /usr/lib/uucp/oldUSERFILE
nuucp, /usr/spool/uucppublic
,      /
# ▮
```

The **USERFILE** in Figure 4-5 permits any system logging in as nuucp to copy files from **/usr/spool/uucppublic**. This is not bad, as long as no administrator adds a new UUCP login without modifying the **USERFILE**. For example, if a new UUCP account is added to the **/etc/passwd** file, say **uunet**, it will not match the entry for **nuucp**, but will match the wildcard entry. The wildcard entry, beginning with the lone comma, permits a system to copy files from anywhere in the file systems. For example, a remote system logging in as **uunet** could use **uucp** to copy the local system's **/etc/passwd** file.

The comma entry is designed to permit *local* users to use **uucp** without restrictions. Since the same effect can be accomplished by following the comma with the system name, the lone comma should never appear in your **USERFILE**.

If a letter **c** follows the login-system name field, this system must be called back. The UUCP callback is similar to the modem security callback. After a system logs in successfully and communicates with the local **uucico**, the local system terminates the conversation. Then, using information in the **L.sys** file, the remote system is called back, with the local system logging in at the remote site.

The purpose for the callback system is to prevent masquerades. UNIX systems keep systems' names stored in the kernel's (operating system's) data region. The name is part of the kernel program, for example, the file **/vmunix** or **/unix**, and is changed by rebuilding the kernel or through a special utility. Since the name can be changed, any user with sufficient privilege can change the system name on a remote system. When the remote system logs into a UUCP account, the current name is the one used. This permits the system to masquerade as some other system, perhaps one with more privileges. (Note that the HoneyDanBer makes masquerading even easier.)

The callback system makes masquerading impossible, since there mote system not only must change its system name, but also appear connected to the same phone number as the authentic system. Version 2 UUCP system cannot use one modem for both incoming and outgoing calls, making the strategy mentioned earlier (not hanging up after calling in) unworkable. The only thing to beware of is that only one system can set the callback flag. (What do you think happens if both systems have the callback flag set for the remote system?)

Controlling Commands, L. cmds   The **L.cmds** file controls which commands can be remotely executed. Typically, the **rmail** (restricted mail) program is the only program you need to include in this file. If you wish to permit users on other systems to use the local print spooler, you might allow **lp** or **lpr** (Figure 4-6), or **rnews** for Usenet news.

Figure 4-6: A minimal L.cmds file permitting the receipt of mail from remote systems.

```
# cat L.cmds
rmail
# ▌
```

Although you can put other commands in the **L. cmds** file, you must be very careful about what commands you include. Commands that permit copy of files, such as **cp**, **sed**, and **cat** must not be included, because these commands can be used to copy *any* file readable by others or the **uucp** account to a remote system. The **uuxqt** program, which carries out remote commands, operates with **uucp** access privileges, and is not restricted by the directories listed in the **USERFILE**. **USERFILE** only limits access for the **uucico** program.

Version 2 Permissions   The files **USERFILE** and **L.cmds** can be readable by all, but must be writeable by the owner, **uucp**, only. One other UUCP configuration file is particularly sensitive. The **L.sys** file contains the names of systems, telephone numbers, login names, and passwords for these accounts. The appearance of phone numbers and passwords makes this file especially dangerous—it must be owned by the **uucp** account, and read and writeable by the owner *only*.

The **/usr/lib/uucp** directory holds both the configuration files and system programs used by the Version 2 UUCP system. This directory must be writeable by the owner (**uucp**) only, and readable and executable by all. The two daemon programs, **uucico** and **uuxqt**, will be executable by all, set-usr-id, and owned by the **uucp** account. Other files in this directory, with the exception of those mentioned, must be owned by **uucp**, writeable by the owner only, and readable by all.

The **/usr/spool/uucp** directory must be owned by **uucp**, writeable by the owner only, and readable and executable by all. The **/usr/spool/uucppublic** directory, as befits a temporary public directory, is readable, writeable, executable by all.

HoneyDanBer Security

HoneyDanBer UUCP has better security than Version 2. The problem with the **uucico** program that could occur during login has been remedied. And the two configuration files for controlling access have been combined into one, easier-to-understand file, **Permissions**. There is a problem with a script that logs unknown systems—this problem must be corrected.

HoneyDanBer takes a stricter approach to security. Generally, default security is tight and privileges are not given without having been explicitly granted in the **Permissions** file. If a remote system does not use a login name in the **Permissions** file, it cannot complete any transactions. With a minimal entry, the only work that can be done is the copying of files to the local system, specifically to the spooling directory.

Unknown Systems   One of the changes made in the HoneyDanBer version prevents systems that do not appear in the **Systems** file (which replaces the Version 2 **L.sys**) from completing a connection with the local system. Version 2 UUCP would permit any system using a login name appearing in the **USERFILE** to carry out UUCP transactions. The older version of UUCP was designed to be used at AT&T Bell Laboratories, where it was desirable for any system to be capable of using UUCP *without* prior setup. The **nuucp** account dates back to these bygone days when any system that could connect to your modem port could be trusted.

As a possible accommodation to the older version, HoneyDanBer will execute a shell script that collects the system name of unknown systems in a file called **Foreign**, which is kept in the **/usr/spool/uucp/.Admin** directory. By examining this file (which is routinely mailed to the **uucp** account), system administrators can determine the names of unknown systems. The system administrator can then decide if a new system should be added to the **Systems** and **Permissions** files and permitted to complete a UUCP transaction.

Unfortunately, there is a problem with the script that handles collecting the names of unknown systems. The **/usr/lib/uucp/remote.unknown** script should either be replaced by a simple program, or have execute permission removed. If the script is not executable, the names of unknown systems will remain unknown. Using a program to replace the script version of **remote. unknown** permits collection of unknown systems in the **Foreign** file. The program version of **remote.unknown** is given in Figure 4-7.

Figure 4-7: The C program for replacing the
remote.unknown *script, along with compilation and installation instructions.*

```
# cat unknown. c
/* remote. unknown replacement program */
#include <stdio.h>
#include  <time.h>
#define FOREIGN "/usr/spool/uucp/.Admin/Foreign"

main (argc, argv)
    int argc;
    char * argv;
{
    FILE * fd;
    time_t gmt;
    char * date, * c;
            /* Must be called with system name */
    if (argc  2) exit(1);
            /* Get current time in seconds */
    time(&gmt);
            /* Convert time to date format */
    date = ctime(&gmt);
            /* Remove new line ('\n') from date */
    for (c = date; *c != '\0'; c++)
        if (*c == '\n') *c = '\0';
            /* Open the Foreign file for append */
    fd = fopen(FOREIGN, "a");
            /* Write message in Foreign file */
    fprintf(fd, "%s: call from system %s\n", date,
        argv[1]);
    fclose(fd);
    exit(0);
}
# cc unknown. c -o /usr/lib/uucp/remote.unknown
# chmod 711 /usr/lib/uucp/remote.unknown
#
```

The easiest thing to do about **remote.unknown** is to make it unexcutable using **chmod -x /usr/lib/uucp/remote.unknown**. Replacing the script with a program that provides the exact same service and output (and which runs faster) is a better solution. Be sure you follow one of these two suggestions, or your Honey-DanBer UUCP system will be remarkably less secure.

Permissions File   The HoneyDanBer **Permissions** file provides a finer degree of control over **uucico** and **uuxqt**. Instead of systems being delivered with the **USERFILE** shown in Figure 4-5, HoneyDanBer systems typically have a much more restrictive **Permissions** file, shown in Figure 4-8.

*Figure 4-8: The default-delivered **Permissions** file is very*
*restrictive. The **uucheck -v** command provides a check of file and*
*directory permissions and an interpretation of the **Permissions** file.*

```
# cat /usr/lib/uucp/Permissions
LOGNAME=nuucp
# /usr/lib/uucp/uucheck -v
*** uucheck: Check Required Files and Directories
*** uucheck: Directories Check Complete

*** uucheck: Check /etc/uucp/Permissions file
** LOGNAME PHASE (when they call us)

When a system logs in as: (nuucp)
        We DO NOT allow them to request files.
        We WILL NOT send files queued for them on this call.
        They can send files to
           /usr/spool/uucppublic (DEFAULT)
        Myname for the conversation will be raven.
        PUBDIR for the conversation will be /usr/spool/uucppublic.


** MACHINE PHASE (when we call or execute their uux requests)


*** uucheck: /etc/uucp/Permissions Check Complete

# ▮
```

The **Permissions** file example in Figure 4-8, although it is the default, may not have been delivered with your system. Some system's vendors have weakened their **Permissions** file before shipping their version. Also, note that with newer releases of the UNIX system, the UUCP configuration files have been relocated. The **/etc/uucp** directory contains the UUCP configuration files with System V Release 4, and SunOS 4.x.

The **uucheck** command performs a check of the UUCP configuration files. The **uucheck** command checks for the existence of three crucial files, **Systems**, **Devices**, and **Permissions**. **uucheck** then interprets the **Permissions** file and displays its interpretation in short phrases.

If a system does not use a login name that appears in the **Permissions** file, the system will be rejected. This is in addition to the rule that a system must appear in the **Systems** file before it can begin a UUCP transaction. And, if the login name is the only rule listed in the entry, the remote system can only transfer files to the public directory. However, mail between the two systems will be exchanged. HoneyDanBer permits a system with the minimum entry to send or receive mail, locally using the **rmail** command.

The default security under HoneyDanBer can be modified considerably by extending the rules governing each entry. Entries in the **Permissions** file are one line long, and lines may be extended by using a backslash to escape the newline. Each entry can define rules for two types of transactions: *LOGNAME* and *MACHINE*.

LOGNAME rules govern when a remote system calls the local system. MACHINE rules control when the local system calls a remote system. The MACHINE rules also control which commands can be executed on behalf of a remote hosts. Since commands can be specified on a per-system level, this is a big improvement over the Version **L.cmds** file. The MACHINE rule can be specified for all systems not covered by other MACHINE rules by using the keyword *OTHER*.

Entries in the **Permissions** file are built from the names of rules, followed immediately by an equal sign (=) and an argument. Figure 4-9 introduces two new rules, and adds a new system with more capabilities to the **Permissions** file.

The *REQUEST* rule permits a remote system to request that a file be copied from the local system. The *SENDFILES* rule allows files that have been queued up for remote copy by local users to be sent to the remote system. Both rules constrain the file transfers to the public directory, **/usr/spool/uucppublic**.

Figure 4-9: The REQUEST and SENDFILES rules
loosen up the default restrictions by permitting a remote
system to request files and to receive files queued for them.

```
# cat /etc/uucp/Permissions
LOGNAME=uurik REQUEST=yes SENDFILES=yes
# /usr/lib/uucp/uucheck -v
. . .
When a system logs in as: (uurik)
        We DO allow them to request files.
        We WILL send files queued for them on this call.
        They can send files to
            /usr/spool/uucppublic (DEFAULT)
        They can request files from
            /usr/spool/uucppublic (DEFAULT)
        Myname for the conversation will be raven.
        PUBDIR for the conversation will be /usr/spool/uucppublic.
. . .
#
```

You might wonder why the defaults prevent sending files to a remote system, even if a local user has requested their transfer. The rational behind this limitation depends on the concept of authentication. When a remote system calls the local system, the only assurance that it is really a particular remote system is the knowledge of the login name and password. It is easy to masquerade as another system by changing the system name, and even easier to do with HoneyDanBer. For maximum security, you do not want to send any files unless you call back the system in question.

There are two ways to increase the assurance that a remote system is not masquerading as another. The *VALIDATE* rule is used in conjunction with the LOGNAME and MACHINE rules. The VALIDATE rule ties a system name with the login name used, much like the older **USERFILE** tied together the login name and system name using a comma. As mentioned, if the login name and password are compromised, it is rather easy to change the system name, so the VALIDATE rule offers little additional protection.

The *CALLBACK* rule is used only with LOGNAME rules. If CALLBACK is set to "yes," the local system terminates the connection with the remote system and calls back, much like Version 2 will do when the callback flag is set. Calling back provides the greatest degree of assurance of a remote system's true identity.

Anytime you call a system, you can be sure you have reached the desired system, unless the phone system has been compromised, or the remote system has been replaced with a usurper. Of course, even if you can now trust the remote system, how does the remote system know it can trust you?

The CALLBACK rule overrides any other rules when used with the LOGNAME rule. Since the connection is terminated, the MACHINE rule controls privileges when the system is called back.

By default, remote systems can write in the public directory, **/usr/spool/uucppublic** when just a LOGNAME rule exists. When the REQUEST rule is present, the remote system can request files also in the public directory. The name of the public directory can be modified with the **PUBDIR** rule. The PUBDIR rule changes the default public directory to the one specified in the rule. The new public directory must be readable, writeable, and executable by all for it to work properly.

The ability to read or write files can be extended beyond the public directory with the *READ* and *WRITE* rules. Each of these rules can be followed by a list of directories, separated by colons, where remote systems can read or write files in addition to the public directory (see Figure 4-10).

Figure 4-10: **Permissions** *file example giving more privileges to the athena system.*

```
# cat Permissions
LOGNAME=uumit MACHINE=athena VALIDATE=yes \
    REQUEST=yes SENDFILES=yes \
    PUBDIR=/usr/spool/mit \
    READ=/u2/share WRITE=/u2/share:/u2/mit \
    NOREAD=/u2/share/yale NOWRITE=/u2/share/yale
# uucheck -v
. . .
When a system logs in as: (uumit)
        We DO allow them to request files.
        We WILL send files queued for them on this call.
        They can send files to
            /u2/share
            /u2/mit
        Except
            /u2/share/yale
        They can request files from
            /u2/share
        Except
            /u2/share/yale
        Myname for the conversation will be raven.
```

Figure 4-10: **Permissions** *file example giving*
more privileges to the athena system (continued).

```
            PUBDIR for the conversation will be /usr/spool/mit.

** MACHINE PHASE (when we call or execute their uux requests)

When we call system(s): (athena)
            We DO allow them to request files.
            They can send files to
                /u2/share
                /u2/mit
            Except
                /u2/share/yale
            They can request files from
                /u2/share
            Except
                /u2/share/yale
            Myname for the conversation will be raven.
            PUBDIR for the conversation will be /usr/spool/mit.

Machine(s): (athena)
CAN execute the following commands:
command (rmail), fullname (rmail)
# ▮
```

In Figure 4-10, the *athena* system is given additional privileges, although it must login as *uumit* when it calls the local system. The public directory has been changed to **/usr/spool/mit**, and a directory tree made accessible. Any file that is readable by others in the **/u2/share** directory tree can be copied out by *athena*, and *athena* can copy files into these directories. The *athena* system can also write in the **/u2/mit** directory tree. For example, athena could send a file to the directory **/u2/mit/widgets**.

The *NOREAD* and *NOWRITE* rules modify the READ and WRITE rules by creating exceptions. In Figure 4-10, the remote system *athena* is prevented from reading or writing in the directory tree beginning with **/u2/share/yale**. The NOREAD and NOWRITE rules cut off branches of directory trees for requesting files and sending files, respectively.

By default, any system listed in either a LOGNAME or a MACHINE rule can request execution of **rmail**. The restricted mail program, unlike the other versions of **mail**, has no shell escapes, menus, or command capability. **rmail** can only be used for sending mail. The only other safe command that can be added is **rnews** (restricted news), which prints files in the **/usr/news** directory.

The *COMMANDS* rule changes the list of permitted commands. The COMMANDS rule works only in conjunction with MACHINE rules. The COMMANDS rule controls **uuxqt**, which is not under the influence of rules controlling the public directory or readable and writeable directories. Any files readable by others can be read by the commands executed by **uuxqt**. For this reason, commands that copy files, such as **cp**, **cat**, **ed**, **sed**, etc., must *not* be included in the list of commands. Even commands that can read files through redirection, such as **mail**, must not be included. The COMMANDS rule could be set equal to *ALL*, meaning all commands—but I do not recommend it.

One possible command that could be added to the list would be **lp**, permitting the use of the line printer spooling system on the local system. With this command, a remote user can print out any file on the local system, as well as files sent from the remote system. Thus, the remote user could print out a wordprocessing file from the remote system, or the **/etc/passwd** file on the local system.

The *MYNAME* rule permits changing the name of the local system while conversing with particular remote systems. The MYNAME rule works with either the LOGNAME or the MACHINE rules. The MYNAME rule makes it very easy to masquerade as another system, and made me wonder why it was included at all. The MYNAME rule is certainly useful while testing or configuring Honey-DanBer, and it also makes it obvious to everyone how easy it is to masquerade as another system. Perhaps that is its purpose.

Table 4-1: Summary of rules for use in the **Permissions** *file (*

Rule	LOGNAME	MACHINE
REQUEST	request that a file be copied (yes or no)	same
SENDFILES	permit queued files to be sent (yes or no)	ignored
READ	add directories that can be written to by the remote system	same
WRITE	add directories that can be written to by the remote system	same
NOREAD	specify exception to READ	same
NOWRITE	specify exception to WRITE	same
COMMANDS	ignored	list of commands for **uuxqt**
CALLBACK	call back remote site (yes/no)	ignored

Table 4-1: Summary of rules for use in the **Permissions** *file (continued).*

Rule	LOGNAME	MACHINE
VALIDATE	remote system must use account (yes or no)	ignored
PUBDIR	changed public directory	same
MYNAME	change local system name for this conversation	same

Use colons to create lists of system names, directories, or commands.
Each entry must be on one line, which may be extended by using a backslash as the last character.
Comment lines begin with the pound sign (#).

The word OTHER can be used to establish default MACHINE rules for all systems not specifically defined by a MACHINE=system-name rule.

The key to maintaining security with HoneyDanBer is to make good use of the **Permissions** file. Do not give privileges to systems unless the system requires the special access. For most systems, a simple **Permissions** file that simply lists login names and has a generic other rule (Figure 4-11) will be sufficient.

Figure 4-11: A minimal **Permissions** *file contains the login*
names for all UUCP accounts and a generic MACHINE rule.

```
# cat Permissions
LOGNAME=uusun:uunet:uworld:uumit

MACHINE=OTHER
# ▮
```

Network Security

Originally a research project of the Defense Advanced Research Association, the Internet has become a mainstay of communication between UNIX systems. Although Internet itself is limited to organizations working on government-sponsored projects, today there are other publicly accessible networks, such as NYSERnet, BARnet, and ALTERnet, that provide essentially the same services—highspeed communications, file transfer, mail, remote login, and remote command execution.

These services are based on TCP/IP, the Transport Control Protocol/Internet Protocol, a specification for moving packets of information around the network and into host computers. Other specifications, such as OSI (Open Systems Interconnection) may become prominent in the future, but the discussion here will be based on TCP/IP.

Along with the service already mentioned, NFS, the Network File System, is also significant. A defacto standard, NFS was originally developed by Sun Microsystems, and the NFS specifications are part of the public domain. A competing specification has been put forward by OSF; however, NFS is already widely available. AT&T also has its own version, RFS, (Remote File System), which is not as widespread because it is proprietary.

NFS and the other network services have some of the same security considerations as ordinary, non-network, services. User accounts, passwords, and file permissions are still relevant and important. However, other configuration files and utilities that do not come into play without networks are also crucial. The Internet Worm relied on the network for its spread, and was totally a creature of the network. Better network security impeded the spread of the Worm on some systems.

This section discusses the configuration files affecting network security. Known problems, and how to check for them on your system, will also be covered. Suggestions for limiting your exposure, while still participating in the network are given.

Network Mechanics

Before discussing problems with software and configuration, it will help to have an understanding of the physical aspects of the network. This brief discussion covers the general makeup of network data and their transmission.

Network data is transmitted in chunks called *packets*. A packet contains the actual data to be transmitted, with a wrapper. The wrapper contains the source and destination address of the packet, and information about the type of packet. You can imagine that as the packet travels through the network media, a wire, fiber optic, or microwave link, hosts connected to the media read the wrapper of each packet to see if the packet is addressed to them.

This brings up the first network issue. Any *host* (a system with network interface and software) can read any packet that passes by on the network. A system that reads data in packets not addressed to it is known as a *promiscuous listener*. Unless the information within a packet is encrypted, the information is potentially available to any host. It is for this reason that most networks are officially not-secure, and do not permit any classified information to reside on any host connected to the network. Only a network where *every* host is trusted could be considered secure.

Practically speaking, data traveling on the net is not encrypted. The shear volume of data makes the task of picking out interesting information difficult. Also, encrypting everything sent on the net would be prohibitively expensive in computing resources. Finally, as mentioned earlier, encryption often draws attention to the data, and there are no available methods of encryption that cannot be broken, given enough time and resources.

Another issue has to do with identifying the source of a communication. TCP/IP uses an Internet Packet address, a quadruple of bytes (values from 0 to 256), that are supposed to uniquely identify each host. In reality, anyone with superuser privilege can alter the Internet address of their own system. The ability to masquerade raises problems when attempting to authenticate requests from other systems. Some attempts to improve authentication have been made, but are not yet universally available.

For example, the Kerberos system, developed at MIT's Project Athena, uses a third party, a special host, to provide authentication. When a user on one host wishes to access a different host, the user must get an authenticator, a "ticket," from the Kerberos host. The ticket is encrypted using a public key known to both hosts and is also time-stamped, so it is good only for a specific transaction or time period. Kerberos definitely increases security, but currently requires the source of many commands and utilities to implement it (besides good programming skills). Kerberos has been accepted by OSF and may become a standard for host authentication.

Sun Microsystems has also offered Secure RPC (Remote Procedure Calls). RPCs form the basis for NFS and other network services. A Secure RPC includes an encrypted time-stamp in the packet, and the ability to decrypt the time-stamp correctly authenticates the packet. Capturing a packet and copying its encrypted key only helps a cracker within the time period valid for the time-stamp. Secure RPC only works among participating systems, that is, Suns with secure networking enabled (it's disabled by default) and licensees of the technology.

Finally, a word about the media. Many networks are based on Ethernet in one of two forms. Thick Ethernet (10Base5) and thin Ethernet (10Base2 or Thinnet) are both well shielded, although thick Ethernet is the better shielded of the two. These systems were designed to prevent emissions that can be picked up by radio receivers and decoded. Fiber-optic based systems have no emissions. Microwave links can be intercepted with sensitive receivers located near enough to the direct line-of-sight. Any of these systems are susceptible to being tapped, and listened to by promiscuous listeners.

Trusted Hosts

Many UNIX systems support what are often called the "r" commands—**rlogin**, **rsh**, and **rexec**. The r commands permit remote users to login or execute commands across the network. The remote users are bound by the same constraints as other users, in that they must first pass a user authentication process by providing a valid login name and password.

The concept of a trusted host is that users calling from a trusted host are *not* required to enter a password. If that user has an account on the local machine, the user is trusted, and permitted to execute commands without providing a password.

While convenient, the concept of trusted hosts is dangerous. The trusted host mechanism was exploited by the Internet Worm in the following fashion. Once the Internet Worm was executing on a system, the Worm checked for trusted hosts, and copied itself to every other system where its user id was trusted. Trust guaranteed the rapid spread of the Worm.

Trusted hosts do not need to be totally eliminated. It's just that you must be very careful in choosing which systems you trust. Because users on systems where there are superuser privileges can easily masquerade, it's dangerous to trust any host. Also, if you choose to trust some hosts, these hosts should be part of the same workgroup or cluster. If a member of a workgroup allows hosts in other workgroups to be trusted, essentially that extends trust to the other workgroups.

Trust is transitive. If host A trusts host B, and host B trusts host C, then host A must trust host C. A user on host C can rlogin into host B, then **rlogin** to host A because the user is currently operating from host B. Even if host A does not explicitly trust host C, there is no way to prevent a user from host C from entering via host B. Thus, for trust to work, each participating host must limit their list of trusted hosts to a common list.

Trusted hosts are defined in two different files on each host. The **/etc/hosts.equiv** file provides a host-wide definition of trusted hosts and **.rhosts** files permit users to define other trusted users and hosts.

/etc/hosts.equiv   The equivalent hosts file, **/etc/hosts.equiv**, permits users working on a listed host to use **rlogin** or **rsh** without providing a password. The user's name must appear in the local host's **/etc/passwd** file, or a login name and password will still be required.

The **/etc/hosts. equiv** consists of a list of names, one per line. The names are taken from the **/etc/hosts** file, which contains IP address quadruples and host names. Besides names, the **/etc/hosts. equiv** can contain group entries. Groups are defined in the **/etc/net group** file (explained on page 144). To trust members in a network group, the line would contain +@*group1*; if a network group is not to be trusted, the line looks like -@*netgroup* instead. Figure 4-12 shows an example **/etc/hosts. equiv** file.

*Figure 4-12: An example **/etc/hosts. equiv** file, permitting*
three hosts, gandhi, dec3100, and piris, and one netgroup
suns-prog. *Hosts in the netgroup marketing are not to betrusted.*

```
# cat /etc/hosts.equiv
gandhi
+@suns-prog
dec3100
piris
-@marketing
# ▊
```

Figure 4-12 shows how specific hosts and groups of hosts are listed as trusted. Listing the *marketing* netgroup as untrusted is unnecessary, since only hosts and netgroups explicitly listed will be trusted. However, the **/etc/hosts.equiv** file is searched from the beginning for the first matching hostname. If the hostname is encountered in an untrusted group before its name appears later in a trusted group, the host will be untrusted.

There is a single wildcard for the **/etc/hosts. equiv** file, the plus sign (+). *If the file contains only a plus sign, all hosts are trusted.* Many Sun systems have been delivered this way—check for this. Remove the plus sign if you find it in **/etc/hosts.equiv** and optionally add trusted hosts.

The **/etc/hosts.equiv** file is not maintained by the Yellow Pages, but the **/etc/netgroup** file is. *Yellow Pages*, also known as the Network Information System, or NIS, was also developed originally by Sun Microsystems. The task of NIS is to maintain current versions of certain files required for smooth functioning of a network of systems. Since users must have accounts on all machines where they can login, it is useful if one machine distributes all changes to the **/etc/passwd** file. NIS consists of server systems, responsible for distributing changes and keeping master copies, and client systems which rely on the server for information. NIS is not considered a secure system. Using either Kerberos or Secure RPC improves authentication, making NIS more secure.

.rhosts   The **.rhosts** file functions as an extension of the **/etc/hosts.equiv** file. The difference between the two is that *any* user on the local machine can have an **.rhosts** file in his or her HOME directory. After the **/etc/hosts.equiv** file has been checked for matching hostnames, the HOME directory of the user logging in is search for a **.rhosts** file. If the file exists and contains the name of the remote host, the remote user will not be prompted for a password. The **.rhosts** file can override the denial of trusted status to netgroups in **/etc/hosts.equiv**.

A user can also list the name of a user on another system as being able to log into the local user's account without a password. Figure 4-13 shows how the user bill has set up his **.rhosts** file.

*Figure 4-13: The **.rhosts** file allows individual users to override the system-wide prohibition on trusting users from other hosts.*

```
# cd bill
# cat .rhosts
achilles
marketing betty
# ▋
```

The **.rhosts** file shown in Figure 4-13 permits any user named "bill" to login from system achilles, even though the host achilles does not appear in the **/etc/hosts.equiv** shown in the earlier example, Figure 4-12. The user betty, coming from any host in the marketing netgroup, will also be allowed to login as "bill" without a password, even though the marketing netgroup is not trusted in **/etc/hosts.equiv**.

Allowing individual users to equivalence hosts and other users is not a good idea. The system administrator should have control over which systems and users can be trusted. If desired, individual users can be equivalenced in **/etc/hosts.equiv**, using the same format of *hostname username* used in **.rhosts**. Unfortunately, the UNIX system contains no automatic mechanisms to prevent the use of individual **.rhosts**. A policy forbidding the use of individual **.rhosts** files should be created.

To enforce this policy, you can have the **cron** program run the script shown in Figure 4-14 every night to collect policy violators and remove any **.rhosts** file which was found.

Figure 4-14: The **no.rhosts** *script can be executed at least nightly by* **cron** *to detect and remove* **.rhosts** *files.*

```
# cat no.rhosts
awk -F: '{print $6}' /etc/passwd |
for home
do
    if [ -f $home/.rhosts ]
    then
        ls -lc $home/.rhosts >> /tmp/rh$$
        cat $home/.rhosts >> /tmp/rh$$
        rm -f $home/.rhosts
    fi
done
if [ -s /tmp/rh$$ ]
then
    mail root  </tmp/rh$$
fi
rm -f /tmp/rh$$
#
```

The **no.rhosts** script searches in the HOME directory of every account entry in the **/etc/passwd** file for **.rhosts** files. If the script finds one, it places the long listing of the file and the file's contents in a temporary file, and removes the **.rhosts** file. At the end of the script, root gets sent mail only if a **.rhosts** file was discovered. If you, working as an administrator, receive such mail, you need to explain the policy to the user.

In the case of root access via **rlogin** and **rsh**, the **/etc/hosts.equiv** file is never searched—only the **/.rhosts** file. The **/.rhosts** file is used to permit a superuser on one host to work as superuser on all hosts without ever entering a password. Needless to say, this is not a secure practice. Convenient, but not secure. The ease of masquerading as a different host makes the use of **/.rhosts** unsafe. If you use **/.rhosts**, a user who can become the superuser on any hosts in the network can become a superuser on your host without a password. Schemes that add authentication, such as Kerberos and Secure RPC help to guard against such masquerades.

NFS Security   The Network File System permits the mounting of file systems across networks. Once a file system has been mounted, most of the familiar access rules still apply. That is, a user must have permission to read a file before the file can be read, or both write and execute permission in a directory before a file can be removed. One of the things that does change, however, is that the root is no longer the omnipotent user. In fact, the root becomes nobody (the user with id -2) by default.

Each system has control over which file systems, or which parts of file systems, are made available for mounting by remote systems. The local system does two things to control remote mounting. First, the local system must support NFS with an appropriately configured kernel and by starting up the network daemons, such as **mountd**. The second thing that the system must do is to *export* file systems.

Exporting file systems actually makes all or part of a file system available for remote mounting. The simplest **/etc/exports** file contains a list, one per line, of directories to be exported. The problem with the simplest **/etc/exports** file is that there are no restrictions placed on who may mount these file systems.

The right way to export file systems is carefully to specify which hosts can mount each file system. The way to do this is to list the trusted hosts on the same line as the file system after the keyword *-access* (Figure 4-15).

*Figure 4-15: An example **/etc/exports** file with a variety of options.*

```
# cat /etc/exports
/usr        -access=suns-prog:gandhi:client1,ro
/var/db     -access=marketing,anon=-1
/u/share   -rw=gandhi
/export/root/client1    -access=client1,root=client1
/export/swap/client1    -access=client1,root=client1
# █
```

The **-access** option controls which hosts may mount each directory. A maximum of 10 host names may follow the access option. (This limitation is one of the reasons netgroups are used.) Host names in a list are separated by colons (:), and options, such as access, anon, or ro, are separated by commas. The first option is preceded by a minus sign, and there cannot be any spaces in the options list.

In Figure 4-15, only one directory tree, **/u/share**, is exported to the world. There is a limitation placed on it, however: only gandhi has read-write access. For the rest of the network, this directory tree will be mount read-only.

The **/usr** directory, which in newer UNIX releases is mounted read-only, can be mounted read-only (the **ro** option) by members of the netgroup suns-prog, the host gandhi, and the host client1. The **/var/db** directory can only be mounted by hosts within the marketing netgroup.

The **anon** option sets the default user id for unrecognized users to -1. By default, the root and users not in the local **/etc/passwd** file are mapped to the user id -2 (often listed in **/etc/passwd** files as *nobody*). However, setting anon=-1 prevents the root or unknown user from having *any* access when this file system is mounted remotely. Thus, a superuser on a marketing host which has **/var/db** mounted will not be able to read, write, or execute any file in that file system. Nor will any user on a marketing group host whose login name does not appear in the local host's **/etc/passwd** file.

The last two export file systems, **/export/root/client1** and **/export/swap/client1** are available only to the host client1. client1 will also have root access on these remote file systems, that is, a user working as root will be mapped to the user id of zero (instead of -2) because of the option *root=client1*.

Another option not appearing in the example is the *secure* option. The secure option forces the local host and the remote host to user Secure RPC when making requests to access this file system.

When file systems are exported to the world, any host, even one that is completely unknown by the local system, can mount that file system. Any file readable or writeable by others could be read or modified by a user on the unknown host. You really do not want just anyone mounting your file systems remotely. Use the **/etc/exports** file to control which hosts can mount which directories, and to set other limitations using the options.

If you do not know who has remotely mounted your file systems, you can use the **showmount** command. The **showmount** command without options displays a list of remote systems that have mounted local file systems. With the **a** option, a somewhat more useful list, consisting of the remote host name, a colon, and the local directory mounted, will be displayed (see Figure 4-16).

The **exportfs** command actually does the work of exporting file systems. Executed without arguments, **exportfs** reports the directories currently exported. If the **-v** flag is added, the options given for each directory are included. The **-u** flag permits the unexporting of a directory. Note, however, that once a directory has been remotely mounted, unexporting will not unmount it. The local system cannot force a remote system to unmount directories short of removing the entry by editing the **/etc/exports** file and rebooting.

Figure 4-16: Use the **showmount** *command to determine which hosts have currently mounted local file systems or directories.*

```
# showmount -a
gandhi:/usr
atlas:/usr
isis:/usr
jpmorgan:/var/db
isis:/u/share
client1:/export/root/client1
client1:/export/swap/client1
# ▮
```

The netgroup File   The **/etc/netgroup** file defines netgroups. Netgroups can be used in place of individual host names in the **/etc/hosts.equiv**, **.rhosts**, and **/etc/exports** files. The **/etc/netgroup** file is distributed by NIS, so it can only be modified on the master server system, and distributed by using the **makedbm** command (which updates the Yellow Pages databases). If you are not using NIS, you can edit your system's copy of **/etc/netgroup** directly.

The format of the **/etc/netgroup** file consists of single line entries starting with a group name, and followed either by other group names or triplets. The triplets are in the form of *(hostname,username,domain)*. Any of the three fields in the triplet can be empty. An empty field represents a wildcard, so the triplet (gandhi,,) means the host named gandhi, any user, and any domain.

Groups in the **/etc/netgroup** file should represent the smallest grouping of related hosts. The smaller group units can be combined to form super groups of related hosts (Figure 4-17).

Figure 4-17: The **/etc/netgroup** *file is used to create groupings of hosts according to affiliations.*

```
# cat /etc/netgroup
suns-prog     (atlas,,) (thor,,) (isis,,)
suns-support  (einstein,,) (freud,,)
all-suns      suns-prog suns-support
marketing     (jpmorgan,,) (rockefeller,,)
# ▮
```

In Figure 4-17, the two groups of Suns, suns-prog and suns-support, are combined into the supergroup all-suns. The supergroup all-suns could be further combined to create a still larger group.

The use of netgroups is not required, but useful. Netgroups help you create an organizational basis for trusting hosts. Also, the **/etc/netgroup** file, unlike **/etc/hosts.equiv**, is distributed via NIS, so that if netgroups are used in **/etc/hosts. equiv**, new trusted hosts can be added through netgroups.

Other Network Services

The TCP/IP network provides other services that are more common than the r commands and NFS. The **telnet** command provides for remote terminal emulation across the network. The **ftp** command uses the File Transfer Protocol for copying files across the network. A simpler version named **tftp** (trivial ftp) works similarly. The **sendmail** program on UNIX systems uses SMTP (Simple Mail Transfer Protocol) to deliver mail across the network. The **finger** command provides information about users on remote hosts.

All of the network services have security problems; some more than others. The **sendmail** program is especially notorious, mainly through undocumented features left in the program during its development. Problems with **telnet** and **ftp** have been minor by comparison. For example, a warning was posted on the network that someone was replacing the **telnet** program with a modified version that copied passwords into a file named "...". This problem had nothing to do with the design of **telnet**, but with the security of the hosts so compromised. Somehow, a user coming in through the network had installed a bogus version of **telnet**. If you don't trust your version of **telnet**, replace it with a copy from your installation tapes.

This next section covers known security problems with network services. The method for setting up your system to use anonymous **ftp** will also be covered.

sendmail   The **sendmail** program was designed to solve a very difficult problem—how to deliver mail. This may not sound difficult, but **sendmail**'s task is to be capable of understanding *any* network addressing scheme so that mail can be correctly routed. The **sendmail** program was designed to be so flexible that it could handle any situation. Its cryptic configuration file provides the flexibility, and although many have complained, no one has produced an acceptable alternative.

The story goes that near the completion of the **sendmail** project, the system administrator deprived the author of root privileges. The author, certainly a clever man, provided himself with a *backdoor*, a method for attaining superuser privilege. The backdoor would be activated when the correct, but unusual, responses were made.

Of course, the backdoor did not stay concealed. The **sendmail** program is distributed as an uncompiled program to source licensees of BSD. Then, word of mouth helped to spread the secret. Eventually, all vendors will have removed this backdoor from their version. You can check your version for the "wizard" password, and make it more secure by removing it if you find it (see Figure 4-18). The **/etc/sendmail.cf** file configures **sendmail**, establishing new methods for expanding addresses and forwarding mail if necessary. This configuration file also contains options for **sendmail**, including a possible "wizard" password.

Figure 4-18: The option for a wizard password,
OW, *has been set to "*", an impossible password.*

```
# grep OW /etc/sendmail. cf
OW*
# ▊
```

The "wizard" password would grant a knowledgeable user a root-owned shell process. Setting the option **OW** to an asterisk prevents use of the wizard password.

The **sendmail** program reads a file containing various aliases. This file, named either **/etc/aliases** or **/usr/lib/aliases**, contains mail recipient aliases. For example, you can create a group alias, so that mail directed to the group is forwarded to all members in the group.

The alias file can also contain names aliased to a command pipeline. Some UNIX systems include the **decode** alias in the alias file, so that **uuencoded** files can be sent to this alias. The **decode** alias should be removed (see Figure 4-19), as it permits the installation of programs by mailing the program to the **decode** recipient.

After editing the aliases file, you must run the **newaliases** command. The **newaliases** command creates and installs the binary files used by **sendmail** for aliasing; simply editing the aliases file does not put the change into effect.

*Figure 4-19: Removing the **decode** alias from the aliases file and creating new aliases.*

```
# grep decode /etc/aliases
decode: "|/usr/bin/uudecode"
# ex /etc/aliases     # remove the decode alias
# newaliases
13 aliases, longest 17 bytes, 153 bytes total
# ▮
```

While editing the aliases file, you should also look for any recipients aliased as commands. Commands that can be coaxed into providing a shell (through a shell escape, for example), must not be allowed.

The ability to alias recipients to commands is considered a feature, not a security problem. The Internet Worm took advantage of another leftover "feature" that is definitely a security problem. The original **sendmail** included a *debug* feature. By invoking the debug feature, the Internet Worm was able to coax **sendmail** into creating and executing a program that copied across the rest of the worm. You can check your version of **sendmail** for the **debug** feature using the example shown in Figure 4-20.

*Figure 4-20: Using **telnet** to check for the debug feature of **sendmail**.*

```
# telnet localhost 25
Escape character is '^]'.
220 s350. Sendmail 4-0/SMI-4-0 ready at Tue, 25 Sep 90 15:45:12
debug
200 Debug set
quit
Connection closed by foreign host
# ▮
```

If **sendmail** fails to recognize the **debug** command, it will report **500 Command unrecognized**. This is what you want to see. If you see something like the "200 Debug set" in Figure 4-20, your **sendmail** has one of the problems exploited by the Internet Worm. Your system is still vulnerable to the very same attack that crippled thousands of hosts on the Internet. You can either get an updated version of **sendmail**, or patch your copy of **sendmail** so that **debug** doesn't work. (Find the string "debug", and replace it with something else.)

ftp   The **ftp** program permits the transfer of files to or from a host on the network. Each host must run the **ftpd** daemon to support **ftp**. If you do not wish to provide this service, you can edit the **/etc/inetd. conf** file and signal the daemon to read this file.

The **ftp** program requires users to have a login name and enter a password. Once authenticated, the user may use the **ftp** program to list directories, change directory, and get or send files. The file access permission functions normally, that is, they are based on the user id of the user that logged in via **ftp**.

It is also possible to allow unknown users to work with a restricted version of **ftp**, called *anonymous ftp*. Anonymous **ftp** provides a change root environment (explained on page 155), a very secure way to work with guests. Using anonymous **ftp** requires some setup (see Figure 4-21).

*Figure 4-21: Steps in setting up an anonymous **ftp** account.*
*Note that the **etc/passwd** copy must have all encrypted passwords removed.*

```
# grep ftp /etc/passwd
ftp:*:127:127:FTP guest Login:/var/ftp:
# mkdir /var/ftp
# cd /var/ftp
# mkdir bin etc pub
# chmod 755 . bin etc pub
# cp /bin/ls bin
# cp /etc/passwd /etc/group etc
# ex etc/passwd          # remove passwords and comments
# cp /u/rik/gift pub
# ▮
```

Figure 4-21 depicts setting up an anonymous **ftp** account. Strangely enough, it is the creation of the pseudo-account *ftp* in the **/etc/passwd** file that enables anonymous **ftp**. The HOME directory for this account becomes the root of the restricted environment. The anonymous user cannot move above this directory, but can change directory to subdirectories, such as **pub**.

The only command necessary is a copy of the **ls** command, placed in **bin**. Copies of **/etc/passwd** and **/etc/group** are copied to the **etc** directory, so that ls will be able to produce long listings (**ls -l**). These copies should be edited to remove *all* passwords, and accounts belonging to users. A script that strips out passwords is provided in the section on change root environments.

The **pub** directory is the customary repository for files that you wish to share. In this example, **pub** is writeable only by the superuser, so only the administrator can install files to be shared. This prevents users from exporting information you would rather not distribute.

Some systems provide a writeable directory so anonymous users can leave files. The problem with this is that you do not have any way of knowing who has left you gifts. Although anonymous **ftp** is a valuable tool, it also provides a way to copy binary executable files to a system. These binary files could be useful utilities. They could also have been infected with a virus, or contain a Trojan Horse, or time bomb. Here's an example of a bad gift: there was a public domain program named "turkey" which was a Trojan Horse. The claim was that "turkey" would draw a picture of a turkey on the user's screen. But what it actually did was remove all files in the user's directory. A simple Trojan Horse.

Trivial ftp   Trivial **ftp**, **tftp**, is the simplified version of ftp. **tftp** permits the copying of files without logging in and is used for booting diskless workstations or downloading server code or fonts to X terminals. **tftp** follows some simple security rules that is supposed to make it safe. One is that it will only copy files readable by all.

The world-readable rule by itself is not very secure. The **/etc/passwd** file is readable by all, and you do not want people copying it. Another rule imposed on some **tftp** daemons is that they can only copy filenames that do not contain slashes. This rule would let a server copy its boot code out of the root directory, but not copy a file in **/etc**. You can test **tftp** for this capability with the commands in Figure 4-22.

Figure 4-22: A flawed version of **tftp**. *It should say "Error code 1: File not found".*

```
# tftp localhost
tftp get /etc/motd
Received 626 bytes in 1 seconds.
tftp quit
# ▮
```

If your version of **tftp** behaves like the one in Figure 4-22, you don't want to let it run. Actually, only systems that work as servers to diskless workstations and X terminals really need to run **tftp** anyway. To turn off **tftp** follow the directions on page 150, "Disabling Network Daemons."

fingerd   The **fingerd** program provides a service to network users. A remote user can use the **fingerd** service to discover if a particular user is at some site. **fingerd**

executes the **finger** command, which produces a report based on the comment field of the matching account in **/etc/passwd**. Such information could be used by someone trying to guess passwords.

There is a greater problem with the **fingerd**, however. Reportedly, when the author of the Internet Worm discovered this flaw, he leaped up on a desk and started screaming. The programmer who wrote **fingerd** had used the wrong function for collecting the string that should contain the local user's name. When the Worm used **fingerd**, it sent information that overwrote part of the program code, and caused **fingerd** to start a shell program instead of **finger** (see the Appendix on the Internet Worm).

If your **fingerd** program predates November, 1988, you can be pretty certain it includes this flaw. You can use the **what** command to view the SCCS date on your version. If you have access to Usenet, you can get fixes to both the **sendmail** bug and **fingerd** from **usr. lib/sendmail/src/srvrsmtp.c**. And, if all you want to do is turn **fingerd** off, try the next section.

Disabling Network Daemons

Perhaps you have decided that you do not want to run some of the network daemons. If you have discovered that you do not need to run **tftp**, or you don't want to allow **ftp** or **fingerd,** you can change the configuration file responsible for starting these daemons.

The UNIX system has an unusual method for launching the network daemons. (*Daemons* are processes that run independently of any terminal or user.) Most UNIX daemons are started during the startup process, by the **rc** scripts. The network daemons get started by a single daemon, **inetd**, the Internet daemon.

The Internet daemon reads a configuration file, **/etc/inetd.conf**, when it starts up. This configuration file tells the Internet Daemon which sockets (virtual connections) to listen to. When the Internet daemon gets awakened by a packet arriving at a socket, it launched the network daemon associated with that socket.

You can prevent the launching of any network daemon by commenting out the line in the **/etc/inetd.conf** file for that daemon. After commenting out the line using the pound sign (#), you must also send a HANGUP signal (**kill -1**) to the **inetd** process (Figure 4-23).

Figure 4-23: Disable network daemons by
commenting out entries in the /etc/inetd.conf file.

```
# grep /usr/bin /etc/inetd.conf
ftp      stream  tcp  nowait  root  /usr/bin/ftpd       ftpd
telnet   stream  tcp  nowait  root  /usr/bin/telnetd    telnetd
shell    stream  tcp  nowait  root  /usr/bin/rshd       rshd
login    stream  tcp  nowait  root  /usr/bin/rlogind    rlogind
exec     stream  tcp  nowait  root  /usr/bin/rexecd     rexecd
tftp     dgram   udp  wait    root  /usr/bin/tftpd      tftpd
# ex /etc/inetd. conf   # comment out undesired damons
# ps -ef | grep inetd
    root    426     1  7 08:53:53 ?     0:00 /usr/bin/inetd
    rik     491   480  7 10:30:33 p0    0:00 grep inetd
# kill -1 426
# ▮
```

Your Internet daemons may be in **/usr/etc** if you work with Suns. When you signal the **inetd** process, you are not killing it, but sending it the signal to look at its configuration files again. Make certain you use signal -1, the hangup.

In particular, you might want to disable some of these daemons on the host that connects to the Internet, or other outside network. The rationale behind this idea is that the host connected to the outside faces the brunt of any outside attack. The host machine might also be configured as a gateway between your internal network and the outside network. Your gateway host can act as a *firewall*, hiding the hosts on the internal network from outside attacks.

The firewall system should not export NFS file systems, or mount any NFS file systems. The firewall system should not be trusted—that is, appear in other hosts' **/etc/hosts.equiv** files. The gateway can be set up so that packets from the outside must stop at the firewall. Users wishing to **telnet** to the outside world must log into the firewall system first. The firewall system also acts as a mail forwarding agent. From the outside world, it looks like every user has an address on the firewall host, when in reality, the firewall host handles distribution of mail. Run frequent checks of the firewall system, looking for modified files, bad passwords, and evidence of break-ins. When possible, turn on auditing or debugging features, and scan the output generated.

Restricted Environments

Restricted environments add some degree of control to what the users within the environments may do. Restricted environments are appropriate for guests to your systems, or even for regular users who are unfamiliar with the UNIX system. There are three different types of restricted environments:

- Replacing the login shell with a special purpose program
- Replacing the login shell with the restricted shell
- Using the **chroot** system call to encapsulate the user's access to a branch of the file system

Each of these three methods has its own benefits and pitfalls. Incorrect use of any one can give you a false sense of security—if you really have not made your system more secure.

Special purpose programs can be the most secure of the three choices. The special purpose program is executed at login time, and totally controls the user's activities. Problems can develop if there are loopholes in the special purpose program that make it more general purpose than planned.

The restricted shell, **/bin/rsh** is linked to the Bourne shell, **/bin/sh**. The restricted shell enforces several rules, which comprise its restrictions. Properly set up, the stricted shell provides a user with a general purpose yet restricted environment. Unfortunately, it is all to easy to make mistakes in the setup for the restricted shell, in which case the restrictions are about as strong as a wet paper bag.

The **chroot** restricted environment provides the strongest protection, and the greatest flexibility for the user. The **chroot** restricted environment is less prone to setup errors than the restricted shell, and provides much stronger protection for your system. It is my preferrence for encapsulating guests that require temporary access to a system.

Special Login Programs

I have already given several examples of special login programs. As the name suggests, special login programs replace the shell in the seventh field of an **/etc/passwd** entry. Several special purpose programs that are not recommended include **who, sync**, and **tty**. For example, if you had an account entry with **/bin/who** as the login program, logging into that account would produce the output of the **who** command, after which you would immediately be logged out.

Using the **who command** was not recommended because it gives away account names.

A better example of a special login program is the **uucico** program, discussed earlier in this chapter. The **uucico** program operates as the authentication and transfer agent for the UUCP system. Properly configured, there is no way to get a general purpose shell from a HoneyDanBer **uucico** program. Logging into a UUCP account with **/usr/lib/uucp/uucico** as the seventh field produces a strange prompt, "Shere." Unless you understand **uucico's** protocol, you are unlikely to get farther.

You can use other UNIX programs as login shells. But most UNIX programs are either too restricted to be of much use, or give access to unrestricted shells. For example, you might at first think that the **/bin/mail** program would provide a user with a mechanism for logging in and reading mail. However, **mail** includes a *shell escape*, a command sequence that can execute any other command, including a shell program. If you decide to use any program as a restricted login program, check for shell escapes. Popular interactive programs, such as mail programs, editors, and wordprocessors, all have shell escapes.

You can also write your own special purpose program. To be secure, your program should follow the general rules for writing set-user-id programs. The comparison between a login program and a set-user-id program may seem unclear, but some of the problems are the same. For example, you may wish to execute a UNIX command to perform some task for your restricted user. However, the restricted user might be able to coax a shell out of your program by the clever use of arguments passed to the UNIX command. Set-user-id programs face similar challenges. See the Appendix on writing set-user-id programs.

Restricted Shell

The restricted shell looks like a good thing. And it actually can carry out its assigned roll quite well, barring mistakes by the administrator and other, non-restricted users. The **rsh** works like the Bourne shell with the following five restrictions:

- User cannot change directory (use **cd**)
- User cannot change **PATH** or **SHELL** environment variables
- User cannot execute a command that includes a slash, for example, . . / . . **/bin/chmod**

- User cannot redirect out (use > or >>)
- User cannot use the **exec** shell built-in

Now, if you give a restricted user the customary **PATH**, for example, **PATH=/bin:/usr/bin:**, then you have done little but inconvenience the restricted user. The key is to set up a directory containing a safe list of commands using the **.profile** setup file for the account.

Unlike an ordinary user, the restricted user does not own the .profile file, or even have write permission in the HOME directory. Instead, the **.profile** contains critical information, and the restricted user gets switched into another directory to perform work. Figure 4-24 depicts an example restricted **.profile**.

Figure 4-24: Example setup for a restricted account that uses the restricted shell, **/bin/rsh**.

```
# cd /u/restrict
# cat . profile
PATH=/usr/rbin export PATH
SHELL=/bin/rsh export SHELL
cd /u/restrict/work
# ls -ld . profile . . /work
drwxr-xr-x  2 root    other      512 Sep 12 15:52 .
-rwxr-xr-x  2 root    other       93 Sep 12 15:54 . profile
drwxr-xr-x  2 ruser   other      512 Sep 12 15:53 . /work
# grep ruser /etc/passwd
ruser:y4Dwk8YeKsdOE:1001:222:rsh user:/u/restrict:/bin/rsh
# ls /u/rbin
cat
ls
mail
red
# ▌
```

The PATH establishes only one directory, **/usr/rbin**, where commands can be found. These commands can actually be links to the real commands (if the commands are in **/usr/bin**). If links cannot be made, copies work fine. The use of links uses less disk space.

The commands in the restricted command directory must be carefully chosen. The restricted shell does not place restrictions on command arguments, so if a restricted user can use an unrestricted editor, like **ex** or **emacs**, they can use it to copy any file into the current directory. The **kermit** program, for example, cannot be included because the restricted user can copy files from anywhere in the file system to a remote computer. The sources for file transfer programs, such as **kermit** and **xmodem**, are readily available and could be modified to create a restricted version that only copies files in the current directory (no directories in the filenames).

Commands to especially avoid are **cp**, **ln**, **chmod**, and **env**. These commands potentially could be used to obtain an unrestricted shell. The **mail** command, although it does possess a shell escape, looks at the SHELL variable, and will give the restricted user another restricted shell.

Perhaps you have noticed what seems to be an inconsistency in the restricted shell. The restricted shell does not permit changing the PATH or SHELL variables, or changing directories. Yet, the **.profile** (in Figure 4-24) does all these things. What happens is that the restricted shell suspends all restrictions while executing shell scripts.

The suspension of restrictions while using shell scripts, and the selection of commands for the restricted account provide loopholes in the restricted shell mechanism. For these reasons, the restricted shell is not considered very secure.

The Change Root Environment

The *change root* environment provides the strongest protection of any restricted environment. The change root environment uses the **chroot** system call to change a process' notion of where the root directory resides. By default, the root directory is fixed, and is always indicated by the slash (/). After the **chroot** call, a new directory is used as the root for locating files.

The easiest way to understand this is to look at a picture. Figure 4-25 depicts a part of the standard UNIX file system, with an additional directory tree beginning with **/restrict**. After the call to **chroot**, with **/restrict** given as the argument, **/restrict** appears as / (slash, the root) to the user working in that environment.

Only the superuser can execute **chroot**. The **chroot** system call modifies the *uarea*, a protected data area associated with every process. The **uarea** also contains other sensitive information about the process, such as the real and effective user and group id of the process. The name of the changed root directory, if any, is kept here, and used as the placement for the true root directory (Figure 4-26).

Figure 4-25: After executing **chroot /restrict**,
the process' view of the file system is changed.

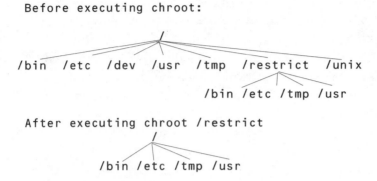

```
Before executing chroot:

                          /
      _____/|_____
     /      /      /      /     \       \         \
  /bin   /etc   /dev   /usr    /tmp   /restrict   /unix
                                      __/|\__
                                     /   |    \    \
                                  /bin /etc /tmp /usr

   After executing chroot /restrict

                  /
          _____/|_____
         /    /      \      \
      /bin /etc     /tmp   /usr
```

Figure 4-26: Using the **chroot** *command.*

```
# ls -C /
bin        etc        lost+found tmp
dev        lib        restrict   unix
# ls -C /restrict
bin        etc        usr        tmp
# chroot /restrict
# ls -C /
bin        etc        usr        tmp
# ▮
```

A **chroot** command is also available to the superuser. The command is not useful for setting up a changed root environment for security purposes, but can be used for other things, as in the case of Figure 4-26. Before executing **chroot**, the root directory is the real root of the file systems, containing other directories, and a copy of the kernel program named **unix**. After the **chroot**, the former **/restrict** directory appears to be the root directory *even to the superuser*.

Getting out of a **chroot** environment is difficult, even for the superuser. If either device file for memory is available (**/dev/mem** or **/dev/kmem**), a specially written program could search out the changed root in the **uarea** and clear it. Once the changed root information is cleared, the process will once again have access to the complete file system hierarchy.

Another way out is to access files directly through the block or character device interfaces to file systems. Another special program, or the System V program

fsdb, must access the file system partitions directly, and then is capable of reading or writing anywhere in the file system hierarchy.

The third means of escape occurs if a hard link has been made from a directory outside the restricted root to one inside the restricted directory tree. Only the superuser can make hard links between directories, which is not normally done. Hard directory links break commands like **find**.

Both of the escape roots require device files. The only device file required in a restricted environment is **/dev/tty**, actually a pseudo-device that is used for collecting passwords and in some shell scripts. Since the **ps** command requires the **/dev/kmem** file, and a copy of the kernel, restricted users will have to live without the **ps** command. Do not provide the **mknod** command, and compilers, such as C or FORTRAN, which include the **mknod** system call.

Although only the superuser can make new device files, a little paranoia is useful. If you do not include device files, and do not include the means for making new ones (with **mknod**), then even if a restricted user becomes superuser, that user is still restricted. The restricted superuser cannot access outside directories to make hard links either.

Because the change root restricted environment is completely cut off from the rest of the file system, everything that the restricted user needs must be included below the changed root. For example, the **ls** command will not provide long listings unless the **/etc/passwd** file is available. This copy of the password file, however, must be edited so only required accounts, without *encrypted passwords*, are included. You do not want to include the accounts for ordinary users (since this gives login names away), or encrypted passwords for any account (to prevent cracking attempts). The script shown in Figure 4-27 removes passwords and comments from a password file.

Figure 4-27: Using a simple **awk** *script to "sterilize" the* **/etc/passwd** *file for use in a restricted change root environment.*

```
# cat pass. fix
:
awk -F: '{ printf "%s:*:%d:%d::%s:%s\n",
      $1,$3,$4,$6,$7 }' /etc/passwd
# pass.fix >/restrict/etc/passwd
# cat /restrict/etc/passwd
nobody:*:-2:-2::/:
root:*:0:1::/:/sbin/sh
sysadm:*:0:0::/admin:/sbin/sh
```

Figure 4-27: Using a simple **awk** *script to "sterilize" the*
/etc/passwd file for use in a restricted change root environment (continued).

```
daemon:*:1:1::/:/sbin/sh
bin:*:2:2::/bin:
sys:*:3:3::/usr/src:
adm:*:4:4::/usr/adm:/sbin/sh
uucp:*:5:5::/usr/spool/uucp:/usr/lib/uucp/uucico
lp:*:6:2::/usr/lib:/sbin/sh
mail:*:8:1::/usr/mail:/usr/bin/mail
yp:*:37:37::/usr/etc/yp:/sbin/sh
nfs:*:38:38::/:/sbin/sh
rik:*:100:100::/u/rik:/bin/sh
canyon:*:101:100::/u/canyon:/bin/sh
rose:*:102:100::/u/rose:/bin/sh
ftp:*:127:127::/var/ftp:/sbin/sh
+:*:0:0:::
# ▮
```

After removing passwords and comments, you will normally also strip out some login names. The login name for regular users do not need to appear in the change root environment, since they only give away information.

When you choose commands for your change root environment, you must also include the supporting files for these commands. For example, a screen-oriented editor might require a copy of **/etc/termcap**. With newer (after 4-0) releases of SunOS, another problem occurs. SunOS 4-x delivers commands that require shared libraries to execute. Without these libraries, copies of the commands are useless. The libraries may be found in **/usr/lib**, and have names like **lib.so4.a**. A way around this problem (besides creating the appropriate directories and copying over the libraries) is to use commands taken from pre-4.0 SunOS tapes. The older versions of commands work just as well as the newer, although they lose the space saving advantages of shared libraries.

Figure 4-28 shows an example set of directories and files that will work with the change root program explained later.

In Figure 4-29, nine commands were copied into the restricted bin directory. You can put many more commands in this directory, leaving out **mknod** and compilers. Of course, if the sole purpose of the restricted environment is to permit an outside contractor to work on your system, you may be forced to include compilers, assemblers, and loaders.

This is not the ideal situation; however, the contractor must become super-user before **mknod** can make device files. The change root environment is the best compromise in this case.

Figure 4-28: The setup for a change root restricted environment.

```
# cd /u
# mkdir restrict
# cd restrict
# mkdir bin dev etc tmp pub
# cp /bin/sh /bin/cat /bin/ls /bin/chmod /bin/mv bin
# cp /bin/date /bin/mkdir /bin/rm /usr/lbin/kermit bin
# ls -l /dev/tty
crw-rw-rw-  1 root    root     2,  0 Sep 23 18:45 /dev/tty
# mknod dev/tty c 2 0
# pass.fix > etc/passwd
# ex etc/passwd    # remove user accounts, except for guest
# cp /etc/group etc
# chown guest pub
# chmod 777 tmp
# ls -l
total 8
drwxr-xr-x  2 root    other      512 Sep 23 18:48 bin
drwxr-xr-x  2 root    other      512 Sep 23 16:39 dev
drwxr-xr-x  2 root    other      512 Sep 23 16:39 etc
drwxr-xr-x  3 guest   other      512 Sep 23 18:16 pub
drwxrwxrwx  2 root    other        0 Sep 23 16:36 tmp
# grep guest /etc/passwd
guest:. k92dKf8c26hg:1002:200::/u/restrict:/usr/lbin/chrt
# ▮
```

Now that you know what files and directories are needed, you will also need a simple program (Figure 4-29). This program is not part of your standard UNIX system, but is simple enough to create on your own. It must be rooted-owned and set-user-id, so beware of making modifications to the program that could compromise its security.

The **/usr/lbin/chrt** program replaces the login program for the guest account. (You do not have to use the **/usr/lbin** directory. Any command directory that is writeable only by the root will work.) The **chrt** program works by getting the real user id which was established during login. Then, the HOME directory is copied to a local variable, and the string "/pub" is appended to it.

Figure 4-29: The chrt.c program must be owned by root and set-user-id.

```
# cat chrt. c
#include <studio.h>
main()
{

    char home[100], newroot[100], *getenv();
    int real_uid;
            /* the real uid set in /etc/passwd */
    real_uid = getuid();
            /* copy the HOME environment */
    strcpy(newroot, getenv("HOME"));
    strcpy(home, newroot);
            /* then concatenated $HOME and /pub */
    strcat(home, "/pub");
            /* change to the $HOME/pub directory */
    chdir(home);
    if (chroot(newroot)) {
            /* chroot returns 1 on failure */
        perror("chroot failed");
        exit(1);
    }


            /* change user id back to real uid */
    setuid(real_uid);
            /* fix user environment variables */
    putenv("HOME=/pub");
    putenv("SHELL=/bin/sh");
            /* start a shell for the guest */
    execl("/bin/sh", "-sh", 0);
            /* only get here if shell fails to execute */
    perror("execute error");
}

# cc chrt. c -o /usr/lbin/chrt
# chmod 4755 /usr/lbin/chrt
# ls -l /usr/bin/lbin
-rwsr-xr-x  1 root    other     51159 Sep 23 18:23 /usr/lbin/chrt
# ▮
```

After changing directory (with **chdir()**), the **chroot()** call changes this process' concept of the root. The **setuid()** call changes the real and effective user id back to that of the guest, and the **putenv()** calls fix the SHELL and HOME environment variables (which contained values put there during login which are no longer appropriate). Finally, the **execl()** call executes **/bin/sh** as a login shell (designated by the "-sh" argument). The shell replaces the **chrt** program, reads the guest **.profile** (if any), and presents a prompt to the user.

Another issue for users of change root environments is that they are also cut off from systems services, such as print spooling and mail. The spooling directories for both of these systems are located outside of the change root environment. If you want your restricted user to have these facilities, you can provide them with shell scripts that mimic the action of **mail**, **lp**, or **lpr**. The shell scripts store the mail message or file to be printed in spooling directories in the change root environment. Then, other shell scripts, started by the **cron** daemon working outside of the restricted environment, routinely check these spooling directories and invoke the real **mail** or line printer programs.

Problems with Restricted Environments

All restricted environments share a common problem—*denial of service*. Denial of service occurs when a user of a computer system abuses his or her privileges in a way that prevents others from using the computer. The denial may be accidental or purposeful. For example, a user might write a program or shell script which creates very large files, filling up the file system. Or, a program which forks multiple copies of itself and uses up process and CPU resources.

Neither of these problems is easy to solve under the UNIX system. The first problem, squandering of disk space, does have a solution under BSD-based version of the UNIX system. BSD UNIX kernels can be built with the QUOTAS switched on, and quotas enabled. Using quotas allows the administrator to set limits on the amount of disk space used by each user in a file system. Setting quotas on guest would prevent a guest from using up all available space in a file system (unless there was only a little space left anyway).

For the quota system to work, the restricted accounts must be confined to particular file systems. Even for non-BSD systems, choosing the right file system is a good strategy. Each file system represents a resource limited by its size. Once a file system is filled, free space can not be taken from other file systems. If possible, put restricted users in a file system of their own. Then restricted users can not effect your other users by depleting disk space. Only the restricted users would be effected.

The second problem is more serious. System V only allows for system-wide limits on the number of processes permitted for each user. BSD-based systems are subject to the same limitation—a system-wide limit on the number of processes owned by each user. However, the BSD system has a means for controlling the amount of CPU time and the size of files created. The **setrlimit()** system calls can be included in the **chrt** program, and used to set reasonable limits on per-process execution time and file creation size. Programmers working in the restricted environment who are aware of this system call can reset these limits to their maximum values (if compilers are provided in the restricted environment).

In the final analysis, even with restricted environments, anyone who you permit to work in your system has the capability to abuse your system. You are ultimately responsible for determining who will be permitted into the system, and for monitoring their use of the system. Chapter 5 explains how to monitor system use. Any user who abuses his or her system privileges should be reprimanded, and, if necessary, barred from the system.

Chapter 5

Stalking the Wily Cracker

Surprise

Somewhere in the arctic, a snowflake falls. A well-mannered intruder may attract about as much notice as that snowflake. The UNIX system has not been rigged with alarms which can warn of intrusion. Your best alarm system is your own, and your users', vigilance, and an awareness of the normal behavior of your UNIX system or network.

Other operating systems, Digital Equipment Corporation's VMS, for example, do include some built-in alarm mechanisms. These mechanisms can detect failed logins or the attempt to access particular files. But if the security violation does not involve these files or a failed login, no alarm is given. The approach used in VMS is like putting an alarm on the front door and one filing cabinet. Someone who has a key (password) and who doesn't touch the filing cabinet doesn't set off any alarms.

UNIX systems can be modified to provide for some alarms. For example, the **login** program can be replaced with a more security-oriented version. Scripts or programs can monitor files, and send warnings when these files are modified, or even accessed.

But that is not how intruders or crackers are caught. Alarm systems only tell you that something is happening. Security problems with UNIX systems are discovered because of alert users and administrators. You must know how to determine if something is awry. You must also discover *who* is the perpetrator, and seal the hole through which the intruder entered.

Clifford Stoll's experience provides the best example of catching intruders that I have seen or heard. Many people are unwilling to disclose the details, or even that they have had a problem. Clifford Stoll, on the other hand, tells an interesting and complete story about discovering an intruder, tracking him down, collecting evidence, and dealing with law enforcement agencies and the phone company. The book, *The Cuckoo's Egg*, is a good primer for anyone interested in what it is like to watch a cracker in action. Stoll has a great deal of perseverance and good record keeping, and is a good example for anyone who wishes to catch computer felons.

Stoll discovered that one of the computers at Lawrence Berkeley Labs was being illicitly used when an accounting discrepancy of less than a dime showed up. The intruder was using a dormant account for which the cracker had discovered a password. The intruder was coming in through a bank of modems connected to a terminal server. A phone trace led to a Tymnet modem in Oakland, California, and from there to Mitre, a military contractor in Virginia. Eventually, Stoll traced the intruder to Hannover, Germany, but only after watching him break into many UNIX and VMS computers on the Internet. West German authorities finally arrested several men and charged them with selling information to the KGB.

Most computer break-ins are not as dramatic as the one depicted by Stoll. But many are found by noticing as small a detail as a 10 cent difference in accounting, a temporary shortage of disk space, or a process using an inordinate amount of CPU time. Although you are concerned with any security violation, the ones involving significant resources will be both the most noticeable and perhaps the most important to solve.

This chapter covers the tools you can use to routinely watch your system. What to do if you discover a break-in, either in-progress or passed, is covered next. You must make your system officially off-limits with a no trespassing notice and a policy statement. To prosecute any abuser of your system, you must know how to collect and maintain evidence.

Tools for Watching Your System

The tools for watching over your computer are not esoteric—they will be familiar to you already. What I'd like to instill in you is a habit of using these tools often.

You can check users or processes while waiting on the telephone. Or you can run your watchdog scripts while you are waiting for someone to join you for lunch. Most importantly, run them anytime you notice anything at all unusual.

who

The **who** command is one of the first commands new UNIX users learn. It is also useful to system administrators. The **who** command displays the user names, port names, and login times in three columns. This information is taken from the **/etc/utmp** file, and is maintained by the **init** program, **login** program, and the **date** command. Changing the date leaves a record that may be viewed with an option available to both System V and BSD variants.

Figure 5-1: Using the **-u** *option with* **who** *displays more information from the* **/etc/utmp** *file. On System V-based computers, the* **-u** *option also displays idle times for users, or a dot if idle less than one minute.*

```
$ who -a
rik          contty        Oct 15 11:00    .    26602
sheri        tty31         Oct 15 08:58   1:14  25434   location 27
rosanna      tty35         Oct 15 09:26    .    25624   location 41
dianne       tty37         Oct 15 09:03    .    12569   location 37
jon          tty38         Oct 15 07:43    .    12378   location 36
dave         tty41         Oct 15 08:18    .    12031   location 39
howard       tty47         Oct 15 09:12   :06   13383   location 40
gary         tty48         Oct 15 10:15    .    26405   location 32
gail         tty57         Oct 15 09:16    .    24943   location 8
$ ▮
```

The **/etc/utmp** file contains current information about recent changes to the system. For example, a record is made when a user logs in. This record gets replaced by a different record, the running of **getty** on that port, when the user logs out. This file contains the boot time, plus the old and new dates when the date is changed by the superuser. Without options, the **who** command only displays currently logged in users.

If present, a cumulative record of all changes made to **/etc/utmp** is kept in the file **/etc/wtmp** (System V) or **/usr/adm/wtmp** (BSD-based systems). If these files do not exist, the cumulative records are not kept. *You want to keep cumulative records.* The **wtmp** file provides the only record of when users were logged in. Without the **wtmp** file, once a user has logged out, you only have indirect information about who was logged in (file modification times or last login times). The only negative side to keeping **wtmp** records is that these files increase in size, so they must be periodically backed-up, compressed, or otherwise truncated.

The information kept in the utmp and wtmp files is in binary form—you can't read it with an editor. You can, however, use the who -a command with a file name to read the binary records and convert them to human readable forms (Figure 5-2).

Figure 5-2: Some of the contents from the **wtmp** *file.*

```
$ who -a /etc/wtmp
getty     tty36        Oct 12 08:56  0:01   7623  id=  36
LOGIN     tty36        Oct 12 08:56  0:01   7623  block 34
rosanna   tty36        Oct 12 08:57  0:01   7623  block 34         $ who
```

Unlike the ordinary display of the **who** commands, the translation of the **wtmp** file is jumbled up. Since **wtmp** represents the cumulative changes to the system's state, users, and date, the changes appear in chronological order. In **utmp**, only the most recent changes are kept. The chronological records in **wtmp** become important when you need to discover which users were logged on during a time period. You will use this information after a break-in is discovered.

The day-to-day use of **who** is intended to help you become accustomed to the pattern of use by your users. If your system has a great number of users, this technique will be less useful because there will be too many users logged in to discern any patterns. When using **who** during regular working hours, you are looking for the unusual—the user who is on vacation and is logged in, the use of a guest account, and activity in accounts that are dormant.

System crackers seem to prefer to use dormant (unused) accounts. One reason for this is that they are less likely to be noticed by the regular user of an account. Another reason may be that crackers using dormant accounts are more noticeable, and more have been caught. Stoll's intruder came to light when a dormant account was used. Break-ins at Columbia University were noticed for a similar reason: a normally unused guest account was being used. For your system's safety, unused accounts should have impossible passwords.

If your system has a night operator, or has users who work into the wee hours, they can watch for unusual activity with **who**. Unusual activity would be seeing the name of a user who never logs in after 5 PM. Another characteristic of crackers is that many prefer to work late hours. This may not be a preference, since they may have other "jobs" during the day. Also, a break-in is less likely to be detected if nobody is watching. Stoll's intruder was very wary, and would log out immediately at the slightest sign that someone might be watching him. He obviously preferred to work at night.

Process Status

The **ps** command reports on current processes. The **ps** command reads information from the kernel's process table and from the user area (*u_area*) of each current process. This information is presented in columns, and always includes the following:

- The process id, the number used to identify the process, or to kill it
- The controlling terminal, the port used by the user initiating the process
- The time, the amount of CPU time used by this process
- The name of the executable file used as the basis for this process

The process id is mainly for identification purposes, although it can also be used to signal a process. Only the owner of a process, or the superuser, can signal a process with **kill**. The controlling terminal indicates which terminal was used to enter the command that started the process. The time represents just the time the process has actually been executing. A user running **vi**, for example, might have started the program hours ago, but only used seconds of CPU time. Finally, the command is the name of the program executed.

A program can change the name of the command that appears in **ps** listings. A much simpler trick is to make a link to a program, or a copy of a program, with a different name and run it. For example, users would copy a game program to a file named **sh** and run it. Even though a game was being used, it appears that the user is running the shell. Disguising the name of the command used is a common ploy. The Internet Worm used the name "sh" for its executable.

When you run the **ps** command routinely, you are looking first for patterns. What commands are your users generally using? By recognizing this pattern, you will be able to pick out unusual commands or programs. Another thing to watch for is large amounts of CPU time. Password cracking programs use enormous amounts of CPU time. Persons trying to crack passwords at Columbia University were discovered because when the system began to slow down someone noticed processes with large amounts of CPU time.

By default, only the processes owned by the user issuing the **ps** command are displayed. Under System V, the **-e** option will display everything (all processes).

To display all process under BSD, the option letters **-ax** are used. The **-l** option adds more information about each process with a long listing.

The long listing adds ten new columns to the **ps** listing, several of which can help you understand what may be happening in your system. The *PPID* column shows the parent process ID, in other words, the process from which this process was executed. Most commands have a shell process as their parent. In Figure 5-3, the **ps** command is a child of the process number 477, a **csh**. Using the parent process ID, the user ID, and the controlling terminal, you can associate processes. Also, by killing the parent process, you can often send the same signal to all the child processes.

*Figure 5-3: Using **ps -l** provides a long listing of the processes associated with the controlling terminal, in this case, **ttyp2**.*

```
$ ps −l
F S    UID    PID   PPID  C PRI NI       ADDR    SZ     WCHAN TTY TIME COMD
2 W    100    475    469  7 200 20  fe00c000    32  7fc419e0 p2  0:00 sh
2 W    100    477    475  7 200 20  fe024000    69  7fc4477c p2  0:00 csh
2 R    100    469      1  7 200 20  fe026000   140           p2  0:28 xterm
2 T    100    528    477  7 200 20  fe02c000    71  7fc4618c p2  0:00 vi
2 R    100    544    477  7 200 20  fe02d000    34           p2  0:00 ps
$ ▮
```

The column labeled *NI* stands for *niceness*. By default, all UNIX processes run with a niceness of 20. This niceness is added to the process' priority and used to determine which process will be schedule to run next. Ordinary users can increase the niceness of their processes by using the **nice** command. This may be done to be nice to others by not hogging the CPU with a calculation intensive task.

Only the superuser may decrease the niceness of a process, making the process more likely to be scheduled to run. This niceness is passed to all sub-processes—so a niced-down shell would also start commands with lower niceness.

The reason that I mention niceness is because I once found that a programmer had written a set-user-id root program that increased the niceness for everyone else's processes, and decreased it for his own processes. Thus, his processes always completed faster. What he had done was noticeable by observing the *NI* column in the **ps** long listing. Every user process had a niceness of 39, while the niceness of his processes was only 1.

On System V-based computers, the command **ps -ef** reports on every process with a "friendly" listing. What's friendly about the listing is a translation of the user id into user names and the display of arguments to commands. In addition to the four standard columns and the user name, the **f** flag also causes **ps** to display the parent process ID, and the start time.

who do and w commands

Both System V- and BSD-based systems provide versions of a command that combines features of **who** and **ps**. The System V **whodo** command provides output that matches a combination of the **who** and **ps** commands when run without options. The BSD **w** command produces a display that looks like the System V "friendly" **ps** listing. The **w** command only displays one line for each user, featuring the process determined to be the most current for that user (see Figure 5-4).

*Figure 5-4: the BSD **w** command combines features from **who** and **ps**.*

```
% w
   9:36pm   up 1 day,   5:21,   8 users,   load average: 0.07, 0.00, 0.00
User      tty           login@  idle    JCPU    PCPU   what
mike      console       Tue 4pm 29:16   21:07   1:31   Mail -N -B -f /tmp/MTda00211
rik       ttyb          9:35pm                  3      3      w
peter     tty02         2:42pm  5:21    44      3      -csh
chris     tty05        10:04am 11:30    8       5      vi hughes.terms
john      tty07         8:44am  5:01    5:36    4      vi uri
mike      ttyp0         Tue 4pm 29:16   6       6      -bin/csh
mike      ttyp1         Tue 4pm  4:28   18:07   8:51   /usr/bin/lockscreen_default
mike      ttyp2         Tue 4pm  5:31   9:21    1:24   -u
mike      ttyp4         Tue 4pm  4:31   10      9      rlogin 426 -l johna
m         ttyp5        11:44am  9:51    4       3      -csh
chuck     ttyp7         9:53am  4:03    19      16     rlogin sl386
bill      ttypd         3:51pm  5:44    8       3      -csh
% █
```

Figure 5-4 tells us some interesting things about the users of this Sun computer. Notice, first, that some users are shown as logged in more than once. For example, "mike" appears to be logged in five times. Mike's first log-in was at the console, and subsequent "log-ins" are through the workstation's windowing system. Ports used for windowing are called *pseudo-ports*, and are indicated with a "p" in the device name. Users logging in over the network, such as "bill", also use pseudo-ports.

The idle time is also useful information. This **w** listing was created after hours, and shows that everybody is idle, but still logged in (except me). Apparently, no one has logged out or logged their terminals or windows, abandoning their account privileges to anyone who can get into the office space. The idle time during the day provides the same type of information—who has walked away from their logged-in terminal. It also gives you a quick snapshot of who is actually active—something the BSD-based **who** does not.

The column labeled "JCPU" is the joint total time used by all the processes started from this port. The "PCPU" is the time for just the current process, the one appearing in the last column.

Above the header to the **w** display, the time the command was issued, the time since the computer was rebooted, and the total number of users logged in is displayed. The last three numbers represent the load average, that is, a measure of how heavily the system's resource are being utilized. Using the **w** command itself only put a .07 load on the system. The other two figures represent load average for the past five minutes and 15 minutes, respectively. A large increase in load average would be seen during password cracking attempts (something the Internet Worm did a lot of).

Process Accounting

The UNIX kernel will optionally produce a report each time a process exits. These reports, called *process accounting*, contain information about the resources used by each process, the command executed, who the user was, and if the process ran set-user-id. One use of the process accounting reports is to charge users for CPU time. Another is to determine which commands a user has executed.

Process accounting is not the same as auditing, where security-sensitive actions are monitored. Process accounting does not preserve the arguments to commands, so it is impossible to tell from process accounting what files may have been modified by the commands, or even if the commands succeeded. It is still a good place to look for clues. For instance, if someone has broken into your system by coaxing the Version 2 UUCP system into providing a shell, there will be commands in the process accounting file executed by a UUCP login. The only command executed by a UUCP login would be **uucico**. Other commands, such as **rmail** or **news**, get executed by the **uucp** administrative account. But never shells, or **ls**.

Process accounting files grow rapidly, with about 128 bytes added for each completed process. It is important to process these files daily so as to reduce the amount of disk space used. System V- and BSD-based UNIX systems take different approaches to process accounting commands and processing, and are covered separately.

System V Accounting   Under System V, process accounting records are kept in the **/usr/adm/pacct** files. If the file grows larger than 500 kilobytes, a script run by **cron** (**ckpacct**) moves the **pacct** file to **pacct***N* and starts a new file. Process accounting is turned on when root executes the **/usr/lib/acct/startup** script. Daily processing, which reduces the sizes of the **pacct** files, is done with the **runacct** script, and monthly processing with the **monacct** script. Both scripts are found in the **/usr/lib/acct** directory.

You can tell that System V process accounting is turned on if the **/usr/adm/pacct** file exists and has a recent modified date. The **acctcom** command can be used to search through this file and produce reports on completed commands. For example, you can discover all the commands executed by the user "bob" during the one hour period between 1700 and 1800 by using the command in Figure 5-5.

Figure 5-5: Using **acctcom** *to display commands completed during the period between five and six PM.*

```
$ acctcom -u bob -s 15:00 -e 16:00
START BEF: Sat Oct  6 18:00:00 1990
END AFTER: Sat Oct  6 17:00:00 1990
COMMAND                     START     END        REAL    CPU  MEAN
NAME       USER   TTYNAME   TIME      TIME      (SECS) (SECS) SIZE(K)
ls         bob    ttyp2     17:03:27  17:03:27   0.10   0.08  0.00
chmod      bob    ttyp2     17:03:36  17:03:36   0.04   0.02  0.00
date       bob    ttyp2     17:03:42  17:03:42   0.08   0.04  0.00
$ ▮
```

The **acctcom** command lets you see what a user has done, not what the user is currently doing. Also, only the command name, no arguments, are shown. Still, activities by an account that is only supposed to run **uucico** could be detected. Or processes using large amounts of CPU time (typically password crackers).

There are other fruits of the System V accounting system. By running the daily **runacct** script, several reports are generated. These reports are stored in the **/usr/adm/acct/sum** directory with a name in the form **rprtMMDD**. The first part of the report contains changes, such as when process accounting was turned on or off (possibly by someone trying to hide activities), or when the date was changed. The next part of the report shows the total number of minutes any user was logged in, plus reports for each port. Also in this report are the number of times on and off for each port. Times on indicate successful logins, and times out indicate both logouts and failed login attempts. A much higher times out may indicate that someone has been trying login name-password combinations. It can also indicate loose wiring or a poorly configured modem.

The last part of each report is the last login. The last login report is cumulative, and displays user names and the last login date, with the oldest account first. This report is good for discovering dormant accounts. You can also look for suprises here, such as someone logging into an administrative account (such as **bin** or **sys**), or someone logging into an account while the owner is out of town.

BSD Accounting   The capability to perform process accounting is not always built into BSD kernels. Look for the line containing the word **SYSACCT** in the kernel configuration file. If this line has been commented out, your kernel will not produce process accounting reports.

BSD process accounting is turned on with the **/usr/etc/accton** program. The default records file is **/usr/adm/acct**, which grows quickly as long as process accounting is turned on. BSD systems have two commands for processing accounting information. The first, **/usr/etc/ac**, processes the information kept in the **/usr/adm/wtmp** file, for login accounting. The second, **/usr/etc/sa**, produces command summary reports which are kept in the file **/usr/adm/savacct**.

BSD systems have a command similar to **acctcom** which is called **lastcomm**. **lastcomm** searches through the **/usr/adm/acct** file, in reverse order, and prints reports similar to the **acctcom** command. The **lastcom** command will limit its reports to particular user, command, or tty by placing one or more of these as arguments on the command line.

The BSD accounting system has the same deficiency (from a security viewpoint) as the System V version—no arguments are saved from commands. BSD account summaries do not include a last login report summary.

Another Way to Watch Commands   Since neither System V nor BSD produce helpful means for watching a particular user execute commands, it is useful to learn another way to do so. Both **ksh** (the Korn shell) and **csh** (the C shell) may keep history files. These history files provide a mechanism for command line editing. For the Korn shell, command line editing relies on the history file. With the C shell, the history file is optional, and is used to extend history over past login sessions.

Korn shell users may either set variables in their **.profile** file, or in a file specified with the variable named **ENV**. In either the **.profile** file or the file named with **ENV**, if the user has set the variable **HISTFILE** to a filename, this file contains a running history of the user's commands *as they appeared on the command line*. This is much more useful than process accounting, because the commands appear with arguments, and can be viewed in context. In the case of the Korn shell, a **tail -f** can be run to follow the Korn shell history file, reporting on commands as they are executed.

C shell users may set the **savehist** variable to indicate how many commands should be saved in the file **~/.history**. This file gets written from the current C shell's memory when the user exits this C shell. Since the file only gets updated after exiting, you cannot follow it using **tail**, but it is still useful for providing a summary of commands, with arguments, for a particular user.

Tapping Ports   People often ask if it is possible to "tap" a port, that is, make everything a user does echo on an eavesdropper's terminal. Although the UNIX kernel can potentially "tap" a port, it is not designed to do so.

When a user logs in, the port, say **/dev/tty11**, used becomes the user's process' standard input, output, and error. The ownership of the port also is set to that of the user. When the user logs out, the connections to the port are dropped, and the ownership generally reverts to the root.

If two processes attempt to listen to (read from) the same port, what happens is that each process takes turns receiving input from that port. Thus, if you as superuser attempt to copy what is entered through a terminal device by, say, using **cat /dev/tty11**, what you get is part of the input. The user's shell gets the other part. And it is obvious to you and the user being "tapped" that something is not right.

The UNIX kernel's tty device drivers can potentially be modified so that they can split the input and/or output stream. For example, a special control flag could be sent to a device driver so that it sends a copy of the I/O of a particular port to a file. This patch is not common in UNIX kernels, and takes a fair amount of expertise to create properly.

The approach used by Clifford Stoll is more mundane, but certainly as effective. After discovering that the intruder was coming in through a 1200 baud modem in a pool of modems, Stoll physically tapped each modem's RS232 cable so that the output transmitted from the host computer was copied to a printer. This involved installing a 1200 baud printer for each modem line, and wading through reems of printouts. While certainly effective, it would have been nicer to use a small UNIX system, with many ports, to monitor the lines and save all text on-line. PC's capable of monitoring 24 ports would cost at least $5000, with a hard disk and a minimal UNIX system installed. Stoll didn't have this type of resource available.

Tapping a user's port or examining files for commands are invasions of privacy. The ethics and correctness of tapping and perusing users' files are covered later in this chapter.

Log Files

Besides the accounting files already mentioned, both BSD and System V maintain other log files. The BSD version, contained in **/usr/adm/messages**, holds a copy of all the messages sent to the console after the kernel has started. Included in this file, is everything which has been logged by the system logger daemon (Figure 5-6).

Figure 5-6: BSD systems keep a log of console messages,
including successful or failed **su** *attempts, in the* **messages** *file.*

```
% sed -n '1,8p' /usr/adm/messages
Oct  5 15:10:20 gandhi su: 'su root' succeeded for peter on /dev/tty02
Oct  5 15:58:22 gandhi su: 'su root' succeeded for m on /dev/ttyp6
Oct  5 16:00:49 gandhi vmunix: mti09: silo overflow
Oct  5 16:18:32 gandhi su: 'su mary' succeeded for m on /dev/ttyp6
Oct  5 16:38:11 gandhi su: 'su root' failed for m on /dev/ttypc
Oct  5 17:52:19 gandhi su: 'su root' succeeded for mike on /dev/ttyp4
Oct  5 17:53:58 gandhi su: 'su john' succeeded for mike on /dev/ttyp1
Oct  5 19:01:54 gandhi vmunix: mti0d: silo overflow
% ▍
```

Interspaced with the **su** reports in Figure 5-6, there are two error messages, as reported to the console. The error log is important for solving system problems, but we are more interested in the logging of **su** activity. By examining the log, we can see who has the root password—any user who can **su** to the root account. We can also see if someone has been trying to guess the root password (indicated by many failed attempts. The **messages** file night also contain reports of bad logins—valid user names combined with failed passwords.

System V does not maintain an ASCII messages file, but does keep a log of **su** attempts, named **/usr/adm/sulog**. Each time any user attempts to **su**, a record is made in the file (see Figure 5-7). Each line indicates whether the attempt succeeded (a plus or a minus), and which user was switching to another account.

Figure 5-7: System V maintains a log of **su** *activities in the*
/usr/adm/sulog *file. This file should be readable only by the superuser.*

```
# sed -n '1,4p' /usr/adm/sulog
SU 10/04 17:40 + ttyq5 m-root
SU 10/05 12:12 + ttyq6 otto-m
SU 10/07 13:55 - ttyq1 rik-root
SU 10/07 13:56 + ttyq1 rik-root
# ls -l /usr/adm/sulog
-rw-------  1 root    root     135 Oct  7 13:56 /usr/adm/sulog
# ▊
```

After the date and time, the **sulog** contains either a plus or minus, indicating either a successful attempt or a failure in switching user. The port and the attempted switch, for example, from "otto-m" are shown last on each line.

Because of the volume of information in either of these files, it is useful to filter out the important information. The System V **sulog**, with its simpler format, is the easiest with which to work. The **fgrep** command can be used, along with a pattern file containing the permitted switches. For example, the root can become any user, but only the users "m" and "rik" can become the root. The pattern file and its use with **fgrep** are shown in Figure 5-8.

Figure 5-8: Using **fgrep** *and a pattern file to pick out unexpected users of the* **su** *command. Only the line containing "otto-m" gets displayed.*

```
# cat patterns
root-
rik-root
m-root
# fgrep -v -f patterns sulog
SU 10/05 12:12 + ttyq6 otto-m
# ▊
```

Filtering the BSD messages file requires longer patterns. Note that the **fgrep** command matches strings exactly, so the entire matching pattern must be spelled out in the patterns file (see Figure 5-9).

Figure 5-9: A similar approach filters out
non-matching patterns from the BSD messages file.

```
% cat patterns
for root
su root' succeeded for peter
su root' succeeded for mike
su root' succeeded for m
su john' succeeded for mike
% grep su: messages | fgrep -v -f patterns
Oct  5 16:18:32 gandhi su: 'su mary' succeeded for m on /dev/ttyp6
Oct  5 16:38:11 gandhi su: 'su root' failed for m on /dev/ttypc
% 
```

The **sulog** and the **messages** file can have other, not so desirable, uses. If someone wants to discover which users know the superuser password, he or she could read these log files and find out. Knowing the possessor of the superuser password is useful to the cracker, because those users are targets for Trojan Horse attacks. For this reason, both the **sulog** and the messages files should be root-owned, and readable by the owner only. Note that these are files that grow, and be certain that the scripts that archive these files maintain the read-only-by-root restriction.

Break-in: What to Do Next

Even if you have properly secured your systems, break-ins are still possible. (I am including abuses of your system by legitimate users in the category of a break-in, since what you should do is similar.) There are really two categories to break-ins: one that is in-progress, and one that was discovered after-the-fact.

Break-in In-Progress

If you notice some abuse of your system, an intruder or an improper use of your system's resource, your first priority is to prevent any damage to your files. This is only common sense, but may prove difficult to accomplish in practice.

For many people, their first impulse is to log off the offender by killing his or her login shell. Although killing the login shell certainly stops most damaging activities, it may prevent other goals from being realized. When you discover an intruder or abuser, you want to

- Identify the person
- Preventing damage to your system's files, and
- Find out how they got in

One common approach is to use the UNIX **write** or **talk** commands to communicate with the user. This approach, sending a message directly to a suspected intruder, is likely to scare off some intruders. I only recommend doing this when you are uncertain of the identity of a user. For example, you have logged into your system late in the evening and notice that a regular nine-to-fiver is also logged in (Figure 5-10).

*Figure 5-10: Using the **write** command in an attempt to verify the identity of a user.*

```
$ who
jim             tty19           Oct  8 19:56
rik             tty21           Oct  8 20:05
$ write jim tty19
Hi Jim. It's nice to notice someone else
working late.
-o-
Message from jim on nomad (tty19) [ Mon Oct  8 20:14:03 ] ...
Hi Rik: Just looking for some e-mail that I
have been waiting for. See you tomorrow.
-oo-
<EOT>
<^D>
$ ▋
```

The exchange show in Figure 5-10 does not really prove that the user "jim" is who he appears to be. Since you cannot *see* the person, or hear his or her voice, you might try to ask some personal question that would definitely identify the user. This relies on your having personal knowledge of the user involved. If you wanted to, you could establish a policy that all users supply their mothers' maiden name, and use this name as a form of authentication, much as banks do. To do this safely, the list of users and maiden names must either be off-line or encrypted.

If you are on-site, and discover a questionable user that is also on-site, the best thing to do would be to have someone locate the user. The **who** command will identify a terminal or host, and if you have mapped out your ports and hosts, it should be easy to approach the user and get physical identification from him or her. Without this identification, discovering who the user is will be much more difficult. Also, you want two people involved in this case, one to watch the system, and another to track down the user in question.

Notice that in the two examples, some level of preparedness is called for. A list of identifying facts for authenticating users with **write**, and a map of terminals and ports have been used. The list of identifying facts could also be used to check for bad passwords. The map is valuable whenever system problems occur. If you do not have these items, perhaps you should.

Network Break-in   If an intruder is coming in over the Internet, the name of the user's host appears in parentheses at the end of the **who** listing. You can use the **finger** command to attempt to get information from this user's host about the user. If **finger** fails, you can also **telnet nic.ddn.mil** to use the **whois** facility. NIC is the Network Information Center at SRI (Stanford Research Institute) in Menlo Park, CA. They maintain an extensive database of all the registered hosts and domains on the Internet. Even if you do not find the user breaking into your system, you can get an administrative contact's name by requesting information about the host or domain, for example, with **whois columbia-dom** you get information about the Columbia University domain. You can get more help with **who is** simply by typing **help**. If you are on the Internet, experiment with **whois** so you know how to use it before you get in trouble.

Once you get a telephone number, call the intruder. If you cannot find a number for the intruder, talk to a local administrator. Tell who you are, and what you know is happening. Many intruders will lie to you—try to get as much information as you can. If you reach the intruder, explain that he or she can be charged under federal law (if the call crossed state boundaries) with a felony. Or, cite whatever local statutes apply. Make certain the intruder understands the gravity of the situation, and that you mean business. If you get the administrator, elicit support. See if the administrator will help you track down the user in question and deal with him or her locally.

Logging Out Intruders   As mentioned earlier, watching what any user is doing is difficult. However, if you feel that your intruder is getting out of hand, you can force the intruder to log out by killing the login shell. The **ps** command with the option letter-**t** and a terminal name prints all processes associated with the named port. Then a **kill** command (see Figure 5-11) can log the intruder out.

*Figure 5-11: Using the device name to discover the login shell and **kill** it.*
*The second **kill** command should fail, proving that the shell has indeed been killed.*

```
# who
jim          tty19        Oct  8 19:56
rik          tty21        Oct  8 20:05
# ps -t19
   PID TTY        TIME COMMAND
  2491 19        0:15 vi
  2480 19        0:00 -csh
# kill -1 2480
# kill -1 2480
kill: 2480: no such process
# ▮
```

Once the intruder has been logged off, it would make sense to invalidate the account's password. As superuser, you can change the password for the account, with **passwd** *username*, to something that only you know. Or, you can choose a different approach. At Columbia University, instead of invalidating the password, the administrator changes the login shell to a special program that prints a message. This program, for example, **/etc/bad/turnedoff**, displays a message to the user, then logs the user out (Figure 5-12).

Figure 5-12: Using a simple program to prevent a user from logging in. Changing
the mode of the user's HOME directory to zero prevents any user from working there.

```
# cat turnedoff.c
char message ▮ = "Your account has expired. Please see \n\
one of the Computer Science Center staff \n\
to have your account reactivated.\n";
main()
{
    write(1, message, sizeof(message));
    exit(0);
}
# cc turnedoff.c -o turnedoff
# ls -l /etc/turnedoff
-rwx--x--x  1 root    staff     7264 Oct  8 15:00 /etc/turnedoff
# vi /etc/passwd # change jim's login shell
```

Figure 5-12: Using a simple program to prevent
a user from logging in. Changing the mode of the user's
HOME directory to zero prevents any user from working there (continued).

```
...
jim:YZVFqjWa7qI6s:152:140:Jim Charles:/u/jim:/etc/turnedoff
...
# chmod 0 /u/jim
# ▌
```

The Columbia administrators also change the permissions on the user's HOME directory to zero. This prevents the user from accessing any files in his or her account, even while working from another user's account. The idea behind this scheme is that the user must talk to a staff member before using the account again. The staff member can verify the user's identity in person, and try to discover if the student was involved in the security problem. Columbia University has put students violating computer services policy on probation.

Break-in in the Past

Administrators at Columbia attributed detecting several break-ins to pure luck— being on the right system at the right time, noticing unusual sluggishness, and investigating the cause. On busy systems, break-ins can occur and easily go completely unnoticed. In fact, whatever brings a break-in to your attention also provides the first clue in tracking down the culprit.

Around 1985, an administrator of a Bell Labs' computer noticed that the **/usr** partition was suddenly very low on disk space. Since the **/usr/spool** directory is used for some temporary files, it was not unusual for the amount of free space to change from day-to-day. The administrator chose to investigate, and discovered that someone had queued up the source files to the UNIX games for transmission via **uucp**.

All **uucp** requests are time-stamped (as were the spooled files), so it was easy to determine when the files had been queued for transmission. By examining the login records kept in **/etc/wtmp**, the administrator was able to narrow down the potential suspects to a handful of users actually logged in during that time.

In a different case, I uncovered a new root-owned set-user-id file, hidden in a system directory, by running security auditing scripts. When I compared the inode change time on the file and the login records, I determined that only one user was logged in the last time that the set-user-id file was modified. Because the user had abused his root privileges, the company that owned the computer made the decision to change the root password and not share it with that user. They also explained to the user why what he had done was a problem.

In both examples, the pattern for sleuthing is the same.

- Check the **inode change time** on the files that aroused suspicion
- Use the **wtmp** file to determine which users were logged in at that time

Inode Change Time   The UNIX system maintains three different times with every inode (file descriptor): the access time, the modify time, and the inode change time. The access time provides the time that the file was created or read. The modify time gives the time that the file was created, written, or changed. These times show only the most recent access to the file—they do not provide a history.

The access and modify time of a file can be changed without reading or modifying the file. The System V **touch** command permits changing these dates to any time in the past (after 1970) or future. Even though BSD systems do not provide the **touch** command, it is possible to change these times by using a system call in a simple program. Because the access and modify times of files can be changed, *you cannot trust these times*.

The inode change time is similar to the modify time. The two differences are that the inode change time includes modification of the inode information and the inode change time cannot be set with the **touch** command or a system call. This makes the inode change time the only accurate means for determining when a file was last changed.

The inode information includes the ownership of the inode, link counts (directory references to this file), permissions, and the other two dates. Modifying a date with the **touch** command sets the inode change time to the time of modification. For example, if someone tried to hide the fact that a file had been edited, he or she could try to use **touch** to set the modify time back—see Figure 5-13. However, the inode change time will reflect the time that the **touch** command was used.

The long listing option to the **ls** command, **-l**, displays the modification time of a file. Using the option letters **-lc** produces the inode change time in the **ls** listing.

*Figure 5-13: The **touch** command can change the*
modification time of a file, but not the inode change time.

```
$ ls -l login.c
-rw-r-----  1 rik    users  11992 Jan 28  1989 login.c
$ vi login.c        # Some change to login.c
$ ls -l login.c
-rw-r-----  1 rik    users  12138 Oct  9 16:56 login.c
$ touch 0128101089 login.c
$ ls -l login.c
-rw-r-----  1 rik    users  12138 Jan 28  1989 login.c
$ ls -lc login.c
-rw-r-----  1 rik    users  12138 Oct  9 16:56 login.c
$ ▮
```

There is a way to modify a file and not change (apparently) change the inode change time. If the intruder gains superuser access, they can use the **date** command to change the system date. The system's notion of time relies on the system date, so changing the date would obscure changes made in the past. Changing the date leaves traces in the BSD **messages** file, and in the **wtmp** file.

Who Was Logged in?   The inode change time can tell you when an event occurred. The **/etc/wtmp** or **/usr/adm/wtmp** file tells you who was logged in during that time. Both these files are binary informat—unreadable without the use of a special program.

BSD-based systems provide the **last** command. The **last** command reads the **wtmp** file in reverse order, showing the last login times and other events (such as reboots) in the **/usr/adm/wtmp** file. **last** formats the output nicely, and also includes the time period that each user was logged in (Figure 5-14).

*Figure 5-14: The **last** command reports on the contents of the*
***/usr/adm/wtmp** file, starting with the most recent login.*

```
% last
rik       ttyb                      Fri Oct 12 10:41    still logged in
recep     tty0d                     Fri Oct 12 10:43    still logged in
lisa      tty09                     Fri Oct 12 10:40 - 10:42 (00:02)
denise    tty0d                     Fri Oct 12 10:39 - 10:43 (00:03)
john      tty05                     Fri Oct 12 10:28    still logged in
m         ttyp1     peacock         Fri Oct 12 10:25    still logged in
uucpNet   ttyb                      Fri Oct 12 09:51 - 09:52 (00:01)
lisa      tty09                     Fri Oct 12 09:31 - 10:31 (00:59)
mike      ttype     ibm1            Fri Oct 12 09:24 - 09:27 (00:02)
```

*Figure 5-14: The **last** command reports on the contents of the*
/usr/adm/wtmp *file, starting with the most recent login (continued).*

```
andrey      tty0a                      Fri Oct 12 09:24    still logged in
m           ttype      ibm1            Fri Oct 12 09:03 - 10:06 (01:03)
johna       ttype      ibm1            Fri Oct 12 08:44 - 08:44 (00:00)
toml        tty02                      Fri Oct 12 08:43    still logged in
andrey      tty0a                      Fri Oct 12 08:41 - 09:16 (00:35)
interrupted Fri Oct 12 08:13
% ▌
```

It is easy to determine who was logged in at a particular time using the output of the **last** command. You can use the **grep** command to filter out **last** output to one day, for example, with **last | grep "Oct 12"**. The **last** command can also be used as a filter by including the name of a port or a user on the command line. Finally, the **last** command can also read from files other than **/usr/adm/wtmp** by using the **-f** option letter and a file name. Since the **wtmp** file grows with every login or logout, you should occasionally truncate the file. I keep old copies around by first renaming the files (for example, *wtmp.1090* for October, 1990), then using **compress** to make the file smaller. Once you have renamed the file, you must create a new **wtmp** file. The file must be owned by the root, writeable by the root only. It should be readable by all, so that **last** will work.

System V does not include the **last** command. Versions of the **last** command for System V are available from Usenet; I suggest you get a copy of one.

System V can use the **who** command with the **-a** option letter to translate the binary **wtmp** file into readable text—see Figure 5-15. The trouble is that the **wtmp** file is a chronological record of many events, and the events that you are interested in usually do not occur sequentially. For example, a user may login at nine in the morning, and not log out again until five in the afternoon. In the mean time, hundreds of other events may have occurred, such as other logins and logouts.

In Figure 5-15, you can see bursts of activity associated with a port. For example, at the beginning of the display, a **getty** on port **tty36** gives way to a **login** process, which is replaced when "rosanna" logs in. What is missing in the figure is the time when "rosanna" logs out. An example of a completed sequence is shown when alan logs into **contty** at ten o'clock, and logs out at 10:07. The **getty** was started at 09:37, shown earlier in the display.

Figure 5-15: The System V **who -a** *command interprets the contents of the* **wtmp** *file.*

```
$ who -a /etc/wtmp
getty       tty36        Oct 12 08:56   0:01   7623   id=  36
LOGIN       tty36        Oct 12 08:56   0:01   7623   block 34
rosanna     tty36        Oct 12 08:57   0:01   7623   block 34
tech        tty44        Oct 12 09:08   .      24622  block 38 (editor)
dianne      tty37        Oct 12 09:14   .      24361  block 37 (spare)
getty       contty       Oct 12 09:32   .      7870   id=  ct
LOGIN       contty       Oct 12 09:32   .      7870
getty       tty31        Oct 12 09:37   .      7885   id=  31
LOGIN       tty31        Oct 12 09:37   .      7885   block 27 (Sheri)
sheri       tty31        Oct 12 09:37   .      7885   block 27 (Sheri)
alan        contty       Oct 12 10:00   .      7870
alan        contty       Oct 12 10:07   .      7870   id=  ct term=0    exit=0
getty       contty       Oct 12 10:07   .      8131   id=  ct
LOGIN       contty       Oct 12 10:07   .      8131
...
$ █
```

You can tell the login times from the logout times by examining the end of each line. When the line reflects a logout, it will include the exit status of the shell program, for example "exit=0". When a user logs in, the comments in the **/etc/inittab** file are displayed after the process id number.

Going through a System V **wtmp** file is a laborious process. You can make it easier by using the **sort** command. The **sort** command will organize the output of **who -a** alphabetically, so that each user's activities appear together. This organization makes it easier to determine when a user was logged in. Even without sorting, you can see that "alan" was logged in from 10:00 to 10:07.

Finding Hidden Files

Anytime that you have a break-in or discover evidence of abuse, you should run your auditing scripts. The auditing scripts, described in Chapter 3, check for the correctness of permissions, ownership, and the contents of system files. A user who has illicitly obtained superuser privilege may seek to maintain that privilege. The most common method is to create a set-user-id file owned by a privileged user. This file is sometimes left in a command directory, but often the user attempts to "hide" the file.

The auditing scripts will pick out new set-user-id files, or modifications to existing system files. You can also search for newly created files by using the **find / -ctime -1 -print** command to find files that have been changed in the last day. The **-newer** *target* option to **find** will pick out all files newer than the target file.

People try to hide files by using tricky filenames. The most common attempt is simply to place a "." (dot) at the beginning of the file name. The dot makes the filename "hidden" in that the **ls** command and shell expansion (with the asterisk) normally will not display that file. However, using the **-a** option letter to **ls** displays all directory entries, regardless of a leading dot. Remember that the file named dot is synonymous with the current directory, and dot-dot with the parent directory. But, "..." is not a special name used by UNIX, but a favorite of crackers.

Another favorite is to create a filename consisting of a space, tab, or other non-printing character. It is possible to create names containing characters not normally acceptable by the shell by quoting the characters. Users sometimes create mysterious filenames because the program they are using passes the name as a quoted string to the UNIX kernel for creation. You can view strange filenames by using the **-b** option letter (System V) or the **-q** letter with **ls**—see Figure 5-16.

Figure 5-16: Viewing examples of "hidden" files with **ls -b** *and* **ls -qa**.
The mysterious character in the filename "hoo?st" is a backspace.

```
$ ls

host
$ ls -b

hoo\010st
$ ls -qa

.
..
...
hoo?st
$ rm " " ... hoo?st
$ ▮
```

Only System V versions of **ls** provide the **-b** option, which displays unprintable characters in octal representation. The **-q** option displays strange characters as question marks, which are also used by the shell to represent any single character. In both cases, the file named by a space does not appear, except as a space in the listing. As far as **ls -aq** is concerned, space is a legal character. You must notice the blank space in the filename.

Removing filenames with strange characters requires special techniques. In Figure 5-16, the space is quoted to protect it from the shell, permitting it to be removed. The dots are easy to move. The filename containing the backspace (which hides the extra "o") can be removed by using the question mark metacharacter in the name (as displayed by **ls -qa**).

If your version of the UNIX system does not provide these options to **ls**, you can pipe the output of **ls** through **sed-n** list which converts non-printing characters to octal representation.

Checking Programs

Because programs are binary files, you cannot view them directly, for example, by using an editor. You can, however, use UNIX utilities to examine parts of executeable files; symbol names and strings of characters. The **nm** command displays the symbols used in an executeable file. Symbols are either variables or function names. The output of **nm** is somewhat arcane. However, a programmer can make inferences about what a program does by examining the symbol table. For example, a password cracker will include **--crypt** in the symbol table, the function call to encrypt passwords. Programs can be stripped of symbols, so **nm** will not always help you.

Binary programs do contain some text. This text makes up the content of error messages and the names of files that are used. A modified version of the **crypt** command was uncovered when someone found the name of a file in the spot where stolen passwords were copied in the text. The **strings** command displays text found in binary files. Most BSD based systems will have **strings.** If your system does not, try Usenet. Also, "UNIX Administrators Guide to System V" has example **strings** programs in an Appendix.

Legal Prosecution

Although computers are no longer new, people are still learning about how to deal with computer crime. If you decide that you need to press charges against an intruder or system cracker, there are certain things which you must do. The legal system has its own standards, based on precedents, of what is considered to be "good evidence". This section explains what you should do when collecting evidence for legal prosecution.

There are also things which you should set up prior to any incident, if you hope to get a conviction. One cracker's lawyer won his case by showing the jury that the system the cracker had logged into had printed a welcome message upon login! You should also establish a policy which defines acceptable use of your system and/or network.

No Trespassing Sign

The UNIX community generally welcomes people who come to share in the collective enterprise of using a computer. The messages displayed during login reflect this welcome. While this is a nice tradition, it has gotten one defendant off the hook, setting a legal precedent that can be used again.

Figure 5-17 shows a "no trespassing sign" that is simply a notice that gets displayed during every login. The **/etc/motd** (Message Of The Day) file is the place to put the no trespassing sign. **/etc/motd** is displayed by the **login** program as part of the login process. Typically, the message of the day includes a welcome, identifying the computer and possibly the release of the operating system (Sun), and sometimes notices about downtime. All these elements can remain. But, a warning message must be added.

Figure 5-17: An example of a no trespassing
sign kept in the /etc/motd file and seen at login.

```
$ cat /etc/motd
#=======================================================#
#                        WARNING                        #
#                                                       #
# ACCESS TO AND USE OF THIS SYSTEM IS RESTRICTED TO     #
#                 AUTHORIZED INDIVIDUALS!               #
#=======================================================#
$ ▌
```

The example shown in Figure 5-17 only contains the no trespassing sign. It is okay to include other information in the login message. But, the message "access to and use is restricted to authorized individuals" must be included, or words to that effect. If your company retains a lawyer, you may ask him or her to provide appropriate wording (but try to keep it short.)

Policy Statement

The policy statement may be more familiar to students than it is to other computer users. The policy statement *defines* what are acceptable uses of the system and any attached network. The policy statement should spell out who can use the system, and what they are permitted to do when using the system. For example, you might allow employees to write personal letters on your system. However, you probably do not want them selling computer time to a bookkeeping service, or running password crackers. Your acceptable use policy spells out what may and may not be done. Since it is difficult to cover all cases, acceptable use policies often permit only uses directly related to the employees' work.

One issue that should be included is sharing the use of the system with unauthorized users. While employees might not allow anyone to use the company truck or car, they have been known to share passwords and phone numbers with non-employees. In some cases, inexperienced system administrators have even created accounts for spouses, family members, and friends, so everyone could communicate via UNIX mail! You want to establish control over your system. This control also reinforces the no trespassing statement.

A policy statement should also provide for penalties for disobeying the acceptable use policy. In a college, for example, running a password cracker could result in probation by the dean of students. In an office environment, prying into other users' files might result in loss of pay, suspensions of computer privileges, or even termination. Whatever remedies are deemed appropriate must be spelled out here.

The policy statement can also define the administrators' behavior. For example, administrators should not abuse their privileges by reading or modifying users' files while working as superuser. On the other hand, administrators should be given full permission to invade users' private files as necessary while tracking down security problems. The policy statement should be read and signed by all computer users. The signed copy of the policy statement can be added to the employee's personnel file, or the student's records. The policy statement helps your users understand what are and are not acceptable uses of your system.

Chain of Evidence

Although Clifford Stoll had tremendous difficulties in convincing authorities to assist him, he had done something right without anyone telling him. Stoll, by attaching printers to the modems used by the cracker, had collected the type of evidence used in court. As he collected the evidence, he signed and dated each sheet of paper. He eventually was told to keep his printed evidence in a locked closet. Authorities in Germany were able to press charges based on his evidence.

The principle behind the chain of evidence is that you must be able to prove control over the evidence from the point in time that it was collected, until it is presented in the courtroom. Minimizing the number of people who have any contact with the evidence is important. Ideally, the evidence is totally under the control of one individual. Practically speaking, there are usually more people involved. But here is how it should be done.

When the evidence is on paper, the person collecting the evidence should sign and date the bottom of each piece of paper. The collection of paper should be locked in a place to which only one person has the key or combination. Ideally, this person is the same person that collected the evidence. In large installations, such as Lawrence Livermore National Laboratories (which shared this information), a computer security officer receives the evidence, provides a receipt to the person who collected it, and locks it up for safekeeping. Having a designated security person helps, because this person should be familiar with rules of evidence and have a safe for keeping evidence.

In the case of magnetic media, the rules are similar. In most of the examples in this chapter, you have learned how to display information found in files in UNIX systems. All the files that you use for gathering evidence should be copied to backup media and preserved. The method used for copying, plus anything else you did to create or collect the files, should be written down. The magnetic media should then be placed in an envelope, which is sealed. You can sign your name and date across the seal of the envelope, along with any witness you might have. The contents of the tape are for use by any expert witnesses that may be called in a trial.

If you have collected evidence on tape, you will also need printouts of the significant information on the tape. Treat these printouts just like other paper evidence. However, make a copy of this evidence. This copy is what you will need to convince a judge or district attorney to actually issue search warrants, or charge someone with a crime.

In California's Silicon Valley, it is relatively easy to get the support of the police and the justice department. A person told me the story of how someone was trying to break into his system through his modem. Every night, around two in the morning, two calls would come in, but fail during login. The system's owner printed out the **wtmp** file, and presented this printout along with explanations to a local district attorney, who presented the information to a judge. The judge issued a search warrant to trap and trace the phone line leading to the modem during the early morning hours. That afternoon, the system's owner got a call from a friend who explained that the friend's computer had been trying to make a UUCP connection at two in the morning. The trace was abandoned.

The elements shown in this example are important. You can ask the phone company to trace a phone call. You must specify a well-defined time period for the trace. However, you cannot have the results of the trace without a search warrant. Your printed evidence, and your explanations of it, must convince a judge, who will issue the search warrant. If your explanation is unclear (remember that judges are lawyers, not programmers), you will probably not get any assistance. Also, you would be more likely to approach the police department first, so make your explanation clear and simple.

If your system has been invaded through a network, or the call into your system comes from (or passes through) another state, your case may be under Federal jurisdiction. It is not your task to determine jurisdiction. Start locally, with the police and the district attorney's office. They will tell you to contact the FBI or other Federal office if appropriate.

Who Else to Call

After the spectacular invasion of the Internet by the Worm, the Computer Emergency Response Team was set up at Carnegie Mellon University in Pennsylvania. CERT's role is to serve as a collection and distribution point for security-related information regarding the Internet. Their number is 412-268-7090, and persons there may be able to help you if you are under attack. Keep in mind that they are paid to protect members of the Internet. If you are not doing government-related research, or are not connected to the Internet, they probably won't be able to help you.

If you have found a security hole in your system, call your system's vendor. Some vendors are growing more responsive to security problems, and will even talk to you without a support contract (but not all). In many cases, you must get help from the vendor, or not use the affected software. So, do not hesitate to call your vendor.

If you are not a UNIX expert yourself, you may wish to locate a consultant with more experience that could help during and after a crises. The key word here is *before* the problem occurs. There is a growing number of people specializing in security, although a good UNIX expert would be just as helpful. There are no standards for determining if your consultant is really an expert. Your experience in dealing with the consultant is your best guide.

Viruses and the UNIX System

Although viruses have yet to be as much as a problem for UNIX systems as they are for personal computers, the potential for trouble is still very present. Viruses have infected Macintoshes at NASA, PC's at other government sites, destroyed or formatted hard disks, and removed files. Viruses are very insidious, because they can be hidden so successfully.

Viruses have not been as much as a threat to UNIX systems because the virus relies on binary compatibility, something that UNIX vendors have yet to perfect. PC's, however, are binary compatible. It is this compatibility that has made PC's so popular, and yet it is one weakness exploited by the computer virus.

Viruses migrate from computer to computer via infected software. The software travels on a diskette that is taken from one PC and inserted into another. Software may also be downloaded from bulletin board services. Most bulletin boards guard against virus infections to prevent becoming the vector for spreading viruses. In the UNIX environment, viruses have been spread via networks.

A computer *virus* is a type of Trojan Horse that spreads itself by copying the virus code into executable programs. The virus gets activated when a program including the virus gets executed by a user. The virus code searches for other executable programs that the user can modify, and copies itself there. To be a true virus, it also checks before making the copy to be sure that the target program is not already infected.

Viruses can be activated in a second way. The first activation involves copying the virus code. The second activation relies on some trigger. The trigger tells the virus that the time has come to carry out its Trojan Horse component. This component may erase files, or enable a trap door granting privilege to the knowledgeable user. Triggers for past viruses have been dates, the existence of files, or the number of generations of the virus (number of times it copied itself).

Viruses can also be benign. One man designed a virus that compressed the program it was attacking. When the program was executed, it would automatically be decompressed and become executable again. Other people may find valid uses for viruses, just as modified forms of the polio virus are used in vaccinations.

When a virus invades a UNIX system, noticeable changes occur. The modify and inode change time of infected files change, the size of the infected file may change, and the checksum may change. If you created auditing scripts based on the information in Chapter 3, you can detect viruses by running these scripts.

This section explains more about how viruses work in PC's, and how UNIX viruses work. You will also learn how to detect a viral invasion, and get some hints on how to best recover from the attack.

PC Viruses

MS/DOS, OS/2, Windows, and the Macintosh Finder provide generic PC environments. These environments are well documented, and also very familiar to thousands of programmers. Add to this the ease with which a programmer can experiment with a PC, and the lack of any security mechanisms, and you have an environment ripe for the creation of viruses.

Not that it is that easy to create a virus. Most viruses are actually mutated copies of other viruses. Writing a "well-behaved" virus is tricky, and not every programmer is capable of creating one. Also, most programmers are not inclined to create what amounts to anti-social programs.

MS/DOS viruses are perhaps the most common, as is MS/DOS itself. MS/DOS viruses have been known to attack the boot program on system disks, COMMAND.COM (the DOS shell), or any program. Some viruses have been designed to live in memory, like a terminate-and-stay-resident (TSR) program, so that the infected computer will continue to infect disks even after a warm reboot.

Macintosh viruses often take advantage of a special feature of the Mac environment. Each application may include resources. These resources contain the text for messages, and any customization that the user of the application desires. Source mechanism permits the addition of program code to an existing application, making this mechanism very useful for writing viruses.

One reason for the quick spread of PC viruses is the sharing of software. The ease with which someone can copy a program to a diskette, carry the diskette to another PC, and copy the program to the new host makes PC viruses especially virulent. So, far, most UNIX software runs on only one type of CPU, and under a particular version of the UNIX operating system. For example, if you buy a desktop publishing package for a Sun 3, it won't work on a Sun 4, a Sun 386i, or on any other manufacturers' system.

UNIX Virus Mechanisms

So far, there have not been widespread UNIX viruses. The Internet Worm, although called a virus by some, did not include two of the defining characteristics of a virus—infecting existing programs and marking the infected programs. People have written and tested UNIX viruses.

Tom Duff, while working as a researcher at AT&T Bell Laboratories, experimented with UNIX viruses. His first experiment was designed to infect programs in the current working directory. Duff installed a version of his virus in a program named **echo** in publicly writeable binary directories, and waited to see what happened. The spread of the infection was slow at first, until an automatic software distribution system copied an infected version of **wc** to 11 other machines. Within a week, there were 466 virus infected programs. Duff had also written a "disinfect" program, which he distributed at the end of the experiment. By the way, his bosses were not pleased by his adventure, and asked him to end the experiment.

A description of the working of Duff's virus will help you to understand how viruses spread.

First, a program infected with the virus is copied to a directory containing other programs. This directory must appear in other users' PATHs, so the infected program will be executed by as many users as possible. Duff installed his virus only in publicly writeable directories because he was mimicking the actions of an unprivileged user. Directories containing commands should never be publicly writeable. Duff also found that some users put these directories *before* the system directories, like **/bin** and **/usr/bin**, in their PATH (also making these users susceptible to Trojan Horse attacks).

When a user executed the program, the virus code runs first. The virus code searches the user's current working directory for writeable and executable files. If any files are found, the virus checks to see if the file contains a program, checks for prior infection, and then checks for enough space in the file to copy in the virus. Duff's virus relied on finding 413 sequential zeroes at the end of the text (executable portion) and before the data portion of the program. On the average, two thirds of the programs in Duff's environment had enough space.

After the virus copied itself into a program, it next modified two addresses. When the kernel executes a program, it uses information contained in a table in the beginning of the program to determine where to start executing the program. The virus changes the start address in the table to point to the virus code. Then, the virus code gets changed so that it runs the program when it completes. Figure 5-18 presents a before and after picture of an infected program.

Figure 5-18: Before infection, the table in the program header points to the starting point of the program in the text region. After infection, the table has been modified to point to the virus code, and the virus code points into the text.

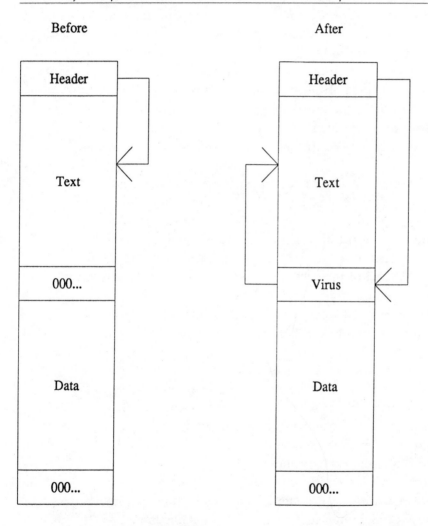

Once the virus code completes execution, it passes control to the original program. Since the virus code does something extra and unexpected, along with the action of the original program, the virus qualifies as a Trojan Horse. Although the virus described here was *not* very fast spreading, a more virulent strain might produce a noticeable delay in program execution that could warn alert users.

Avoiding UNIX Viruses

You certainly want to avoid getting a virus in your system or network of systems. There are several things you can done to help prevent acquiring a virus, and helping it spread.

- Beware of gifts. Any binary program, even one that you purchase, has the potential of carrying a virus.
- Put system directories first in your PATH. Only system programmers have any need to put other directories first, and even that is a questionable practice.
- Do not allow directories containing programs or the programs themselves to be writeable. If only root can write in these directories, no one else will be able to put infected programs (or Trojan Horses) there. And only the root can infect a program.

The first point is the hardest to follow. How can you operate a computer without software? Most UNIX systems today are loaded with application software—software for wordprocessing, financial analysis, graphics display, communications, and so on. I am not suggesting that you never purchase software, only that you be aware of the danger that you may have introduced a virus to your system. Ideally, new software should be tested by using it in an isolated system—no network connections to any other system. Any changes in other executable files would point to the newly installed software. If your installation has good reasons to be paranoid, test your software first. Don't forget to advance the date during testing—some viruses have time-delay triggers, and won't go into action until some time in the future.

The other two points have already been made, in Chapters 2 and 3. I am repeating them here because a bad PATH and writeable directories make your system more susceptible to viruses. Also, if superusers always use a safe PATH, and only root can write to system directories and commands, then you are much less likely to suffer infection of your command directories, or a root writeable file.

Once a virus gains root privilege to infect a file, it has succeeded anyway. Protecting your system directories and commands makes this less likely.

In SunOS 4.0 and in System V release 4, all the commands that were in **/bin** have been moved into **/usr/bin**. Commands found in **/etc** we removed when possible to **/usr/etc**. The directories in **/usr** that contained temporary files, such as **/usr/spool**, were moved under the **/var** directory. Symbolic links were used to make everything appear as it did formerly, so that programs that expect to find the shell in **/bin** could continue to do so.

Having done all this, SunOS 4.0 can now mount the **/usr** partition as **read-only**. Even the superuser can not write in a file system that is mounted read-only. By placing commands in a read-only file system, SunOS 4.0 has substantially increased its resistance to virus infection.

Detecting UNIX Viruses

Often, a virus will go undetected unless the virus was poorly written, or until it causes some damage. A viral attack can be very subtle. The small amount of extra time to execute a command might very well go unnoticed in a busy system. So the best way to detect a virus attack is by monitoring your system.

Viruses introduce noticeable changes in programs. Not changes that you can see directly, since programs are binary (machine language) files. But other changes that can be detected with UNIX commands. Here are the things that a virus may change when it infects a program.

- The inode change time will definitely change, while the modify time might change.
- The size of the file might change, depending on the type of virus.
- The virus will change the checksum of an infected file.

The permset and permck scripts presented in Chapter 3 are well suited for uncovering a viral attack. The permset script is used to set up a database of permissions, sizes, and checksums, which can be used to determine if a program has been infected. The size of a file may or may not change, but the checksum will change. For example, if a virus has infected several files in the **/usr/bin** directory, running the permck script would produce the results shown in Figure 5-19.

*Figure 5-19: Running the permck script produces the file "fixes",
containing commands to fix permissions and names of files to replace. In this
example, permck turned up three programs whose size and checksums have
changed. Using ls -lc shows that these files have been recently modified.*

```
# permck
...
Working in /usr/bin
...
# cat fixes
# permck run on Sun Oct 14 11:46:09 PDT 1990.
# /usr/bin/acctcom: size and/or checksum have changed.
# Replace /usr/bin/acctcom from backups.
# /usr/bin/admin: size and/or checksum have changed.
# Replace /usr/bin/admin from backups.
# /usr/bin/asa: size and/or checksum have changed.
# Replace /usr/bin/asa from backups.
# ls -lc /usr/bin
-rwxr-xr-x  1 bin      bin      119470 Oct 10 19:23 /usr/bin/acctcom
-rwxr-xr-x  1 bin      bin      118878 Oct 12 08:41 /usr/bin/admin
-rwxr-xr-x  1 bin      bin       30286 Oct 14 11:45 /usr/bin/asa
-rwxr-xr-x  1 bin      bin       27912 Jul 15 13:37 /usr/bin/banner
-rwxr-xr-x  1 bin      bin        1206 Jul 15 13:37 /usr/bin/basename
-rwxr-xr-x  1 bin      bin       49432 Jul 15 13:37 /usr/bin/bc
-rwxr-xr-x  1 bin      bin       39288 Jul 15 13:37 /usr/bin/bdiff
...
# ▌
```

The permset script does not record the inode change time, but does pick out the changes in checksums and sizes. If Duff's virus had been present, there would have been no change in file sizes, but the checksum would still have changed.

By looking at the output of **ls -lc**, most files in the **/usr/bin** directory have the inode change time of July 15. The infected files, however, have much more recent inode change times. There is even a pattern here, with the first file in this directory having the earliest of the inode change times of the infected files.

When a virus strikes your system, you can determine approximately when it began working by looking for the earliest inode change time of an infected file. Since most viruses will begin infecting files in programs owned by users, it might be much more difficult than it is in this example to find the first infected file. Still, the inode change time provides a key for determining how far back in time the virus first entered your system.

Recovering from a Virus Attack

If your system has been attacked by a virus, you have got a problem. Although the permck script can uncover infection in system files, just replacing these files will probably not solve your virus infection. Most likely, the virus was introduced through a user program. The virus might also have been introduced through some newly installed software.

The first step is to backup your entire system in a way that permits you to recover individual files. Next, you need to reinstall your operating system from backups or the installation tape or media. You may be able to replace just the infected commands from a backup tape, but this depends on the degree of infection. If your version of **tar** is infected, then using **tar** to replace infected files will reintroduce the infection. Or, your shell program may be infected. If you must use an infected program during the restore process, you will reinfect your system. One way around this would be to boot an alternate root file system that has not been infected, and work from there.

Once you have recovered your operating system base, you must start recovering other files. Installing application programs from their original media is the safest route. Another solution would be to restore only the executable programs that are part of applications. Only the executable programs can be infected, and restoring other files from backups will preserve your installation and any customization made to configuration files.

One approach to restoring your users' files would be to restore all their files from the most recent backup, then to remove all programs. Presumably, if your users have executable programs, they also have the source code to replace them. You can use the pipeline shown in Figure 5-20 to find executable programs.

Removing your users' programs may seem draconian, but if you have been invaded by a virus, you will be ready to do so. Recovering from a virus attack is very difficult, and you may spend days doing so. Your users will be aware of what has be going on, and are more likely to be sympathetic than angry. And, finally, if you have set up your system correctly and, working as system administrator, have not introduced the virus yourself, some one of your users introduced the virus. It is important and necessary to "sterilize" your system by removing programs.

Figure 5-20: Using a pipeline to collect a list of executable programs. These programs can be removed outright, making the assumption that their owners can recompile them.

```
# file 'find /u -perm -100 -print' | grep executable |
sed 's/:.*$//'   /tmp/programs
# cat /tmp/programs
/u/rik/Chap03/fix
/u/rik/Chap03/guess
/u/rik/Chap03/checker
/u/rik/Chap03/fcheck
/u/rik/Chap03/pwage
/u/rik/X/Src/Space/spaceout
/u/rik/Hsh/listener
/u/rik/C/kermit
/u/rik/C/xmodem
/u/rik/C/u2dos
/u/rik/C/compress
/u/rik/Dcopy/dcopyu
/u/rik/RS6000/c-ibm
# rm 'cat /tmp/programs'
# ▮
```

Once you have restored your system, watch it like a hawk for the next week or so. If you have failed to remove all traces of virus infected programs, it will start to be reinfected again. One way of watching the system would be to use a script to collect the inode change times of all programs. Use the pipeline shown in Figure 5-20, but run it for the entire file system to collect a list of all executable programs. Then, build a list of inode change times using **ls -lc** and save this output. Routinely recreate the output of the **ls -lc** command, and use **diff** to compare it to the original. If the inode change times start changing, your system is still infected. At least this time you will have almost immediate notification, and won't have to remove every file. Hopefully, you will also be able to pin down the offending program by examining the output of process accounting, and seeing which programs were run at the time of each infection.

Summary

This chapter has focused on what you can do to detect and catch intruders in your system. Although the focus has been on break ins, abuses of your system, and viruses, there are other things with which you must also be concerned.

One of the greatest problems in computer security today are the programmers and administrators charged with creating and maintaining systems. In

Chapter 4, you read about the author of the **sendmail** program, and in this chapter, there was the administrator who created a set-user-id shell for himself. The programmer who leaves "trapdoors" for himself is certainly a problem, especially since only another equally skilled programmer could examine the source to the program and detect the trapdoor code.

Programmers have done other deeds. One programmer, although not working on a UNIX system, modified the payroll accounting program so that it checked to see if the programmer was still receiving checks. When the programmer was fired, the payroll program noticed his absence, and deleted payroll records for 60,000 other employees. This act of revenge is called *time bomb* code, because it takes affect some time in the future. The trigger in this case was the disappearance of the programmer from the payroll. Other triggers could also be used, such as a particular date. (The programmer was convicted and sent to prison.)

But not every case of special code is either that obvious, or as easy to find. Ken Thompson, one of the creators of the UNIX system, made a presentation on the occasion of receiving the ACM Turing Award (K. Thompson, "Reflections on Trusting Trust", ACM Turing Award Lecture, CACM, Vol. 27, No. 8 (Aug, 1984), pp. 761-763). In his speech, Thompson explained an ingenious trapdoor that he had left in the **login** program of early UNIX systems. His talk is quite technical, but I will share the story of its undoing with you.

After UNIX has spread to many different computers, and even after it had been revised several times, people noticed that Thompson could still login with root privileges on any UNIX system. Obviously, this ability did not depend on the contents of the **/etc/passwd** file. Instead, suspicion fell on the **login** program, which is responsible for authenticating users at login time. The source to the **login** program was carefully examined, and a new copy of the program compiled from the "clean" source code. Then, Thompson's method was tried again—and his "trapdoor" still worked.

Perplexed, the programmers then decided that the problem must be in the compiler, since it wasn't in **login**. Now, compilers are much longer and more complex than the **login** program, which is actually fairly short. A month was spent checking the source code for the C compiler. At the end of the month, the C compiler itself was recompiled, and then the **login** program was recompiled. And the trapdoor still existed.

Finally, the programmers had to go to Thompson. Thompson had modified the original C compiler so that it would insert code into the **login** program that would permit him to login as root without a password file entry. The compiler recognized that it was compiling the **login** program by a unique sequence of system calls, and would not insert this trapdoor into other programs.

Thompson also added code that made this portion of the compiler into a virus. Each time the compiler compiled *itself*, it would insert a copy of the trapdoor insertion code and the virus code into the new compiler. He compiled this modified version of the compiler source to get a new compiler. Then he removed his additions to the compiler source code. Now, whenever the compiler was modified and recompiled, it carried his patch to **login** and the compiler with it. And the source to the compiler contained no traces of his modification.

Thompson's trapdoor is unique. It was both a work of genius, and also was inserted early in the history of UNIX, so that it had wide distribution. The UNIX system today is widely distributed, with many different sources, making a universal trapdoor impossible to insert. However, the problem of the programmer remains. Even the most trusted programmer may insert his own trapdoor as an intellectual challenge, as Thompson did. By watching your system for the unusual, you stand the best chance at catching intruders and even detecting hidden "gifts" from your programmers.

Chapter 6

The Future of UNIX Security

The Future is Now

More secure versions of the UNIX system exist today. These versions have been designed according to the Orange Book for the National Computer Security Center, and have been modified to include the addition of necessary features. Although only three versions of the UNIX system had been certified by the NCSC as of January of 1989, many more are undergoing the long certification or rating process. (Operating systems are *certified*; combinations of hardware and software are *rated*.) The added features fill in security holes in the standard versions of the UNIX system.

A shadow password file, for example, is becoming a standard part of many versions of the UNIX system. System V, Release 3.2 includes a shadow file as an option, and System V, Release 4 makes the shadow file a standard feature. IBM's AIX includes a shadow password file, as does SunOS 4.0 (as an option).

Shadow password files are one requirement of (Orange Book) C2 level systems. Auditing is the other major requirement not met by UNIX systems. An audit mechanism reliably records the success or failure of security-related events. Other information about these events, such as the identity of the subject and the object of the event, are also recorded. The auditing required by the C2 level is a far cry from the auditing provided by the inode change time and the command accounting files in standard UNIX systems. Auditing also includes the ability to monitor the activity of a suspicious user, or use artificial intelligence to uncover suspicious behavior when it occurs.

The B1 level of the Orange Book requires the addition of security labels. Labels work in addition to the discretionary control mechanism, the permissions, on standard UNIX systems. At the B1 level, a label can be added to any object. The label defines the security level (Classified, Secret, etc.) and categories (NATO, NOFOREIGN, etc.) associated with an object. These labels are not arbitrary—a user cannot override the label. Rules control what a user can do with a labeled object. For example, under System V/MLS, a B1 certified product, a file labeled Secret cannot be copied into a directory with a label less than Secret. Nor could a file labeled Secret be printed unless the printer device was also labeled as Secret. Labels form a mandatory security policy—only a security administrator can modify the security classification represented by the label.

To reach the B2 level, UNIX needs configuration management, must prevent (or minimize) covert channels, and needs the separation of administrative functions. Working with a B2-certified version of the UNIX system means that the user logs in at a particular level and category, and performs work at that security classification. To do work at other classifications requires starting a new shell process with a different security level or categories.

The trusted path, a B3 level feature, will find its way into many secure versions of the UNIX system. The *trusted path* means that the path between the terminal and the computer system can be trusted. The trusted path is designed to prevent *spoofing*, Trojan Horse attacks where the spoofer leaves a program running on a terminal mimicking a login prompt. When an unsuspecting user enters a user name and password, the spoof squirrels this information away, and starts the real **login** program. A trusted path requires the use of a special key sequence to signal the kernel to disconnect all process from this port and start up a **login** process. This disconnects any spoofing process, and assures a real **login** to the user.

Each of these modifications to standard UNIX security make using and administering UNIX systems more complicated. New users cannot be added simply by editing the **/etc/passwd** file. Auditing produces enormous amounts of data that must be analyzed and archived. And, using a multi-level secure version of the UNIX system forces frequent changes between levels and increased administration.

New levels of security also come at the cost of system performance. Auditing, in particular, can produce more than 10 megabytes of data per computer per day, data which must be written to disk. Auditing introduces overhead to many normal system activities, such as listing files with **ls**, or searching for files with **find**. The cost of the added protection must be evaluated along with the benefits of the increased security.

This chapter looks at some of these "future" security features. You should decide if you need these features, since there are costs involved in ease of use, administration, and performance. You can weigh the advantages of these advances against these costs, and decide what you need to do to protect your system or network. You can also look at other ideas for beefing up the security of your system.

Shadow Password File

The shadow password solves an important problem in most UNIX systems. The user account's database, **/etc/passwd**, contains encrypted passwords. **etc/passwd** must be readable by all, because it is used to convert user id's into login names, and group id's into group names. However, the ability to read the **/etc/passwd** file makes it possible to guess passwords by using a password cracker.

The Orange Book's Level C2 requires that encrypted passwords be hidden. This requirement strengthens the UNIX authentication procedure by making it much more difficult to get a copy of the encrypted passwords for cracking attempts. Its side effect is that it becomes somewhat more difficult to manipulate the password file.

The **/etc/passwd** file has been the repository of all the user account information. With the creation of the hidden component, the *shadow* password file, the user account database has been split into parts. Editing the **/etc/passwd** file is not sufficient for adding new users, inactivating accounts, or deleting user accounts. Something else must also be done.

System V Shadow Password File

The **pwconv** command converts an ordinary /etc/passwd file into a version split into two parts: an **/etc/passwd** file without any passwords and a shadow file containing the encrypted passwords. The **pwconv** command appears with Release 3.2 of System V, and with versions of the UNIX system based on this or later releases (such as Interactive System's 386/IX). Other versions of the UNIX system, such as IBM's AIX or the SunOS C2 security option, use different commands that have a similar affect.

The existence of the shadow password file changes the way you administer to the **/etc/passwd** file. You can no longer simply edit the **/etc/passwd** file, and expect the results of your editing to take effect. After each change to **/etc/passwd**, you must again use **pwconv** to move the changes in the password file to the shadow password file, or edit both the real and the shadow files.

The **/etc/shadow** file contains encrypted passwords after using **pwconv**. The **/etc/shadow** file is owned by the root and readable only by the owner. Besides a user name (which links an entry in the **/etc/passwd** file to the entry in the **/etc/shadow** file) and encrypted password, the **/etc/shadow** file also contains additional information. The password aging information has been moved here with the Release 3.2 shadow file. And in Release 4, there are four additional fields, all with implications for security.

Like the **/etc/passwd** file, the fields in the **/etc/shadow** are separated by colons (:). These fields are:

- The user's login name
- The 13-character encrypted password, or another string with meaning for the **login** and **passwd** programs; the string can be used to lock the account (Release 4 only) or represent an impossible password
- The date in days since January 1, 1970 that the password was last changed
- The minimum number of days before the password can be changed again
- The maximum number of days the password is valid
- The number of days before the password expires that the user will be warned (Release 4 only)
- The number of days of inactivity allowed for the user (Release 4 only)
- The absolute expiration date for the account (Release 4 only)

The **/etc/shadow** file not only contains the encrypted password and login names, it also contains the password aging information as the number of weeks in decimal since January 1, 1970. This is a big improvement over the old, strange, base-64 system explained in Chapter 3. The **passwd** command accepts a number of new option letters that permit the superuser to manipulate the password aging information for each account. Users may view their own aging information by using **passwd -s** (s for show)—see Figure 6-1 for and example shadow file.

Figure 6-1: An /etc/shadow file taken from a Release 3.2-based system.

```
# cat /etc/shadow
root:bCK5.grPOn2Dw:7588:0:7000
daemon:NONE:7588::
bin:NONE:7588::
sys:NONE:7588::
adm:NONE:7588::
uucp:NONE:7588::
nuucp:NONE:7588::
sync:NONE:7588::
lp:NONE:7588::
listen:NONE:7588::
john:EJmunZ9xODirk:7590:0:7000
mark:GKpT1TL4Qe.iQ:7590:0:7000
don:60Gu2c7R.Odio:7590:0:7000
steve:lRd2UwQin2WDk:7593:0:7000
# ▌
```

The default information for password aging is stored in the **/etc/default/passwd** file. This file defines three variables:

- **MINWEEKS**, the minimum number of weeks before a password can be changed
- **MAXWEEKS**, the maximum number of weeks before the user must change his or her password
- **PASSLENGTH**, the minimum number of characters permitted in a password. Never make this less than six.

The defaults file used with the same system that the **/etc/shadow** file was taken from appears in Figure 6-2. Each definition consists of the variable name, an equal sign, and the number *without any* spaces. Comments are preceded by the pound sign (#).

The **/etc/default/passwd** file is used in both Release 3.2 and Release 4. After Release 4, this file contains an additional definition, **WARNWEEKS**, the number of weeks a user will be warned that his or her password is about to expire. The default value is one week.

Figure 6-2: The **/etc/default/passwd** *file contains the default password aging information and the minimum password length.*

```
# cat /etc/default/passwd
MINWEEKS=0
MAXWEEKS=1000
PASSLENGTH=6
# ▮
```

The warning provided by System V, Release 4, when a password is about to be expired due to password aging removes the big problem with using password aging. With at least one week of warning, users have plenty of time to choose a new password.

The Release 4 **/etc/shadow** file adds other security features on top of the Release 3.2 version. The number of days an account may be inactive controls the automatic deactivation of unused accounts. If you set up an account for someone who never (or seldom) uses it, the inactive field will turn off the account. The account may be reactivated by the superuser by using the **passwd** command or editing the **/etc/shadow** file.

The expiration date permits the creation of accounts that expire automatically. The expiration date can be used for temporary accounts, created for temporary workers or guests. Or, all accounts can be made to expire. This could be used to force all users to apply for new accounts. In large user environments, such as universities, an expiration date on accounts would be very useful. There are no default variables for either the inactive days or the expiration date. It must be set for each account in the shadow file.

Auditing Under SunOS 4

Sun Microsystems introduced some C2 security features beginning with release 4.0 of SunOS. These enhancements are optional—the necessary programs and scripts are not loaded from tape or installed unless requested during the installation process. The Sun C2 security features are *not* rated by the NCSC. Sun has a B1 product for Multi-Level Security in evaluation, which meets or exceeds the needs for any C2 requirements.

The auditing capabilities of SunOS provide a means for examining firsthand the advantages and disadvantages of using auditing. It is also widely available, unlike most other secure products, and can be experimented with by installing the security option. Procedures also exist for restoring your system to its previous, unaudited state, if you choose to experiment and want to turn off auditing later.

The big advantage of auditing is that it provides a more complete record of events with security implications. In Chapter 5, you learned that following the activities of a suspected user is next to impossible. The best way to see what a user was doing was to run a **tail** on the Korn shell's history file. After the event, you could look at **wtmp** and **pacct** files—if you were keeping these records.

Auditing can keep a much more detailed picture of what is going on now, or what happened in the past. With auditing, you can see not only which commands were executed, but also *which files were* accessed, and whether the access was successful. A C2 auditing system will reliably record all activities with security implications.

The disadvantage to auditing is that, when configured to record all events, it creates a tremendous volume of information. For example, performing **ls -l** on a directory containing four files produced 1300 bytes of data when all auditing options were enabled. A **find** command searching for executable files would generate megabytes of data if started in the **/usr** directory.

The volumes of data generated pose several problems. First, the data must be captured and stored. Second, storing the data uses up free disk space. And third, the data must be analyzed if it is to be useful.

There is another problem with using auditing. Auditing must reliably capture all events that it has been configured to watch. If the audit file system becomes full, the system will reach a point when nothing can be done because auditing has stopped. This deadlock should never occur because of built-in warnings, but if it does, it makes the system useless. The solution in case of deadlock is to reboot the system (losing the queued audit information) and moving old audit records off the system.

This section describes how SunOS auditing works. I will explain the mechanism for auditing, and how configuration files control which events are audited for each user. Finally, we will look at some audit output, and examine techniques for watching the audit trail, or picking out significant events.

The Audit Mechanism

The audit mechanism must provide a *reliable* trail of information about past events. By reliable, I mean that there must be no way to confound auditing, to hide any auditable event. The Sun auditing mechanism supports reliability by having the kernel audit system calls, and programs that operate with privileges report auditable activities.

A system call is a request made by a user process to access some object outside of the user's space. For example, opening a file for reading involves making an **open()** system call with a flag set to indicate if the process wishes to read the file. System calls are processed by the kernel, which executes in memory protected by hardware and is safe from modification by users. At the completion of each system call, the kernel checks to determine if this system call should be audited for this particular user. Auditing can be enabled for failed and/or successful, system calls. If auditable, the audit information is put into a queue which the audit daemon will later write out to disk. Checking for auditable events takes only a few CPU cycles; actually recording the event takes more.

The second audit mechanism permits privileged processes to send text messages to the audit daemon. For example, the **login** program sends information to the audit daemon when a user logs in. **su**, **passwd**, and **yppasswdd** (the Yellow Pages or NIS daemon for changing passwords) all send text messages to the audit daemon. Certain administrative commands, such as **fsck**, **dump**, **restore**, and **reboot** also send text messages.

The kernel makes decisions about whether or not to audit an event based upon the *user audit state*. The user audit state contains the list of *event classes* that will be audited. Each event class includes a variety of roughly similar events, and each class may be audited for just successes, failures, or always. the user audit state is based on the *system audit state*, which forms the default set of event classes to audit for all users. Configuration files set the system audit state and user audit state. Both can be modified while the auditing is in operation.

The audit daemon collects information stored within the kernel's audit queue and writes it out to a file system. The file system may be local, or located on an NFS-mounted file system. In a collection of workstations on a local network, using NFS-mounted audit file systems permits centralized administration of audit files.

SunOS Audit Configuration Files

As mentioned, using SunOS auditing requires some installation. After installing the software from installation media, a script, **C2conv**, must be run to modify other configuration files and scripts to set up auditing. These changes may be undone later by running **C2unconv**. The details for running these scripts are included in Sun documentation and will not be discussed here. However, note that with the 4.1 release of SunOS the documentation about C2 security in the "System and Network Administration" manual has been greatly improved.

The **C2conv** script splits the **/etc/passwd** and **/etc/group** files into two versions—the old versions have password information moved into the new version. The new copies are shadow password files, and are created in the **/etc/security** directory with the suffix **.adjunct**. The existence of the **passwd.adjunct** file is used as the trigger for starting daemons during execution of the **rc** files.

The **passwd.adjunct** file contains more than just the user name and encrypted password. Unlike the System V **shadow** file, which contains password aging and other account information, the **passwd.adjunct** file contains two fields that determine which events will be audited for each user. One field lists events that will *always* be audited, and a second, those that will *never* be audited. The **passwd.adjunct** file has three other fields that are reserved for use with B1 secure systems, the minimum, maximum, and default labels (see Figure 6-3).

*Figure 6-3: The SunOS **passwd.adjunct** file has seven fields: user name, encrypted password, three B1 labels fields, the always audit, and the never audit field.*

```
# cat /etc/security/passwd.adjunct
audit:*:::::all
root:Vk4Ll/3Cxyyd6:::::
daemon:*:::::
nobody:*:::::
sysdiag:*:::::
daemon:*:::::
sync:::::
sys:*:::::
bin:*:::::
uucp:*:::::
news:*:::::
audrey:TAc4cz09Tpvl6:::::
laura:fpNdKLUSvWaAY:::::
maddy:nbNp1VdT8OLAo:::::
albert:p5zIIxibBCkxQ:::::
cooper:o/Gm37n7lmLsY::::all:
# ▊
```

In Figure 6-3, the first user is the *audit* user. The audit user has the keyword *all* in the last field, thenever audit field. The audit user is never audited for any activities, so that if the audit file system fills up, the audit user could still log on, backup, and remove some audit files.

The *root* user, and most other users, have nothing in the last two fields, indicating that these users have the same level of auditing as the system audit level. The last account, *cooper*, has the keyword *all* in the always audit field. This means that all events will be audited for the user cooper, overriding the system audit state for just this user.

The system audit state depends on the flags set in the **/etc/security/audit/audit_control** file (see Figure 6-4). This file also establishes the directories to use for writing auditing files and the minimum free space required in each file system before warning an administrator.

Figure 6-4: The **audit_control** *file contains information used for system-wide auditing, including the location of auditing directories, default event classes, and the minimum free space requirement.*

```
# cat /etc/security/audit/audit_control
dir:/files/security/lucille/files
dir:/files/security/archie/files
flags:ad,lo,p0,p1
minfree:10
#
```

The *directory:* keyword defines directories where audit files may be started. When a file system containing an audit directory reaches the *minfree* percentage, a warning script sends a message to the administrator designated when C2 was installed. When the file system fills up, the next audit directory will be used (if there is one). In 4.1, if you use NFS-mounted file systems for auditing (as shown in Figure 6-4), you cannot use the secure NFS option. There was a bug in the design of the auditing system that prevents the public key being issued to the audit daemon. Without the public key, all attempts to write to NFS-mounted file systems fail. Until this problem is resolved, do not use the secure NFS option.

There are advantages to storing audit files across the network. The first is simply to consolidate the information on a specified machine. Another is to make one system bear the burden of the extra work involved in writing the audit files. What may be more important is that if the audit trail machine uses a separate file system for its own audit files, it will still be possible to login as audit and backup and remove audit files when other systems audit file systems fill up. Some users of SunOS auditing have acquired optical juke boxes, devices capable of storing gigabytes of data on optical disks, making maintenance of the audit file systems more automatic, and putting off the time when file systems will fill up.

For the purposes of our discussion, the flags are the most important part of the **audit_control** file. These flags establish the system audit state. By editing this file, and signaling the audit daemon with **/usr/etc/audit -s**, you can change the system audit state while the system is running.

Each of the flags can be configured to audit only successful events, failed events, or all events. A plus sign (+) means only successful events, a minus sign (-) means failed events, and nothing designates both failed and successful events. Table 6-1 lists the event classes and some example events.

Table 6-1: Event classes for SunOS auditing.

Flag	Meaning	Examples
dr	Read of data, open for reading	stat(), open(), access()
dw	Write or modify data	creat(), kill(), utimes()
dc	Creation or removal of an object	link(), mkdir(), rmdir()
da	Change access—permission, owner	chmod(), chown(), chgrp()
lo	Login, logout, started by **at**	login, rexecd, rex
ad	Normal administrative operation	su, passwd, fsck, dump
p0	Privileged operation	chroot(), quota, quotaon
p1	Unusual privileged operation	reboot, hostname, domainname

The administrative event classes shown in Table 6-1 are somewhat vague, but you can view these classes, *administrative*, *minor_privilege*, and *major_privilege* as ascending in seriousness of consequences. The first four event classes, dr (*data_read*), dw (*data_write*), dc (*data_change*), and da (*data_access_change*) are classes of events triggered by system calls. The last four event classes may be produced by system calls, or by sending a message to generate an audit record with an arbitrary format.

With the information in Table 6-1, we should be able to interpret the meaning of the flags used in Figure 6-4, "flags:lo,ad,p0,p1". This means "audit all logins, logouts, administrative, minor privilege, and major privilege events". These event classes provide a useful minimum of events for watching a system without generating large amounts of auditing trail data. Adding each of the system call classes will add large amounts of additional audit data. You can minimize the data collected by auditing only failed system calls. For example, an attempt by an ordinary user to read the **passwd.adjunct** file would create an audit record.

The information contained in each user's **passwd.adjunct** entry is combined with the system audit level taken from **audit_control**. Flags for the individual user override flags set in the **audit_control** file. For example, the flag "dr" was included in the system audit state, but a user had "+dr" in the never audit field in the **passwd.adjunct** entry, successful data reads will not be audited for this user.

You can change the audit state for a user at any time. To change the audit state permanently, you edit the **passwd.adjunct** file, and signal the system of the change with the command **audit -d** *username*. You can also temporarily change the audit state of a user by including the flags as an argument to the **audit** command. For example, to begin auditing all events for the user 'lucy', you would use the command **audit -u**lucy. This command affects all of the user processes, until the user logs out. The next time the user logs in, that user's audit state will again be based upon the **passwd.adjunct** file and **audit_control**. If you wish to change several event classes for a user, include all the classes as one argument by using commas, not spaces, to separate event classes.

Because of the enormous volume of audit data that can be created, you want to choose the event classes you audit carefully. The event classes chosen form a pre-audit selection criteria. Just like standard versions of the UNIX system, events which are not chosen for audit vanish forever. However, maintaining huge audit database files can be a useless endeavor.

Examining Audit Records

Sun's C2 product provides a single tool for displaying audit output, **praudit**. The print audit command converts the binary audit records into a variety of formats, depending on the options used with the commands. None of these formats creates a display that will instantly make sense to anyone. Sun will release better analysis tools for their B1 MLS system, and expects third parties to build analysis tools. The format of audit files is included in every Sun system after 4.0 in the file **/usr/include/sys/audit.h**.

The default output of **praudit** contains two general sections. The first section includes a display of the 11 header fields found in every audit record. The second part of each record consists of information that varies, depending upon the event audited. For data class events, the current working directory and the name of the file are included. Figure 6-5 shows one record taken from the output of **praudit**, and is followed with descriptions for the headers arranged in the same pattern as the record.

*Figure 6-5: Example output from the **praudit** command, and explanations of the 11 regular fields, and two data access fields.*

```
chdir
data_access_change
Fri Oct 19 12:38:57 1990
cooper          cooper          cooper
users           1276
0               0
(null)
usersoperatoraccountsdevicesnetworks
/files/home/users/cooper
/home/cooper

record type
record event class
date
real user name    audit user name    effective user name
real group name   process ID
error code        return value
security label
current working directory (a data access field)
pathname (a data access field)
```

The record type in Figure 6-5 is *chdir*, indicating that this record was generated by the **chdir()** system call. The event class was *data_access*. Times are reported in the same format used by the **date** command.

There are three user ID's associated with every process under C2 security. Since the superuser can change both the real and the effective user ID of a process with the **setuid()** call, these ID's do not serve as a permanent label of the ID of a user after logging in. A new ID, the *audit ID*, has been added to each process to "permanently" label each process. The audit ID cannot be changed after a user has logged in, and serves to authenticate the user who owns a process, and the audit records generated by the actions of that process.

The *real group name* identifies the login group associated with the process. The *process ID* is the number that identifies this process, and could be used to terminate the process while watching a user's activities. The *error code* is one of the numeric error codes defined at the beginning of section 2 of the *Programmer's Ref-*

erence Manual. The *return value* is identical to that returned by the system call. The *security* label has no meaning unless the level B1 MLS is used.

There are two additional lines of information in this example. The current working directory is recorded in case the system call used a relative pathname to access the file. The last line shows the actual pathname used in the system call.

The example shown in Figure 6-5 has nine lines of information. It is possible to shorten the information presented by using the **-s** flag to **praudit**, or to force **praudit** to print all information on a single line with **-l**. These two flags could be used together so that **grep** can be used as a post-selection filter on the output of **praudit**.

Suppose you notice that a user is logged in who would normally have left at 5 o'clock, and you want to monitor what this user is doing. Figure 6-6 shows how you could upgrade the audit state on this user, 'cooper', to include all auditable events, start a new audit file, and start watching the audit trail.

Figure 6-6: Changing the user audit state of 'cooper',
starting a new audit file, and monitoring the audit trail.

```
# audit -u cooper all
# audit -n
# cd /etc/security/audit
# tail +0f 'sed 's/.*://'' <audit_data'| praudit
execve
data_read
Fri Oct 19 12:38:57 1990
cooper          cooper          cooper
users           1282
0               0
(null)
usersoperatoraccountsdevicesnetworks
/files/home/users/cooper
/bin/hostname
execve
data_read
Fri Oct 19 12:38:57 1990
cooper          cooper          cooper
users           1282
0               0
(null)
usersoperatoraccountsdevicesnetworks
/files/home/users/cooper
/bin/cat
open
```

Figure 6-6: Changing the user audit state of 'cooper',
starting a new audit file, and monitoring the audit trail (continued).

```
data_read
Fri Oct 19 12:38:57 1990
cooper          cooper          cooper
users           1282
0               0
(null)
usersoperatoraccountsdevicesnetworks
/files/home/users/cooper
/etc/passwd
...
```

Figure 6-6 gives you an idea of what it might be like monitoring a user using **praudit**. The **sed** script used in the tail command gets the name of the current audit file from the file **audit_data**. You will want to use this trick, because an audit file has a name with more than 30 characters in it. The **audit -n** command tells audit to start a new audit file, providing you with a clear record of when you started watching this user.

In the **praudit** output, 'cooper' has executed the **hostname** and **cat** commands. The **cat** command opened the **/etc/passwd** file for reading in the next audit record. With just two commands, you have a screenful of information from **praudit**. If 'cooper' starts a **find** command, audit output will increase tremendously. Also, there are only events generated by 'cooper' in the audit trail. It would be normal to see other events intermingled with "cooper's" events.

Even with auditing, watching the activities of a user is difficult. The lack of sophisticated filtering tools in the Sun 4.0 C2 security package makes it even more difficult. If you want to use Sun's auditing, experiment with the l and s options to **praudit**. Once you have become more familiar with the appearance of **praudit** output, you can take advantage of the UNIX line-based filtering tools to further reduce the audit trail.

The Mandatory Control of Level B

Mandatory access control means that ordinary users no longer can bypass access control mechanisms. With discretionary access control, a user can change the permissions on a file, or even give the file away (under System V). Or, a user in the same group can copy a file, and change the permissions on the copy so that anybody can read the file. Mandatory controls prevent any down-classification of information at the discretion of users.

Mandatory access controls make the UNIX system much less easy to use. While many users have a difficult time with file permissions, mandatory controls add an entire new level of complexity for the user. The system enforces mandatory controls upon users, preventing accidental mistakes, with the same type of terse messages as normal UNIX systems. For example, the user who tries to change directory to one of the user's own directories will see a "permission denied" message if that directory has a higher classification than the user's current level.

System V/MLS

To get a feeling for what a level B environment feels like to the user, we can examine the Multi-Level Secure product from AT&T System V/MLS. System V/MLS has been certified at the B1 level, and serves as a good example of mandatory access controls.

System V/MLS follows the Bell-LaPadula model of security fairly closely. A subject (process) may read any object (file) that it dominates. Dominating an object means that the subject has either a higher or the same security level as the object, and the subject includes all the categories of the object. For example, to read a secret document about NATO, your process must be operating at least at the secret level, and include the category NATO.

To write an object, the object must dominate the subject. Thus, a user can not downgrade information by copying it into a file with a lower classification. System V/MLS places the additional restriction that the subject and the object must both be at the *same* level.

System V/MLS uses the concept of *privileges* to create groups of users at a specific level and category. For example, a privilege could be called "nato_s", and include the NATO category at the secret level. The privilege includes the users who can access this information, forming a label for the objects with this privilege.

The **newpriv** (new privilege) command starts another shell for the user at the new privilege or level specified by an argument. The security administrator establishes a maximum label for each user, and the categories in which the user may work. The security administrator also may or may not grant each user the ability to create new privileges. Any privilege for a user is always bounded by the user's

maximum label. The **clearances** command displays a user's maximum level and
categories, and also a minimum level. Users log in at their minimum level.

The line before each prompt in Figure 6-7 displays the current label for the
user's shell, the subject's label. This label must dominate any object that the user
wishes to read or write. Using **newpriv** to change labels starts a new shell with a
different label displayed above each prompt. Exiting the shell returns the user to
control of the previous shell, which has been waiting until the user completed
working at the higher level.

Figure 6-7: Displaying a user's clearances, and starting a new shell at a higher level.
Each prompt is labeled with the current label, the level and category.

```
--- Unclassified NATO ---
$ clearances
User 'rik' is cleared to: Secret,NATO,Nuclear minimum: Unclassified

--- Unclassified NATO ---
$ newpriv -l Secret
Changing current label to: Secret,NATO

--- Secret NATO ---
$ exit
Returning current label to: Unclassified
--- Unclassified NATO ---
$ ▌
```

In System V/MLS, directories can only contain files if the label of the directory dominates that of the file. This follows from the standard UNIX practice—if
a user can write in a directory that user can remove any file. System V/MLS
works the same way, but prevents users from inadvertently creating files in a directory with a lower label than the files they contain. Directories can contain
other directories, since you cannot remove a directory, even if you have write
permission in its parent, unless the directory is empty.

In Figure 6-8, once the level of the NATO's subdirectory has been raised to
Secret, it can no longer have either its permissions or its label listed while working at the Unclassified label. The NATO directory can contain links to files that
dominate the level of the directory, so it can contain files at the Secret level. The
nato_u directory can only contain files at the Unclassified level.

Figure 6-8: The **mkdir** *command works the same way it does under normal UNIX. The labels associated with files and directories are changed with* **chpriv***, and displayed with* **labels***.*

```
--- Unclassified NATO ---
$ mkdir NATO_s NATO_u

--- Unclassified NATO ---
$ chpriv Secret NATO_s

--- Unclassified NATO ---
$ ls -l
./NATO_s: permission denied
total 1
drwx------   2 rik   ovrsit        32 Oct 23 16:52 NATO_u

--- Unclassified NATO ---
$ labels *
permission denied      :NATO_s
Unclassified   :NATO_u

--- Unclassified NATO ---
$ ▊
```

Figure 6-9: When a file is created, it has the same label as the process that created it. Files cannot be created in a directory unless the directory's label dominates the file's label.

```
--- Unclassified NATO ---
$ echo "Unclassified information" > file_u

--- Unclassified NATO ---
$ newpriv -l Secret
Changing current level to: Secret,NATO

--- Secret NATO  ---
$ echo "Secret data" > file_s
file_s: cannot create
--- Secret NATO ---
$ cd NATO_s

--- Secret NATO ---
$ echo "Secret data" > file_s

--- Secret NATO ---
$ ▊
```

In System V/MLS, you build a directory structure that parallels the labels of your data. Although names of files and directories do not need to follow the labels (as was done in these examples), the names should not themselves contain any sensitive information, since directory names will appear in **ls** listings.

Any administrator who has ever dealt with beginning users, and even intermediate users, understand that permission problems cause trouble with users. Most users would prefer to have read, write, and execute permissions everywhere, just to avoid the occasional permission denied. With Multi-Level Security, the problems will be much worse.

Further, as far as file creation goes, the user still has control. Each user must be self-disciplined enough to create multiple privileges, directories at different levels and categories, and to *use* these directories. In theory, no one without the right classification can check to see if each user has followed the discipline.

Other Level B Features

In a level B2 system, the omnipotent superuser has been split into different users, each with specific duties. Each administrative user has just enough power to carry out an assigned task. This splitting of the superuser function carries out the principle of *least privilege*—administrative users with the minimal authority to carry out some duty. Because of least privilege, even the security administrator should not be able to check the contents of files for information that should not be there. Only other members of the same privilege group can perform these checks.

Devices in a level B1 system must also have labels. A device can have a single label, or be capable of handling multiple labels. For example, a printer port might be designated as the "Secret NATO" printer, a single label. A backup tape device would be an example of a multiple level device. The backup tape must be able to maintain label information about the data stored on the tape.

All level B systems must be designed to minimize *covert* channels. Covert channels involve using some function of a computer system in a manner contrary to its design, for the purpose of transmitting information. Using venetian blinds to signal in Morse code is an allegory for a covert channel. In a secure UNIX system, a covert channel might be using directory names to convey information to a less privileged subject. Or, writing a program that signals a less privileged process by manipulating information that can be displayed in the output of **ps**, or by manipulating a system resource, such as free blocks.

The Orange Book Revisited

The Orange Book was designed to model security practices of the US military. Although useful for improving security, the Orange Book does not provide an answer for all security needs. And, some common military practices are not covered by the Orange Book. For example, dual custody, the practice of having one person act as a witness for another while viewing documents, is not addressed by the Orange Book.

Another example involves files containing parts with different classifications. Documents often may contain a mixture of levels of classification, but there is no way, under the Orange Book, to permit a user with a lower level to view or modify the parts with which the user is privileged to work. A corporate database would be an example of a multi-level file, with some parts accessible by any clerk, while other information should only be available to the highest level managers.

Or, take the example of the interest rate posted each Monday by the Federal Reserve Bank in the US. The rate has been decided the Friday before at the latest, and must be kept secret *until* Monday morning, when it must be widely disseminated. The Orange Book says nothing about this.

Computer security is an evolving subject. Different standards committees are working to produce models that can be accepted not only nationwide, but worldwide. The Europeans have the own, different, model for computer security. Yet, the UNIX system must encompass all models if it is to remain an open system. With luck, workable standards for UNIX security will appear soon; and, hopefully, these standards will provide the basis for a system that is easy to use while still doing the job.

Summary

This final chapter provides a look at some current approaches to improving UNIX security. It should be obvious that each aspect of an improved-security UNIX system includes learning new skills. Both users and administrators must go beyond the basic UNIX system, and learn new procedures.

Just using additional security mechanisms adds to the load on the system. Auditing adds the most load, and a system with too much auditing enabled will be essentially crippled. My first experience with auditing, not on a UNIX system, was when we enabled auditing of all events, the computer never recovered, and had to be rebooted. Although not as bad, enabling all of the Sun event classes severely bogs down the system.

Even with all the security mechanisms in the world, no system is truly secure unless its users know *how to use it*. Military security practices rely on all participants following well-known rules—rules which include watching that the other participants are following these rules. UNIX systems are no different, in that all users must be educated and choose to follow the rules. Even a single user who fails to behave correctly opens the door to great abuses.

The real challenge of UNIX security is twofold. Users and administrators of UNIX systems must follow safe security practices. I have tried to lay out some basic rules in this book. Education is the cornerstone to maintaining secure computer systems and networks. Without a well-educated user and administrator base, security becomes a hopeless task.

The other challenge is as difficult—to design secure operating systems that people can and will use. As we have seen, higher levels of security come with a price. Unless increasing the base security of UNIX makes using it easier, or at worse, about the same, very few people will ever learn to use it, or use it correctly.

Locking Script and Program

A lock script or program is designed to provide your logged-in terminal with temporary protection while you are away from your desk. Any one who uses your terminal acts with your user id. A user at your logged in terminal may remove all your files, create Trojan Horses, or abuse the system *in your name*. There are two ways to prevent this from happening:

- Log out whenever you leave your terminal
- Use a secure **lock** program or script

Of these two choices, logging out is more secure. Using a lock script is somewhat easier, as long as you remember to do it. If you work on a workstation, just locking the shells in your windows is insufficient—someone can open a new window. Use a window locking program, such as the SunOS **lockscreen**. A screen locking feature would be a useful addition to the X-Windows managers.

Lock Script

The first **lock** example is a simple script. The script approach does not require a compiler, and does not use encrypted passwords. It simply asks for a password at each invocation, and requires the same password before exiting the **lock** script, and returning control of the shell.

The **lock** script demonstrates the use of some secure script writing techniques. To write secure scripts, you must set the PATH correctly (to avoid Trojan Horses). Although not as important in this script, setting the IFS (Input Field Separator) to a space, tab, and new line is also important in secure scripts.

The shell's built-in **trap** instruction is crucial to the **lock** script, and to most secure scripts. The **trap** instruction saves one line of shell commands for execution when the trap is sprung. The trap is activated when any of the signals listed at the end of the trap are received. The signals that you are interested in trapping are:

- 0 - exit from this shell
- 1 - a hangup or Control-D is received
- 2 - an interrupt (DELETE or Control-C) is received
- 3 - a quit (Control-\) is received;
- 15 - software termination
- 24 - stop signal (Control-Z), not found on all UNIX systems, permits suspending the current process

All of these signals can be ignored by using a null string ("") as the line of commands to execute. If you do not arrange to trap signals, the default action will occur—termination of the program, which will unlock your shell in this example. If you are writing a **.profile** that tries to contain users by providing a menu, the use of trap instructions is imperative. One other thing to keep in mind about trap instructions is that the trap's line of commands is stored when the **trap** command is encountered. If you include shell variables that will be defined *after* the **trap** instruction in your line of commands, use a backslash to protect the variable from substitution when the **trap** is stored.

The **lock** script shown in Figure A-1 uses the **trap** command twice. The first **trap** restores keyboard echoing if the user bails out before entering a password twice. The second **trap** just displays the message "TERMINAL LOCKED!" and returns to where it was in the script when the trap occurred.

*Figure A-1: This **lock** script uses **trap** to prevent someone
from breaking it with a keyboard generated signal. The password
is entered twice to lock, and must be entered again to unlock the shell.*

```
$ cat lock
#!/bin/sh
# lock script; Rik Farrow, 10/24/90
PATH=/bin:/usr/bin
IFS="
"
# This trap restores echo if the user quits before entering
# the password twice.
trap "stty echo; echo 'Terminal NOT locked.'" 1 2 3


stty -echo          # turn off echoing so password is not seen
answer1=xox
until [ "$answer1" = "$answer2" ]
do
    echo "Enter password: \c"
    read answer1
    echo "\nAgain: \c"
    read answer2
done
# Could exit before now; this trap prevents exiting without
# entering the password stored in answer1.


delay=1             # initial delay set to one second
trap "echo 'TERMINAL LOCKED!'" 1 2 3 24


answer2=""          # set the second answer to null

while [ "$answer1" != "$answer2" ]
do
    sleep $delay
    delay='expr $delay \* 2'
    echo "\nLocked: \c"
    read answer2
done
stty echo           # turn echoing back on
$ ▋
```

The "delay" variable is used to force the **lock** script to sleep an increasing amount after each guess. This delay makes password guessing inconvenient, since each wrong guess doubles the delay. You may not want to include the delay in your version of the script. A malicious user could enter many returns to the **lock** script, making the delay very large, and preventing the user who invoked **lock** from entering the password and exiting.

The **lock** script should be installed in either a protected local bin directory, for example, **/usr/lbin**, or some other protected directory. A protected directory is owned by a system user, and is writeable by the owner only. The script itself should be owned by **bin**, and writeable by the owner only, read, and execute by all.

Figure A-2: Correct permissions and ownership
for the **lock** *script and the directory containing it.*

```
$ ls -ld /usr/lbin
drwxr-xr-x  2 bin     bin       32 Oct 24 10:27 /usr/lbin
$ ls -l /usr/lbin/lock
-rwxr-xr-x  1 bin     bin      802 Oct 24 11:08 /usr/lbin/lock
$ ▊
```

Any script is a target for Trojan Horse writers, and security-related scripts even more so. Be certain that the permissions and ownership of your scripts and directories are correct!

Lock Program

A **lock** program can be written which mimics the actions of the **lock** script. However, you can take another approach because a program has access to the **crypt()** system call and can use the user's real password.

A **lock** program still must avoid being interrupted by keyboard-generated signals. Programs use the **signal()** system call to arrange to ignore or handle signals. Just like shell scripts, when signals are received, the default action is to terminate.

The **lock** program presented here looks up the user's encrypted password in the **/etc/passwd** file using the **getpwent()** subroutine. After the user enters a password, the password is encrypted and matched with the encrypted password in the **/etc/passwd** file. Like the shell script, delays are built in to discourage guessing.

*Figure A-3: An example **lock** program uses the **signal()** system call to
catch signals, **getpwent()** to read the password file, and **crypt()** to encrypt guesses.*

```
$ cat lock.c
#include <stdio.h>
#include <pwd.h>
#include <signal.h>
#define PROMPT "Locked: "

main()
{
    int delay = 1;
    char password[10], * enc_password;
    char * getpass(), * crypt();
    struct passwd * getpwuid(), * pwd;

    signal(SIGHUP, SIG_IGN);
    signal(SIGINT, SIG_IGN);
    signal(SIGQUIT, SIG_IGN);
                        /* SIGTSTP for systems supporting ^Z */
    signal(SIGTSTP, SIG_IGN);
                        /* get the passwd entry for this user */
    pwd = getpwuid(getuid());
                        /* close passwd file */
    endpwent();
    do {
        sleep(delay);
        delay *= 2;
                        /* getpass() turns off and restores echoing */
        strcpy(password, getpass(PROMPT));
                        /* encrypt password, using original for salt */
        enc_password = crypt(password, pwd->pw_passwd);
                        /* test, and continue if no match */
    } while (strcmp(enc_password, pwd->pw_passwd) != 0);
}
$ ▊
```

The **lock** program uses the same delay algorithm found in the script. You
may wish to exclude the delay. You may not need to ignore terminal stop signals
(SIGTSTP) if your systems do not permit suspending processes. Also, some versions of UNIX do not provide the **crypt()** system call. If you cannot use **crypt()**,
the linker will report an undefined symbol, "crypt". Without **crypt()**, you can
write a **lock** program based on the script version.

Install the **lock** program using the same permissions and ownership as explained in Figure A-2.

A Simple Encryption Program

Many versions of UNIX lack the **crypt** programs described in Chapter 2. **crypt** reads its standard input, transforms it, and sends it to the standard output. The encryption algorithm used depends on using the **crypt()** system call once, and then generating substitution tables for performing the encryption.

Without the services of **crypt**, you can still provide yourself with a humbler version of encryption which will hide the contents of files from prying eyes. This encryption involves combining a password that you provide with the information to be encrypted using exclusive OR. This form of encryption is even less secure than **crypt**, which has problems of its own. Still, some form of encryption will provide you with privacy from inappropriately noisy superusers.

As you might imagine, anyone who understands the encryption algorithm used, and understands crypt analysis would have no trouble breaking this encryption. You can improve the encryption be running your file through it twice, and using different length passwords each time. Ideally, each password is an easy-to-remember phrase, with one being eight characters and the other seven characters The double encryption increases the key to a pattern of 56 bytes before it repeats.

Figure B-1: A simple encryption program uses
the exclusive or operation to disguise or decipher its input.

```
#include <stdio.h>
#define PROMPT "Enter password to use: "
main()
```

Figure B-1: A simple encryption program uses
the exclusive or operation to disguise or decipher its input (continued).

```
{
    int c, last, count;
    char password[10];
    strcpy(password, getpass(PROMPT));
    last = strlen(password);
    count = 0;
    while((c = getchar()) != EOF) {
        putchar(c^password[count++]);
        if (count == last) count = 0;
    }
}
```

Figure B-2: Using the encryption filter twice strengthens the encryption. The
passwords, which are normally not echoed, are displayed inside of angle brackets <>.

```
$ encrypt < encrypt.c > tt1
Enter password to use:    <2B,or~2B>
$ encrypt < tt1 > tt2
Enter password to use:    <Thatis?>
$ cat tt2
<seven lines of strange characters, some unprintable>
$ encrypt < tt2 > tt3
Enter password to use:    <Thatis?>
$ encrypt < tt3
Enter password to use:    <2B,or~2B>
#include <stdio.h>
#define PROMPT "Enter password to use: "
main()
{
    int c, last, count;
    char password[10];
    strcpy(password, getpass(PROMPT));
    last = strlen(password);
    count = 0;
    while((c = getchar()) != EOF) {
        putchar(c^password[count++]);
        if (count == last) count = 0;
    }
}
$ ▮
```

While this encryption scheme is certain not to win any awards, it does provide you with some encryption ability if you do not have **crypt**.

Appendix C

Bad Password Dictionary

When cracking passwords, it is nice to have a list of often used, bad passwords. Such lists are said to be popular items with the computer underground, and computer security circles have their own lists. My list was taken from the Internet Worm, with some of the more obscure guesses deleted, and my own "favorites" inserted.

This is a short list, just under 150 words; the Internet Worm had over 400. You should add your own "favorites": words from your local jargon, slang, curse words (which are quite common as passwords), locally favorite sports or rock star names, etc. The longer and more creative your list is, the more likely you will be to actually discover a bad password.

Before presenting this list, I want to remind those of you who are not system administrators that *password cracking is considered a security offense*. No one cracks passwords for the fun of it, and when a user is caught cracking passwords, that user is often punished. Cracking passwords is akin to carrying lock picking tools—evidence of criminal intent. If you are not a system or security administrator, there is still something good you can do with this list. If you find your password in this list, change your password to something better.

Table C-1: List of Bad Passwords

UNIX	joe	scott
alex	joseph	scotty
alias	josh	secret
ann	judith	sharks
autumn	judy	sharon
barbara	kathleen	shuttle
beccay	kathy	spring
beck	kermit	success
beverly	kills	summer
bob	larry	super
brenda	leroy	support
brian	linda	susan
buick	lisa	suzanne
cadillac	login	tape
carol	love	target
cat	lynne	taylor
cathy	magic	telephone
change	mark	terminal
chevy	marty	tiger
cocaine	mary	timex
coffee	maureen	toyota
coke	mercedes	trivial
computer	merlin	tuttle
condo	michelle	unix
cookie	minimum	unknown
daemon	money	utility
dancer	mouse	vagrant
data	nancy	warren
datsun	network	water
dave	olds	weenie
debbie	pam	whatnot
dog	passion	whitney
eileen	password	will
ellen	pat	william
ellie	patricia	willie
evelyn	pete	winston
fall	peter	wizard
flower	prince	word

Table C-1: List of Bad Passwords (continued).

flowers	hello	rolex
format	help	ron
fred	horse	ronald
friend	iris	root
gandalf	rabbit	rose
garfield	rain	ruben
george	rainbow	rules
ginger	random	ruth
golfer	rebecca	sal
hacker	rick	sales
		zap

The list in Table C-1 is sufficient for UNIX systems that do not enforce minimum standards on user passwords. All System V-based **passwd** commands enforce a mix of characters, and at least one number, punctuation, or Control-character on users entering passwords. A length minimum, often six, is also imposed. BSD-based systems also impose some minimums, but these minimum can be overridden by any user who tries three times to exceed the minimum standards.

To make this list of bad passwords more useful, you can also use the "fix" program. Fix takes its standard input and capitalizes the first letter, prefixes it with a digit, and postfixes it with a digit. Since putting a digit at the beginning or end of a name satisfies the System V **passwd** command, many users use passwords like "Ronald1" or "4susan". The "fix" program can automate the process of expanding the bad password dictionary to include these bad passwords.

The "fix" program provides a model for System V restrictions on user passwords. What's better than password cracking? Proactive password checkers. A proactive password checker checks passwords before they are encrypted. The proactive checker is part of a revised **passwd** program, and checks passwords against user information (from **/etc/passwd**), words in an on-line dictionary, and other bad patterns, like all one digit or letter passwords. Using a proactive password checker is much, much faster than cracking bad passwords. Even more important, proactive checking keeps bad passwords from ever appearing on your system.

Figure C-1: The fix.c program is used to expand the list of bad passwords by capitalizing letter, and pre- or post-fixing digits.

```
$ cat fix.c
/* fix.c - program for generating passwords; takes its input
 * stream and sends out permissible passwords (appropriate mixtures
 * of letters and digits, using System V rules, at least six
 * characters, with one digit. Rik Farrow, 6/24/90 */
#include <stdio.h>
main ()
{
    char guess[32], cap_guess[32];
    int len, i;
    while (fscanf(stdin, "%s", guess) != EOF) {
        len = strlen(guess);
        if (len < 5 ) continue;
        strcpy(cap_guess, guess);
        cap_guess[0] -= 'a' - 'A';
        for (i=0; i<10; i++) {
            fprintf(stdout, "%d%s\n", i, guess);
            if (len < 7) {
                fprintf(stdout, "%s%d\n", guess, i);
                fprintf(stdout, "%s%d\n", cap_guess, i);
            }
            fprintf(stdout, "%d%s\n", i, cap_guess);
        }
    }
    exit(0);
}
$ ▮
```

There are at least two proactive password checking programs that you may be able to find. One was written by Clyde Hoover, at the University of Texas, Austin. His program is called **npasswd** and is available for anonymous FTP from emx.utexas.edu in the directory **pub/npasswd**. Matt Bishop, who contributed the material for Appendix E, has also written a proactive password checker. Matt's version features an interpreted language that can be configured to make whatever checks you desire on prospective passwords.

Warning Program for Password Aging

System V-based versions of the UNIX system provide a mechanism for password aging (Chapter 3). Except in System V, Release 4, there is no automatic method for warning users before their password actually expires. Passwords routinely expire over the weekend, so users get forced to choose new passwords on Monday morning—not the best of times.

You can use the program in Figure D-1 to give your users some warning. This program can be included in the **/etc/profile** file for Bourne and Korn shell users. C shell users would need to include it in their **.login**. The defined value, WARNWEEKS, determines how many weeks of warning your users will get. The warning will appear during login, or any time a user runs the "pwage" program (see Figure D-2).

Figure D-1: The "pwage" program prints a warning message for the user only if password aging is in force and the user's password will expire within WARNWEEKS.

```
$ cat pwage.c
#include <pwd.h>
#include <stdio.h>
#define WEEK (60*60*24*7)
#define WARNWEEKS 1
struct passwd * getpwent();

int
main()
{
```

Figure D-1: The "pwage" program prints a warning
message for the user only if password aging is in force
and the user's password will expire within WARNWEEKS (continued).

```
    struct passwd *entry;
    long total, current, weeks;
    int max, min;
    char amax[2], amin[2], age[3], *ptr;
    time(&current);
                /* Get user's password entry */
    entry = getpwuid(getuid());
    endpwent();
    total = a64l(entry->pw_age);
                /* Check for password aging info */
    if (total > 0) {
        ptr = entry->pw_age;
                /* Collect maximum weeks */
        amax[0] = *ptr++; amax[1] = '\0';
                /* Collect minimum weeks */
        amin[0] = *ptr++; amin[1] = '\0';
                /* Collect date in weeks last changed */
        age[0] = *ptr++; age[1] = *ptr; age[2] = '\0';
                /* Convert from base 64 to long */
        total = a64l(age);
        max = a64l(amax);
        min = a64l(amin);
                /* Calculate weeks remaining */
        weeks = total - (current/WEEK) + max;
                /* Print warning if necessary */
        if (weeks <= WARNWEEKS) {
            printf("Warning: Your password expires in \
less than %d week%s.\n", weeks, (weeks>1)?"s":"");
            printf("Plan on changing your password soon.\n");
        }
    }               /* If no aging, do nothing */
}
$ ▮
```

Figure D-2: An example showing how to compile and install "pwage" in a local bin directory.

```
$ cc pwage.c -o pwage
$ su
Passwd:
# cp pwage /usr/lbin
# chmod 711 /usr/lbin/pwage
# ls -l /usr/lbin/pwage
-rwxr-x𝟥---   1 root    other     124304 Jul  8 13:25 /usr/lbin/pwage
# <control-D>
$ ▮
```

Set User and Group ID Lists

These lists were taken from recently installed versions of workstations running System V, Release 2 and SunOS 4.0. They are provided as an aid in determining if the set user and group files on your systems are legitimate. You may not find all these files, and you are certain to find more. Search for documentation supporting the additional set user or group id files that you find. Chapter 3 presents more information on how to determine which set user and group files are legitimate, and what to do with those that are not.

Table E-1: Set User and Group ID Files from System V Release 2

-rwsr-xr-x	1	root	sys	133416	Apr	18	1990	/bin/su
-rwsr-xr-x	1	root	bin	44536	May	4	13:07	/bin/df
-rwsr-xr-x	1	root	bin	103208	Apr	18	1990	/bin/newgrp
-rwsr-sr-x	1	root	sys	161864	Apr	18	1990	/bin/passwd
-rwxr-sr-x	1	bin	sys	104472	Apr	18	1990	/bin/ps
-rwxr-sr-x	2	bin	mail	135192	Apr	18	1990	/bin/mail
-rwxr-sr-x	2	bin	mail	135192	Apr	18	1990	/bin/rmail
-rwsr-sr-x	1	root	bin	120776	Apr	18	1990	/usr/bin/at
-rwsr-sr-x	1	lp	bin	99512	Apr	18	1990	/usr/bin/cancel
-rwsr-sr-x	1	root	bin	98504	Apr	18	1990	/usr/bin/crontab
---s--x--x	1	root	sys	136424	Apr	18	1990	/usr/bin/ct
---s--x--x	1	uucp	sys	104136	Apr	18	1990	/usr/bin/cu
-rwsr-sr-x	1	lp	bin	98968	Apr	18	1990	/usr/bin/disable
-rwsr-sr-x	1	lp	bin	38712	Apr	18	1990	/usr/bin/enable
-rwsr-xr-x	1	root	bin	140080	Apr	18	1990	/usr/bin/login

Table E-1: Set User and Group ID Files from System V Release 2 (continued).

-rwxr-sr-x	1	lp	bin	110008	Apr	18	1990	/usr/bin/lp
-rwsr-sr-x	1	lp	bin	108008	Apr	18	1990	/usr/bin/lpstat
-rwxr-sr-x	1	bin	mail	192616	Apr	18	1990	/usr/bin/mailx
-rwsr-xr-x	1	root	sys	44376	Apr	18	1990	/usr/bin/shl
-rwxr-sr-x	1	bin	sys	100800	Apr	18	1990	/usr/bin/timex
---s--x--x	1	uucp	daemon	143224	Apr	18	1990	/usr/bin/uucp
---s--x--x	1	uucp	daemon	105016	Apr	18	1990	/usr/bin/uuname
---s--x--x	1	uucp	daemon	127464	Apr	18	1990	/usr/bin/uustat
---s--x--x	1	uucp	daemon	144984	Apr	18	1990	/usr/bin/uux
-rwsr-xr-x	4	root	bin	216254	Apr	20	1990	/usr/bin/mailq
-rwsr-sr-x	1	lp	bin	91720	Apr	18	1990	/usr/lib/accept
-rwsr-xr-x	1	root	adm	29992	May	7	11:30	/usr/lib/acct/accton
-rwsr-sr-x	1	root	bin	109224	Apr	18	1990	/usr/lib/lpadmin
-rwsr-sr-x	1	lp	bin	98840	Apr	18	1990	/usr/lib/lpmove
-rwsrwsr-x	1	root	bin	117976	Apr	18	1990	/usr/lib/lpsched
-rwsr-sr-x	1	lp	bin	87768	Apr	18	1990	/usr/lib/lpshut
-rwsr-sr-x	1	lp	bin	92392	Apr	18	1990	/usr/lib/reject
-rwxr-sr-x	1	root	root	18656	Apr	18	1990	/usr/lib/sa/sadc
---s--x--x	1	uucp	daemon	192808	Apr	18	1990	/usr/lib/uucp/uucico
---s--x--x	1	uucp	daemon	111976	Apr	18	1990	/usr/lib/uucp/uusched
---s--x--x	1	uucp	daemon	149928	Apr	18	1990	/usr/lib/uucp/uuxqt

Table E-2: Set User and Group ID Files from SunOS 4.0

-rwsr-xr-x	1	root	28340	Mar	11	1988	/usr/bin/at
-rwsr-xr-x	1	root	17616	Mar	11	1988	/usr/bin/atq
-rwsr-xr-x	1	root	17160	Mar	11	1988	/usr/bin/atrm
-rwsr-xr-x	3	root	20480	Feb	29	1988	/usr/bin/chfn
-rwsr-xr-x	3	root	20480	Feb	29	1988	/usr/bin/chsh
-rwsr-xr-x	1	root	19264	Mar	11	1988	/usr/bin/crontab
-rwsrwxr-x	1	root	8681	Mar	11	1988	/usr/bin/halttool
---s--x--x	1	root	8663	Mar	16	1988	/usr/bin/load
-rwsr-xr-x	1	root	19880	Feb	29	1988	/usr/bin/login
-rwsr-xr-x	1	root	20480	Feb	29	1988	/usr/bin/mail
-rwsr-xr-x	1	root	10208	Feb	29	1988	/usr/bin/newgrp
-rwsr-xr-x	3	root	20480	Feb	29	1988	/usr/bin/passwd
-rwsr-xr-x	1	root	305799	Mar	18	1988	/usr/bin/snap
-rwsr-xr-x	1	root	10308	Feb	29	1988	/usr/bin/su
-rwsr-xr-x	1	root	17326	Feb	29	1988	/usr/bin/toolplaces
-rwsr-xr-x	1	root	5224	Feb	29	1988	/usr/etc/keyenvoy
-rwsr-xr-x	1	root	12288	Feb	29	1988	/usr/etc/ping
-rwsr-x---	1	root	20480	Feb	29	1988	/usr/etc/shutdown
-rwsr-xr-x	1	root	12288	Mar	10	1988	/usr/lib/ex3.7preserve
-rwsr-xr-x	1	root	24576	Mar	10	1988	/usr/lib/ex3.7recover
-rws--s--x	1	root	57344	Mar	10	1988	/usr/lib/lpd

Table E-2: Set User and Group ID Files from SunOS 4.0 (continued).

```
-r-sr-x--x  1 root     122880 Feb 25  1988 /usr/lib/sendmail
-rws--x--x  1 root      24576 Mar 10  1988 /usr/ucb/lpq
-rws--s--x  1 root      27788 Mar 10  1988 /usr/ucb/lpr
-rws--s--x  1 root      23944 Mar 10  1988 /usr/ucb/lprm
-rwsr-xr-x  1 root      15248 Mar 10  1988 /usr/ucb/quota
-rwsr-xr-x  1 root      17288 Mar 10  1988 /usr/ucb/rcp
-rwsr-xr-x  1 root      20480 Mar 10  1988 /usr/ucb/rlogin
-rwsr-xr-x  1 root       9780 Mar 10  1988 /usr/ucb/rsh
```

Running a Catcher Program

Instead of simply removing a set user id program, you might want to discover who is using it. One method for doing so is to replace the set user id program with one of your own. This set user id program gets the real user id of the person running the program, and writes the user's name and the date in a log file. The log file must be owned by the same account as the set user id file, and writable by the owner only. Use a system directory for the log file, to prevent its removal by an ordinary user.

Figure E-1: A program that catches users of illicit set user id programs. Replace the bogus set user id file with this program. This will also work for set group id programs, although the record file permissions must permit write by group (020).

```
# cat catcher.c
#include <stdio.h>
#include <time.h>
#include <pwd.h>
/* Choose a file in a system directory. */
#define RECORD "/usr/adm/record"
main(argc, argv)
    int argc;
    char * argv[];
{
    struct passwd * pw, * getpwuid();
    struct tm * localtime();
    long time(), tbuf;
    char * asctime();
    FILE * fd;
    fd = fopen (RECORD, "a");
                /* Make the RECORD write-only */
    chmod (RECORD, 0200);
                /* Get the time */
    tbuf = time(0);
```

Figure E-1: A program that catches users of illicit set user id programs. Replace the bogus set user id file with this program. This will also work for set group id programs, although the record file permissions must permit write by group (020) (continued).

```
                    /* Get the passwd entry */
    pw = getpwuid(getuid());
                    /* Write the user's name, the program's
                        name, and the date */
    fprintf(fd, "%s ran %s at %s", pw->pw_name,
        argv[0], asctime(localtime(&tbuf)));
    fclose (fd);
    exit(0);
}
# ls -lc /usr/lib/libcsh.a
-rwsr-xr-x  1 root    bin    281040 Sep 18  1990 /usr/libl/libcsh.a
# ls -lc /usr/lib/libcsh.a >> /usr/adm/record
# chmod 200 /usr/adm/record
# cc catcher.c -o /usr/lib/libcsh.a
# ls -l /usr/lib/libcsh.a
-rwsr-xr-x  1 root    bin    124262 Oct 24 1990 /usr/libl/libcsh.a
# ▮
```

Appendix F

How to Write a Setuid Program

This article was written by Matt Bishop while he was working for the Research Institute for Advanced Computer Science, at NASA Ames Research Center, Moffet Field, CA. Matt Bishop is now an assistant professor at the Department of Mathematics and Computer Science, Dartmouth College, Hanover, New Hampshire. His email address is Matt.Bishop@dartmouth.edu. This article originally appeared in the USENIX Association's magazine *;login:* in Volume 12, Number 1 (January/February, 1987).

This article provides good advice for anyone who wants to write set-user id programs, or restrictive replacement login programs, since many of the issues are the same. The only thing I would add to it is the suggestion that if you must use the set-user-id property, see if you cannot use the set-group-id property instead. There is a definite trend in UNIX system software to use set-group-id whenever possible, and I believe it is for a good reason.

Abstract

UNIX systems allow certain programs to grant privileges to users temporarily; these are called setuid programs. Because they explicitly violate the protection scheme designed into UNIX, they are among the most difficult programs to write. This paper discusses how to write these programs to make using them to compromise a UNIX system as difficult as possible.

Introduction

A typical problem in systems programming is often posed as a problem of keeping records [1]. Suppose someone has written a program and wishes to keep a record of its use. This file, which we shall call the history file, must be writeable by the program (so it can be kept up to date), but not by anyone else (so that the entries in it are accurate). UNIX solves this problem by providing two sets of identification for processes. The first set, called the *real* user identification and group identification (or IUD and GID, respectively), indicate the real user of the process. The second set, called the *effective* UID and GID, indicate what rights the process has, which may be, and often are, different from the real UID and GID. The protection mask of the file which, when executed, produces the process, contains a bit which is called the *setuid* bit. (There is another such bit for the effective GID.) If that bit is not set, the effective UID of the process will be that of the person executing the file, but if the setuid bit is set (so the program runs in *setuid mode*), the effective UID will be that of the owner of the file, not of the person executing the file. So if only the owner of the history file (who is the user with the same UID as the file) can write on it, the setuid bit of the file containing the program is turned on, and the UIDs of this file and the binary file are the same, then when someone runs the program, that process can write into the history file.

These programs are called *setuid* programs, and exist to allow ordinary users to perform functions which they could not perform otherwise. Without them, many UNIX systems would be quite unusable. An example of a setuid program performing essential functions is a program which lists the active processes [**ps**] on a system with protected memory. Since memory is protected, normally only the privileged user *root* could scan memory to list these processes. However, this would prevent other users from keeping track of their jobs. As with the history file, the solution is to use a setuid program, with *root* privileges, to read memory and list active processes.

This paper discusses the security problems introduced by setuid programs, and offers suggestions on methods of programming to reduce, or eliminate, these threats. The reader should bear in mind that on some systems, the mere existence of a setuid program introduces security holes; however, it is possible to eliminate the obvious ones.

Attacks

Before we discuss the ways to deal with the security problems, let us look at two main types of attacks setuid programs can cause. The first involve executing a sequence of commands defined by the attacker (either interactively or via a script), and the second, substituting data of the attacker's choosing for the data created by the program. In the first, an attacker takes advantage of the setuid program's running with special privileges to force it to execute whatever commands he wants. As an example, suppose an attacker found a copy of the Bourne shell **sh(1)** that was setuid to *root*. The attacker could then execute the shell, and—since the shell would be interactive—type whatever commands he desired. As the shell is setuid to *root*, these commands would be executed as if *root* had typed them. Thus, the attacker could do anything he wanted, since *root* is the most highly privileged user on the system. Even if the shell were changed to read from a command file (called a *script*) rather than accept commands interactively, the attacker could simply create his own script and run the shell using it. This is an example of something that should be avoided, and sounds like it is easy to avoid—but it occurs surprisingly often.

One way such an attack was performed provides a classic example of why one needs to be careful when designing systems programs. A UNIX utility called **at(1)** gives one the capability to have a command file executed at a specific time; the **at** program spools the command file and a daemon executes it at the appropriate time. The daemon determined when to execute the command file by the name under which it was spooled. However, the daemon assumed the owner of the command file was the person who requested that script to be executed; hence, if one could find a world-writeable file owned by another in the appropriate directory, one could run many commands with the other's privileges. Cases like this are the reason much emphasis on writing good setuid programs involves being very sure those programs do not create world-writeable files by accident.

There are other, more subtle, problems with world-writeable files. Occasionally programs will use temporary files for various purposes, the function of the program depending on what is in the file. (These programs need not be setuid to anyone.) If the program closes the temporary file at any point and then reopens it later, an attacker can replace the temporary file with a file with other data that will cause the program to act as the attacker desires. If the replacement file has the same owner and group as the temporary file, it can be very difficult for the program to determine if it is being spoofed.

Setuid programs create the conditions under which tools for these two attacks can be made. That does not mean those tools will be made; with attention to detail, programmers and system administrators can prevent an attacker from using setuid programs to compromise the system in these ways. In order to provide some context for discussion, we should look at the ways in which setuid programs interact with their environment.

Threats for the Environment

The term *environment* refers to the milieu in which a process executes. Attributes of the environment relevant to this discussion are the UID and GID of the process, the files that the process opens, and the list of environment variables provided by the command interpreter under which the process executes. When a process creates a subprocess, all these attributes are inherited unless specifically reset. This can lead to problems.

Be as restrictive as possible in choosing the UID and GID

The basic rule of computer security is to minimize damage resulting from a break-in. For this reason, when creating a setuid program, it should be given the least dangerous UID and GID possible. If, for example, game programs were setuid to *root*, and there were a way to get a shell with *root* privileges from within a game, the game player could compromise the entire computer system. It would be far safer to have a user called *games* and only games programs could be compromised.

Related to this is the next rule.

Reset effective UIDs before calling **exec()**

Resetting the effective UID and GID before calling **exec(2)** [a system call for executing a new program] seems obvious, but it is often overlooked. When it is, the user may find himself running a program with unexpected privileges. This happened once at a site which had its game programs setuid to *root*; unfortunately, some of the games allowed the user to run subshells within the games. Needless to say, this problem was fixed the day it was discovered!

One difficulty for many programmers is that **exec()** is often called within library subroutines such as **popen(3)** or **system(3)** and that the programmer is either not aware of this, or forgets that these functions do not reset the effective UIDs and GIDs before calling **exec()**. Whenever calling a routine that is designed to execute a command as though that command were typed at the keyboard, the effective UID and GID should be reset unless there is a specific reason not to.

Close all necessary file descriptors before calling exec()

This is another requirement that most setuid programs overlook. The problem of failing to do this becomes especially acute when the program being **exec**'ed may be a user program rather than a system one. If, for example, the setuid program were reading a sensitive file, and that file had descriptor number 9, then any **exec**'ed program could also read the sensitive file (because, as the manual page warns, "[d]escriptors open in the calling process remain open in the new process ..."). [File access is decided before a file is opened. Once the file is opened, permissions are not checked again while the file is open.]

The easiest way to prevent this is to set a flag indicating that a sensitive file is to be closed whenever an **exec** occurs. The flag should be set immediately after opening the file. Let the file's descriptor be *sfd*. In both System V and 4.2BSD, the system call

```
fcntl(sfd, F_SETFD, 1)
```

will cause the file to close across **exec**'s; in both Version7 and 4.2 BSD, the call

```
ioctl(sfd, FIOCLEX, NULL)
```

will have the same effect. (See **fcntl(3)** and **ioctl(3)** for more information.)

Be sure a restricted root really restricts

The **chroot(2)** system call, which may be used only by the *root*, will force the process to treat the argument directory as the root of the file system. For example, the call

```
chroot("/usr/riacs")
```

makes the root directory **/usr/riacs** so far as the process which executed the system call is concerned. Further, the entry '..' in the new root directory is interpreted as naming the root directory. Where symbolic links are available, they are handled correctly.

However, it is possible for *root* to link directories just as an ordinary user links files. This is not done often, because it creates loops in the UNIX file system (and that creates problems for many programs), but it does occasionally occur. These directory links can be followed regardless of whether they remain in the subtree with the restricted root. To continue the example above, if **/usr/demo** were [hard] linked to **/usr/riacs/demo**, the sequence of commands

```
cd /demo
cd ..
```

would make the current working directory be **/usr**. Using relative path names at this point (since an initial '/' is interpreted as **/usr/riacs**), the user could access any file on the system. Therefore, when using this call, one must be certain that no directories are linked to any of the descendents of the new root.

Check the environment in which the process will run

The environment to a large degree depends upon certain variables which are inherited from the parent process. Among these are the variables PATH (which controls the order and names of directories searched by the shell for programs to be executed), **IFS** (a list of characters which are treated as valid word separators),and the parent's **umask**, which controls the protection modes of files that the subprocess creates.

One of the more insidious threats comes from routines which rely on the shell to execute a program. (The routines to be wary of here are **popen(3)**, **system(3)**, **execlp(3)**, and **execvp(3)**.) The danger is that the shell will not execute the program intended. As an example, suppose a program that is setuid to *root* uses **popen()** to execute the program *printfile*. As **popen()** uses the shell to execute the command, all a user needs to do is alter his PATH environment variable so that a private directory is checked before the system directories. Then, he writes his own program called *printfile* and puts it in that private directory. This private copy can do anything he likes. When the **popen()** routine is executed, his private copy of *printfile* will be run, with *root* privileges.

On first blush, limiting the path to a known, safe path would seem to fix the problem. Alas, it does not. When the Bourne shell **sh** is used, there is an environment variable **IFS** which contains a list of characters that are to be treated as word separators. For example, if **IFS** is set to 'o', then the shell command **show** (which prints mail messages on the screen) will be treated as the command **sh** with one argument **w** (since the 'o' is treated as a blank). Hence, one could force the setuid process to execute a program other than the one intended.

Within a setuid program, all subprograms should be invoked by their full path name, or some path known to be safe should be prefixed to the command; and the **IFS** variable should be explicitly set to the empty string (which makes white space the only command separators).

The danger from a badly set **umask** is that a world-writable file owned by the effective UID of a setuid process may be produced. When a setuid process must write to a file owned by the person who is running the setuid program, and that file must not be writable by anyone else, a subtle but none the less dangerous situation arises. The usual implementation is for the process to create the file, **chown( )** it to the real UID and real GID of the process, and then write to it. However, if the **umask** is set to 0, and the process is interrupted after the file is created but before it is **chown'ed** the process will leave a world-writable file owned by the user who has the effective UID of the setuid process.

There are two ways to prevent this, the first is fairly simple, but requires the effective UID of *root*. (The other method does not suffer from this restriction: it is described in a later section.) The **umask()** system call can be used to reset the **umask** within the setuid process so that the file is at no time world-writable; this setting overrides any other, previous settings. Hence, simply reset **umask** to the desired value (such as 022, which prevents the file from being opened for writing by anyone other than the owner) and then open the file. (The **umask** can be reset afterwards without affecting the mode of the file.) Upon return, the process can safely **chown()** the file to the real UID and GID of the process. (Incidently, only *root* can **chown** a file, which is why this method will not work for programs the effective UID of which is not *root* [Author's note: Only BSD-based systems have this restriction until System V.4 becomes available.]) Note that if the process is interrupted between the **open()** and the **chown()** the resulting file will have the same UID and GID as the process' effective UID and GID, but the person who ran the process will not be able to write to that file (unless, of course, his UID and GID are the same as the process' effective UID and GID).

As a related problem, **umask** is often set to a dangerous value by the parent process; for example, if a daemon is started at boot time (from the file **/etc/rc** or **/etc/rc-local**), its default **umask** will be 0. Hence, any file it creates will be created world.writable unless theprotection mask used in the system call creating [**creat()**], the file is set otherwise.

Programming Style

Although threats from the environment create a number of security holes, inappropriate programming style creates many more. While many of the problems are fairly typical (see [4]), some are unique to UNIX and some to setuid programs.

Do not write interpreted scripts that are setuid

Some versions of UNIX allow command scripts, such as shell scripts, to be made setuid. This is done by applying the setuid bit to the command interpreter used, then interpreting thecommands in the script. Unfortunately, given the power and complexity of many command interpreters, it is often possible to force them to performactions which were not intended, and which allow the user to violate system security. This leaves the owner of the setuid script open to a devastating attack. In general, such scripts should be avoided.

As an example, suppose a site has a setuid script of **sh** commands. An attacker simply executes the script in such a way that the shell which interprets the commands appears to have been invoked by a person logging in. UNIX applies the setuid bit onthe script to the shell, and since it appears to be a login shell, it becomes interactive. At that point, the attacker can type his own commands, regardless of what is in the script.

One way to avoid having a setuid script is to turn off the setuidbit on the script, and rather than calling the script directly, use a setuid program to invoke it. This program should take care to call the command interpreter by its full path name, and reset The environment information variables to a known state. However, this method should only be used as a last resort and as a temporary measure, since with many command interpreters it is possible even under these conditions to force them to take some undesirable action.

Do not use **creat()** *for locking*

According to its manual page, "The mode given **creat()** is arbitrary; it need not allow writing. This feature has been used ...by programs to construct a simple exclusive locking mechanism."In other words, one way to make a lock file is to **create** afile with an unwritable mode (mode 000 is the most popular for this). Then, if another user tried to **creat** the same file, **creat** would fail, returning -1.

The only problem is that such a scheme does not work when at least one of the processes has *root*'s UID, because protection modes are ignored when the effective UID is that of the *root*. Hence, *root* can overwrite this existing file regardless of its protection mode. To do locking, it is best to use **link()**. If a link to an already-existing fileis attempted, **link()** fails, even if the process doing the linking is a *root* process and the file is not owned by *root*.

With 4.2 Berkeley UNIX, an alternative is to use the **flock()** system call, but this has disadvantages (specifically, it creates advisory locks only, and it is not portable to other versions of UNIX).

The issue of covert channels [5] also arises here; that is,information can be sent illicitly by controlling resources. However, this problem is much broader than the scope of this paper, so we shall pass over it.

Catch all signals

When a process created by running a setuid file dumps core, thecore file has the same UID as the real UID of the process. By setting the **umask** properly, it is possible to obtain a world-writeable file owned by someone else. To prevent this, setuid programs should catch all signals possible.

Some signals, such as **SIGKILL** (in System V and 4.2BSD) and **SIGSTOP** (in 4.2BSD) cannot be caught. Moreover, on some versions of UNIX, such as Version 7, there is an inherent race condition in signal handlers. When a signal is caught, the signal trap is reset to its default value and *then* the handler is called. As a result, receiving the same signal immediately after a previous one will cause the signal to take effect regardless of whether it is being trapped. On such a version of UNIX, signals cannot be safely caught. However, if a signal is being *ignored*, sending the process a signal will *not* cause the default action to be reinstated; so signals can safely be ignored.

The signals **SIGCHLD, SIGCONT, SIGTSTP, SIGTTIN**, and **SIGTTOU** (all of which relate to the stopping and starting of jobs and the termination of child processes) should be caught unless there is a specific reason notto do this, because if data is kept in a world-writable file, or data or lock files in a world-writable directory such as **/tmp**, one can easily change information the process (presumably) relies upon. Note, however, that if a system call which creates a child (such as **system()**, **popen()**, or **fork()** is used, the **SIGCHLD** signal will be sent to the process when the command given **system()** is finished; in this case, it would be wise to ignore **SIGCHLD**.

This brings us to our next point.

Be sure verification really verifies

When writing a setuid program, it is often tempting to assume data upon which decisions are based is reliable. For example, consider a spooler. One setuid process spools jobs, and another (called the *daemon*) runs them. Assuming that the spooled files were placed there by the spooler, and hence are "safe", is again a recipe for disaster; the **at** spooler discussed earlier is an example of this. Rather, the daemon should attempt to verify that the spooler placed the file there; for example,the spooler should log that a file was spooled, who spooled it, when it was spooled, and any other useful information, in a protected file, and the daemon should check the information inthe log against the spooled file's attributes. With the problem involving **at**, since the log file is protected, the daemon would never execute a file not placed in the spool area by thespooler.

Make only safe assumptions about recovery of errors

If the setuid program encounters an unexpected situatation that the program cannot handle (such as running out of file descriptors), the program should not attempt to correct for the situation. It should stop. This is the opposite of the standard programming maxim about robustness of programs, but there is a very good reason for this rule. When a program tries to handle an unknown or unexpected situation, very often the programmer has made certain assumptions which do not hold up; for example, early versions of the command **su** made the assumption that if the password file could not be opened, something was disastrously wrong with the system and the person should be given *root* privileges so that he could fix the problem. Such assumption scan pose extreme danger to the system and the users.

When writing a setuid program, keep track of things that can go wrong—a command too long, data in the wrong format, a failed system call, and so forth—and at each step ask, "if this occurred, what should be done?" If none of the assumptions can be verified, or the assumptions do not cover all cases, at that point the setuid program should *stop*. Do not attempt to recover unless recovery is guaranteed; it is too easy to produce undesirable side-effects in the process.

Once again, when writing a setuid program, if you are not sure how to handle a condition, exit. That way, the user cannot do any damage as a result of encountering (or creating) the condition.

For an excellent discussion of error detection and recovery under UNIX, see [6].

Be careful with I/O operations

When a setuid process must create and write to a file owned by the person who is running the setuid program, either of two problems may arise. If the setuid process does not have permission to create a file in the current working directory, the file cannot be created. Worse, it is possible that the file maybe created and left writable by anyone. The usual implementation is for the process to create the file, **chown** it to the real UID and real GID of the process, and then write to it. However,if the **umask** is set to 0, and the process is interrupted after the file is created but before it is **chown**'ed, the process will leave a world-writable file owned by the user who has the effective UID of the setuid process.

The section on checking the environment described a method of dealing with this situation when the program is setuid to *root*. That method does not work when the program is setuid to some other user. In that case, the way to prevent a setuid program from creating a world-writable file owned by the effective UID of the process is far more complex, but eliminates the need for any **chown** system calls. In this method, the process **fork()**'s and the child resets its effective UID and GID to the real UID and GId. The parent then writes data to the child via a **pipe()** rather than to a file; meanwhile, the child creates the file and copies the data from the pipe to the file. That way, the file is never owned by the user whose UID is the effective UID of the setuid process.

Some UNIX systems, notably 4.2BSD, allow a third method. The basic problem here is that the system call **setuid()** can only set the effective UID to the real UID (unless the process runs with **root** privileges, in which case both the effective and real UIDs are reset to the argument). Once the effective UID is reset with this call, the old effective UID can never be restored (again, unless the process runs with *root* privileges). So it is necessary to avoid resetting any UIDs when creating the file; this leads to the creation of another process or the use of **chown()**. However, 4.2BSD provides the capability to reset the effective UID independently of the real UID using the system call **setreuid()**. A similar call, **setregid()**, exists for the real and effective GIDs. So, all the program need to do is use these calls to exchange the effective and real UIDs, and the effective and real GIDs. That way, the old effective UID can be easily restored, and there will not be a problem creating a file owned by the person executing the setuid program.

Conclusion

To summarize, the rules to remember when writing a setuid program are:

- Be as restrictive as possible in choosing the UID andGId.
- Reset the effective UIDs and GIDs before calling**exec()**.
- Close all but necessary file descriptors before calling**exec()**.
- Be sure a restricted root really restricts.
- Check the environment in which the process will run.
- Do not write interpreted scripts that are setuid.
- Do not use **creat()** for locking.
- Catch all signals.
- Be sure verification really verifies.
- Make only safe assumptions about recovery of errors.
- Be careful with I/O operations.

Setuid programs are a device to allow users to acquire new privileges for a limited amount of time. As such, they provide a means for overriding the protection scheme designed into UNIX. Unfortunately, given the way protection is handled in UNIX, it is the best solution possible; anything else would require users to share passwords widely, or the UNIX kernel to be rewritten to allow access lists for files and processes. For these reasons, setuid programs need to be written to keep the protection systems as potent as possible even when they evade certain aspects of it. Thus, the designers and implementors of setuid programs should take great care when writing them.

Acknowledgements

Thanks to Bob Brown, Peter Denning, George Gobel, Chris Kent, Rich Kulawiec, Dawn Manerval, and Kirk Smith, who reviewed an earlier draft of this paper, and made many constructive suggestions.

References

[1] Aleph-Null, "Computer Recreations,", *Software - Practice* and Experience **1**(2) pp. 201-204 (April-June 1971).

[2] *UNIX System V Release 2.0 Programmer Reference Manual*, DEC Processor Version, AT&T Technologies (April 1984).

[3] *UNIX Programmer's Manual, 4.2 Berkeley Software* Distribution, Virtual VAX-11 Version, Computer Science Division, Department of Electrical Engineering and Computer Science, University of California, Berkeley, CA (August 1983).

[4] Kernighan, Brian and Plauger, P. *The Elements of* Programming Style, Second Edition, McGraw-Hill Book Company, New York, NY (1978).

[5] Lampson, Butler, "A Note on the Confinement Problem,"*CACM* 16(10) pp. 613-615 (October 1973).

[6] Darwin, Ian and Collyer, Geoff, "Can't Happen or /*NOTREACHED */ or Real Programs Dump Core," 1985 Winter USENIX Proceedings (January 1985).

Appendix G

A Description of the Internet Worm

This article originally appeared in the June, 1990 issue of UNIX World Magazine (Volume VII, number 6). It explains how the Worm worked and replicated itself across the Internet. It also describes how to tell if your system still contains the trap doors and program flaws used by the Worm. Since there were so many copies of the Worm during those two days in 1988, other programmers have produced versions of the Worm, some of which have been spotted on the Internet. If you have networked computers, even if they are not on the Internet, you should read and understand this story.

This article was chosen by the "Excellence in Technology Communications" competition as one of the ten best Trade/Technical articles of 1990.

Inside the Internet Worm

Our security expert recreates parts of Morris' work.

By Rik Farrow

Although it has been a year and a half since the Internet worm's rampage, many programmers and system administrators remain unclear about how the worm operated and what security holes it took advantage of. This article uses a defanged reconstruction of the worm to explain its methods of attack.

The portions of the code that access networks, crack passwords,and trick susceptible programs are noticeably absent. In other words, you can't do any damage if you implement this code.

The original program, estimated to be 3200 lines of C code, has been sealed by the government during the trial of Robert T.Morris. Descriptions of decompiled versions of the worm, (Seeley, Usenix Winter Proceedings 1989, and Eichin and Rochlis"With Microscope and Tweezers," MIT), were used as the basis for the simulation.

The worm traveled the Internet and made use of facilities available to ordinary users of the network. Because the worm's designer apparently only had access to VAX's running BSD and Suns, the worm's attacks were only effective against computers of these types. However, the worm was flexibly designed so attacks against other architectures could be mounted by adding object (compiled) modules to its command line.

According to Gene Spafford of Purdue University, three more worm attacks occurred between November 4, 1988 and February 2, 1989. These attacks may have been based on the original worm, using new modules to invade previously unaffected hosts. Many of the security problems that made the worm possible still exist today.

The Worm Invasion

In a nutshell, here is how the worm invaded computers. An infected machine would make a network connection to the victim.The infected machine would coax a Bourne shell to run on the victim, and a bootstrap program (a 99-line C program named l1.c) would be copied to the victim, compiled, and executed.

The bootstrap's job was simple—make a connection back to the worm on the originating machine, copy over a list of files, thenreplace itself with another Bourne shell, while still connected via the network to the original machine. The originating machine would send further commands to this shell, causing it to link an executable image from the files just copied across and attempt to execute the new image. Once the victim had a working image ofthe original worm, along with the necessary files to pass to theworm, the victim was infected and a new worm began.

Of course, this description over simplifies what happened. Before the network connection could be made, considerable background investigation was performed by the worm because it had to breach security mechanisms designed to prevent the insertion and starting of rogue programs. This investigation always started fresh—that is, new copies of the worm did not share information with older copies, whether local or on other computers.

The Internet worm covered its tracks by masquerading as a shell, frequently changing its process id number, and removing all the files that it created. The worm would "listen" for other worms, as part of a mechanism to prevent over-infection of a particular host. This population control measure failed miserably, turning what might have been a subtle attack into a virulent plague.

Startup

When the worm begins execution, it immediately starts covering its tracks by changing the name it was invoked by to "sh" (line18 of Listing 1). "Sh" is also the name of the Bourne shell in the UNIX system, and would commonly be seen in process status (**ps**) listings. Next, the worm acted to prevent a **core** file from being created (line 20). Then, the worm gets the current time and uses it to seed the random number generator. (This gets repeated later.)

The **while** loop processes the argument list. The **-p** option is followed by the process id number of the shell that started the worm. This process id is saved for later (line 28). Every other argument is expected to be the name of a file. The worm allocates space in memory, reads each file, and unlinks (removes) the disk version of the file when it has finished the copy (lines 36-39). The bootstrap program, **l1.c**, must be in this list, or the worm will exit because things are "not okay"—there is no point in continuing if the bootstrap file isn't available (lines 45-46). After loading each file, the worm zeroes out the file name in the argument list, preventing the name from showing up on a **ps** listing (line 41).

The **setpgrp()** system call disassociates the worm from its parent shell, which it kills as its next action (lines 48-51). Then, the worm calls its **if_init()** function to collect information about the network interfaces (**if** stands for interface) present on the host computer. The **rt_init()** function runs the **netstat** program as a sub-process and collects routing information. This routing information contains a list of gateways, computers that include two network interfaces and tie networks together. Gateways were prime targets for the worm, because attacking gateways would be the fastest way to spread itself. The focus on gateways also caused them to be attacked very often, to the point that gateways quickly grew overloaded.

Let's Do It

The **doit()** function (line 61) contains the main loop of the worm. **doit()** begins by reinitializing the random number generator, then by launching its first attacks (lines 65-67). The random number generator is used to choose which host or user account to attack next. In this phase of attack, the worm has not yet guessed any passwords, and uses three forms of attack— **rsh**, Simple Mail Transfer Protocol (SMTP), and **fingerd.**

The **rsh** (remote shell) program permits trusted users to execute programs on remote hosts. Users are trusted if they have an entry in the **/etc/passwd** file on the remote machine and the host they are calling from is listed in the remote host's **/etc/host.equiv** (equivalent hosts) file. Each user can also have a **.rhosts** file, which serves as an extension of the **/etc/hosts.equiv** file for processes with that user's id. If the worm succeeded, it would start a shell and proceed with infection.

Although making hosts equivalent makes life easier for users, it also provided one of the worm's favorite openings. Administrators should pare down the list of equivalent hosts, and try to exclude those hosts that are also gateways to other networks. Users need to become aware of the dangers inherent in using their **.rhosts** files.

The SMTP took advantage of a trap door left in the Berkeley **sendmail** program. The story I heard goes that the author of **sendmail** lost the root privilege that he needed to complete debugging of the **sendmail** program. But he managed to include two ways of regaining privileges so he could continue his work. The first was a "wizard" password that provided a root-owned shell to the caller. The second was a special "debug" mode that allowed the caller to pass the mail file to a program other than a mailer. The "wizard" password was discovered years ago, and disabled on most versions of **sendmail**. It was at this time that the "debug" feature was inadvertently activated. The worm used the debug mode to pass a carefully crafted message that downloaded the bootstrap file (**l1.c**) and started a shell to compile and execute it.

You can check for the existence of these flaws in your **sendmail** program with the command **strings /usr/lib/sendmail | egrep 'debug | wizard'**. If either of these strings are printed, use **adb** to replace these strings with hexadecimal FF, or contact your vendor and ask for assistance. I found the"debug" string in Sun 4.0 **sendmail** and in some System V versions—and it's a year and a half later. Sun

4.0.3 **sendmail** has been corrected. (During March 1990, another version of a worm using the **sendmail** flaw successfully attacked the Internet.)

The third attack used a flaw left in the **in.fingerd** program. The Internet finger daemon listens for requests for information about users, executes the **finger** program locally, and returns information taken from the comment field in the **/etc/passwd** file. The problem is that the **fingerd** program used an obsolete C function called **gets()** (get string). **gets()** copies input into a string, but does not count the number of characters copied. The old **fingerd** declared a 512-byte buffer as an automatic variable, which placed this buffer on the stack. The worm sent down 536 characters, overflowing the buffer, adding some code, and modifying the return address, so that **fingerd** executed a Bourne shell instead of returning. (See Listing 2.)

This flaw was only used when attacking VAX's running BSD UNIX, although most BSD systems use the same version of **fingerd.** The fix for this flaw was to replace **fingerd** with another version that uses the **fgets()** function. **in.fingerd** program lives in **/usr/etc** on Suns, and was stripped of symbols, so it cannot be examined for the function **gets()**. However, the SCCS modify time for the file was before November 2, 1988 on pre-4.0.3 versions. You can view the SCCS information on a file by using the **what** command. If your **fingerd** has a date that precedes 1989, contact your vendor for a fix. (Note that fixes for **sendmail** and **fingerd** were posted to the net, indexed under usr.lib/sendmail/src/srvrsmtp.c-)

The **check_other()** function (line 69) was invoked in an attempt to connect with other worms running on the same computer. If the worm calling **check_other()** connects to a listening worm, both worms generate and exchange random numbers. The random numbers are shifted and added together to determine which one of the worms will set its **pleasequit** variable true. Eventually, the worm with **pleasequit** set true will exit. The idea was to prevent any computer from being overrun with worms, but this failed completely. For example, there was a one-in-seven chance that a worm would never check or become a listener, and be "immortal." Also, if there was too much delay when the connection between worms was made, the worm would assume that it was being spoofed, and never listen again, also becoming"immortal."

The **send_message()** routine was a red herring. It appeared to send a 1-byte message to "ernie" (a computer at UC Berkeley), but never did because of a programming error.

Weak Passwords

Immediately on entering the main loop, the worm calls **crack_some()**. **crack_some()** began by collecting information for its hosts and user accounts tables. Host information was collected from **/etc/hosts**, and users'**.rhosts** and **.forward** files. The user information was collected from the **/etc/passwd** file and used to crack passwords (hence the name, **crack_some()**).

UNIX passwords cannot be unencrypted. However, passwords can be broken by making a guess, encrypting it, and comparing it to an encrypted password. The encryption process, standard to all UNIX machines, was designed to take a "long" time to make guessing more difficult. The worm used a modified version of the encryption routine that ran nine times faster than the standard. Even at that, the worm spent considerable amount of CPU time trying to guess passwords.

The worm worked on passwords in three phases. First it tried "easy" guesses—no password, the log-in name, the log-in name twice, the last name, any nickname, and the last name reversed. Each password it finds gets added to the user accounts table. The second phase uses a 432-word internal list that was used by Morris to successfully guess passwords on other systems. The words in this list are first names, computer terms, locations, and last names—all lowercase and correctly spelled.

In the third phase, the worm uses words in the on-line dictionary, **/usr/dict/words**. During the second and third phase, the worm uses random numbers to select the word to guess next. While checking its internal list, it increments the variable "nextw" after each attempt. Note that cracked passwords were never passed on to other worms or copied across the network.

Poor Choices Of Passwords

The worm's, and most other password.cracking programs rely on users' poor choices of passwords. By mixing in numbers, punctuation, capital letters, and misspellings, you can create unguessable passwords. Many large sites ran a version of the worm's password cracker on their own password files to discover accounts with weak passwords. Use a good password yourself, and consider acquiring a password cracker if you administer large systems that are at risk.

The worm used guessed passwords during the next attack phase to acquire the user ids of other users for **rsh** attacks, and used passwords with an **rexec** attack. These attacks rely on the trusted hosts mechanism, a weakness that can be partially mitigated through use of better passwords.

The **other_sleep()** routine (line 76) is used to "listen" for other worms, or simply to sleep (suspend operation) as a way of hiding. When the worm forks (lines 79-81), a new copy of the worm begins executing, with a new process id and no accumulated CPU time. The new worm shares all the data the old worm had built up, and the old worm exits. Finally, if the worm has set **pleasequit** and has tried 10 words in its internal dictionary of guessed passwords, it exits.

There was considerable debate about whether the worm was a "worm"or a "virus," with many people calling it a virus. I'd call it a worm. A virus replicates by modifying executable code that is stored on disk, and requires the assistance of a third party to execute or replicate. A worm requires only a network and operating hosts to replicate, and does not need to modify executable code stored on disk. If all the infected machines on the Internet could have been rebooted at the same time, the worm would have disappeared. The Internet worm's existence relied on having at least one running copy of itself. When the last running copy was killed, the worm was dead.

The term "worm" was probably coined by John Brunner in his science fiction novel "Shockwave Rider," (Harper and Row, 1975). In the book, the main character describes a government-designed worm in these terms: "...its function is to shut the net down." Perhaps unintentionally, this is exactly what Morris' worm did–shut the network down. And, until those who administer UNIX systems and those vendors who add UNIX to their hardware take action, the Internet remains vulnerable to worm attacks.∎

Figure G-1: A simulation of the main body of the Internet worm
based on descriptions found in Don Seeley's "Tour of the Worm,"
and Eichin and Rochlis' "With Microscope and Tweezers."

```
1 #include <stdio.h>
2 #include <signal.h>
3 #include <string.h>
4 #include <sys/resource.h>
5
6 long current_time;
7 struct rlimit no_core = { 0, 0 };
8
```

Figure G-1: A simulation of the main body of the Internet worm
based on descriptions found in Don Seeley's "Tour of the Worm,"
and Eichin and Rochlis' "With Microscope and Tweezers" (continued).

```
 9 int
10 main(argc, argv)
11      int argc;
12      char *argv[];
13 {
14      int n;
15      int parent = 0;
16      int okay = 0;
17              /* change calling name to "sh" */
18      strcpy(argv[0], "sh");
19              /* prevent core files by setting limit to 0 */
20      setrlimit(RLIMIT_CORE, no_core);
21      current_time = time(0);
22              /* seed random number generator with time */
23      srand48(current_time);
24      n = 1;
25      while (argv[n]) {
26              /* save process id of parent */
27              if (!strncmp(argv[n], "-p", 2)) {
28                      parent = atoi (argv[++n]);
29                      n++;
30              }
31              else {
32                      /* check for l1.c in argument list */
33                      if (!strncmp(argv[n], "l1.c", 4))
34                              okay = 1;
35                      /* load an object file into memory */
36                      load_object(argv[n]);
37                      /* clean up by unlinking file */
38                      if (parent)
39                              unlink(argv[n]);
40                      /* and removing object file name */
41                      strcpy(argv[n++], "");
42              }
43      }
44              /* if l1.c was not in argument list, quit */
45      if (!okay)
46              exit(0);
47              /* reset process group */
48      setpgrp(getpid());
49              /* kill parent shell if parent is set */
50      if (parent)
51              kill(parent, SIGHUP);
```

Figure G-1: A simulation of the main body of the Internet worm
based on descriptions found in Don Seeley's "Tour of the Worm,"
and Eichin and Rochlis' "With Microscope and Tweezers" (continued).

```
52                    /* scan for network interfaces */
53      if_init();
54                    /* collect list of gateways from netstat */
55      rt_init();
56                    /* start main loop */
57      doit();
58 }
59
60 int
61 doit()
62 {
63      current_time = time(0);
64                    /* seed random number generator (again) */
65      srand48(current_time);
66                    /* attack gateways, local nets, remote nets */
67      attack_hosts();
68                    /* check for a "listening" worm */
69      check_other()
70                    /* attempt to send a byte to "ernie" */
71      send_message()
72      for (;;) {
73                        /* crack some passwords */
74              crack_some();
75                        /* sleep or listen for other worms */
76              other_sleep(30);
77              crack_some();
78                        /* switch process id's */
79              if (fork())
80                        /* parent exits, new worm continues */
81                        exit(0);
82              /* attack gateways, known hosts */
83              attack_hosts();
84              other_sleep(120);
85                        /* if 12 hours have passed, reset hosts */
86              if(time(0) == current_time + (3600 * 12)) {
87                        reset_hosts();
88                        current_time = time(0); }
89                        /* quit if pleasequit is set, and nextw>10 */
90              if (pleasequit && nextw > 10)
91                        exit(0);
92      }
93 }
```

Figure G-2: VAX assembly-language code used to subvert the finger
daemon. Arguments to call **execve** *are pushed onto the stack and*
the **execve** *system call is made when the finger program returns.*

```
nop                             400 no op's (do nothing)
...
pushl    $68732f                store '/sh[NULL]' on stack
pushl    $6e69622f              store '/bin' on stack
movl     sp,r10                 save stack pointer in r10
pushl    $0                     store 0 on stack (arg 3)
pushl    $0                     store 0 again (arg 2)
pushl    r10                    store string address (arg 1)
pushl    $3                     store argument count
movl     sp,ap                  set argument pointer to stack
chmk     $3b                    system call to execve
```

Bibliography

Wood, P. and Kochan, S., "UNIX System Security", Hayden Book, New Jersey, 1985.

Thomas. R. and Farrow, R., "UNIX Administration Guide to System V", Prentice Hall, New Jersey, 1989.

Kernighan, B. and Ritchie, D., "The C Programming Language",Prentice Hall, New Jersey, 1978.

Kernighan, B. and Pike, R. "The UNIX Programming Environment", Prentice Hall, New Jersey, 1984.

Morris, R. and Thomson, K, "Password Security: A Case History", UNIX Programmer's Manual, Section 2, AT&T Bell Laboratories.

Grampp, F. and Morris, R., "The UNIX System: UNIX Operating System Security," AT&T Bell Laboratories Technical Journal , Vol. 63,No. 8, Part 2 (Oct. 1984), pp. 1649-1672.

"Network and Communications Administration", Sun Microsystems Inc., revision A of 27 March, 1990.

Farrow, R., "Further Cures for Business Ills, Part 2B," UNIX/World ,Vol III, No. 5, (May 1986), pp. 65-70.

Farrow, R., "What Price System Security?", UNIX/World ,Vol IV, No. 6, (June 1987), pp. 54-61.

Witten, I., "Computer Insecurity: Infiltrating Open Systems",Abacus , Volume 4, No. 4, Summer 1987.

McIlroy, M. D. and Reeds, J. A-, "Multilevel Security with Fewer Fetters", (paper), AT&T Laboratories, Murray Hill, NJ 07974, 1988.

Curry, D. "Improving the Security of Your UNIX System", SRI International, ITSTd.721-FR-90-21, April, 1990.

Stoll, Clifford, "Stalking the Wily Hacker", Communications of the ACM,Volume 31, Number 5, pages 484-497, May 1988.

Stoll, Clifford, "The Cuckoo's Egg", Doubleday, 1989.

Baran, S. Kaye, H. Suarez, "Security Breaks: Five Recent Incidents at Columbia University", USENIX Security Workshop Proceedings II, pages 151-171, 1990.

Duff, T. "Viral Attacks on UNIX System Security", USENIX Conference Proceedings, pages 165-172, Winter 1989.

Index

Police, 189-190
Policy statements, 187-188
Popular passwords, 76, 77
Ports
    modem, 117-119
    pseudo-ports, 169
    tapping, 173-174
Pound sign (#)
    disabling network daemons and,
      150
    passwords and, 22
praudit, 214-215, 216, 217
praudit -l, 216, 217
praudit -s, 216, 217
Princeton University, 122
Privacy, invasions of, 174
Privileges
    B level systems and, 221
    System V/MLS and, 218-219
Process accounting, 170-174
Processes, 10
.profile
    correcting permissions and, 47, 49
    file permissions and, 33
    history files and, 173
    restricted Bourne shells and, 154,
      155
    restricted environments and, 160
    startup files and, 40, 42
    system files database and, 97, 98
Programmers, 6, 56
Programs. *See* Software *or specific program*
Project Athena, 137
Promiscuous listener, 136
Prosecution, 186-190
Protection, data/system, 5, 9
ps, 167-169
    device files and, 96
    restricted environments and, 157
    set user and group property and,
      107
ps -ax, 168
ps -e, 167
ps -ef, 169
Pseudo-ports, 169
ps -l, 168
pub, 148-149
PUBDIR, 132, 135
putenv(), 160
pwadmin, 78
pwage, 80
pwck, 66, 67, 69
"pwck.out", 69
pwconv, 205, 206
pwdck, 66, 67
pwdck -y ALL, 73
pwguess, 77

Question marks, 185, 186
QUOTAS, 161
Quotas
    file permissions and, 32
    restricted environments and, 161

Random passwords, 20-21
Rated, 203

Raw device files, 94. *See also* Device files
rc
    auditing and, 211
    disabling network daemons and,
      150
    read access and, 93
    startup files and, 44
"r" commands, 138
READ, 132, 134
Read access, 26-27
    directory permissions and, 36-39
    file permissions and, 28-34
    system ownership and, 92-94
Read-down, 15
Real user/group id, 106
reboot, 210
Redirect out (), 154
Redman, Brian, 122
Red teams, 7-8
Reference monitor, 10, 11, 12
Reliable, 209
Remote File System (RFS), 136
Remote Procedure Calls (RPCs). *See*
    Secure RPC
remote.unknown, 128, 129
REQUEST, 130-131, 132, 134
Resources, 192
restore, 210
"restore" file, 103-104
/restrict, 155, 156
Restricted Bourne shell (**rsh**), 152, 153-155
    /etc/hosts.equiv and, 139
    .rhosts and, 141
    trusted hosts and, 138
    user id and, 60
    See also Bourne shell
Restricted environments, 152-162
    change root environment and,
      155-161
    problems with, 161-162
    restricted Bourne shells and,
      153-155
    special login programs and, 152-153
rexec, 138
RFS (Remote File System), 136
.rhosts, 138
    trusted hosts and, 140-141
rikf, 125
rlogin
    /etc/hosts.equiv and, 139
    .rhosts and, 141
    trusted hosts and, 138
rm, 35, 37
rmail
    HoneyDanBer UUCP security and,
      130, 133-134
    process accounting and, 170
    Version 2 UUCP security and, 126
rnews, 134
ro, 143
Root, 60
root
    modem security and, 117
    system ownership and, 81
RPCs (Remote Procedure Calls). *See* Se-
    cure RPC

rprt, 171
rsh. *See* Restricted Bourne shell
runacct, 171
Runs, 116-117

Safe paths, 95
savehist, 173
SCOMP, 18
Scripts
    auditing, 184, 191
    checking password file and, 69-70
    startup, 91-92
    See also specific script
Search permission. *See* Execute access
Search warrants, 189
Secrecy, 222
secure, 143
Secure RPC, 137
    /etc/hosts.equiv and, 140
    .rhosts and, 141, 143
Security, 4-12
    categories of, 13, 14-15, 27
    cost of, 5-6
    ease of use and, 6
    levels of, 12-13, 14-15, 27
    modem, 116-122
    multilevel, 17
    network, 135-151
    programmers and, 6
    simple, 15
    UUCP, 122-135
    See also specific topic
Security administrators, 55-57
    passwords and, 64
    See also System administrators
Security Administrator's Workbench, 74
Security domains. *See* B3 level systems
Security labels. *See* Labels
sed
    auditing and, 217
    HoneyDanBer UUCP security and,
      134
    system files database and, 100
    Version 2 UUCP security and, 126
    write access and, 91
sed -n l, 186
Seed, 70
    encrypted passwords and, 71
Self-locking terminals, 25
SENDFILES, 130-131, 134
sendmail, 145, 199
    fingerd and, 150
    other network services and, 145-147
Services
    denial of, 5, 14, 161
    network, 145-150
set, 47, 48
setenv, 41
"setfiles" list, 110, 112
set-group-id, 105-112
setrlimit()
    chrt and, 161
    restricted environments and, 161
setuid()
    auditing and, 215
    restricted environments and, 160